WHY RELIGION IS GOOD FOR AMERICAN DEMOCRACY

Why Religion Is Good for American Democracy

ROBERT WUTHNOW

PRINCETON UNIVERSITY PRESS
PRINCETON & OXFORD

Published by Princeton University Press
41 William Street, Princeton, New Jersey 08540
6 Oxford Street, Woodstock, Oxfordshire OX20 1TR

press.princeton.edu

All Rights Reserved

Library of Congress Cataloging-in-Publication Data

Names: Wuthnow, Robert, author.
Title: Why religion is good for American democracy / Robert Wuthnow.
Description: Princeton, New Jersey : Princeton University Press, [2021] |
    Includes bibliographical references and index.
Identifiers: LCCN 2021018383 (print) | LCCN 2021018384 (ebook) |
    ISBN 9780691222639 | ISBN 9780691222646 (ebook)
Subjects: LCSH: Democracy—United States—Religious aspects. | Religion and
    politics—United States. | Political participation—United States—Religious aspects. |
    Religious pluralism—Political aspects—United States. | Political culture—United
    States. | United States—Religion. | BISAC: SOCIAL SCIENCE / Sociology of
    Religion | POLITICAL SCIENCE / Civics & Citizenship
Classification: LCC JK1726 .W87 2021 (print) | LCC JK1726 (ebook) |
    DDC 322/.10973—dc23
LC record available at https://lccn.loc.gov/2021018383
LC ebook record available at https://lccn.loc.gov/2021018384

British Library Cataloging-in-Publication Data is available

Editorial: Fred Appel and James Collier
Production Editorial: Mark Bellis
Jacket Design: Karl Spurzem
Production: Erin Suydam
Publicity: Kate Hensley and Kathryn Stevens
Copyeditor: Laurel Anderton

This book has been composed in Arno

Printed on acid-free paper. ∞

Printed in the United States of America

10 9 8 7 6 5 4 3 2 1

CONTENTS

WHY RELIGION IS GOOD FOR
AMERICAN DEMOCRACY

Introduction

RARELY IN OUR NATION'S HISTORY have so many thoughtful observers voiced so many urgent messages about the need to understand and better protect the foundations of American democracy. To the familiar challenges of partisan polarization and gridlock has now been added the troubling prospect of cherished democratic traditions being subverted by far-right nationalistic extremism, plutocracy, self-dealing, and sheer incompetence. The warnings are credible. Democracy is in danger unless the citizens it seeks to protect work for its preservation.

Religion—how it is practiced, what it impels people to do—is again at the center of debate about our collective well-being. We are a nation of many religions and of many views about religion. Some of America's faith communities imagine God to be visiting us with difficulties to teach us a lesson. Others hope for an end to the nonsense they see perpetrated by religious leaders. And if religion is troubling, some argue, things could be much worse without it. Democracy would wither, they contend, without the leavening influences of faith.

How do the diverse practices that characterize religion in the United States strengthen democracy? Or do they strengthen it? What do these practices contribute, if anything, to public advocacy about democracy's basic principles—fair representation, liberty of conscience, freedom of assembly, human dignity, and equality?

The claim I make in the following pages is that religion is good for American democracy less because of the unifying values it might provide and more because of religion's capacity to bring diverse values, interests, and moral claims into juxtaposition with one another. Through its diversity, religion contributes to the contending beliefs, values, arguments, and counterarguments that constitute the debate about how to order our lives together. People who care about religion—including those who doubt its value—vehemently disagree with one another and take adversarial positions toward one another. This diversity—these diverging practices and the moral convictions they imply—animates American democracy, sometimes in ways that pose questions about whether we can agree on anything, but more often with robust outcomes that reflect advocacy and counteradvocacy. Contention about what we hold dear is central to democratic processes: voicing strong convictions about what is unequivocally right, advocating for conflicting definitions of the common good, affirming and modifying basic points of agreement, and refining the procedures that make living together possible. Religious diversity is woven into this contention, augmenting it and supplying it with competing ideas, practices, and values.

Conceived in this manner, religious groups' potential to benefit American democracy occurs in several ways. They can mobilize resistance to the authoritarian threats of autocratic leaders, support efforts to uphold freedom of conscience, organize voluntary associations, and defend these associations' independence. Additionally, religious groups can advocate for human dignity, provide social services and support, champion the value of inclusive orientations, and address the threat to democracy of economic inequality. The key to understanding these potential benefits is how religious groups with diverging convictions understand their civic roles and relate to one another. Differing groups bring multiple perspectives to bear on social issues, articulate claims and counterclaims, mobilize in opposition to one another, check one another's aspirations, and give voice to constituencies with differing values and interests. None of this follows a set pattern. It happens in historical contexts—where religion's diverse contributions are most clearly seen.

The historical episodes I discuss begin with an examination of how the most influential religious groups in the early 1930s—predominantly

Protestant, Roman Catholic, and Jewish organizations—drew on their differing locations and beliefs to warn constructively about the imminent threat of authoritarianism. I then discuss religious diversity's role in redefining freedom of conscience in the late 1930s and early 1940s. In the 1950s we see religious groups advocating for freedom of assembly and from the 1960s through the end of the century contending about human dignity and welfare provision. In recent decades a further role of religious diversity is evident in discussions of immigrant rights, the wealth gap, and the response to COVID-19. In each instance, the details of what happened are broadly familiar, documented by journalists and social scientists. Building on this information, I show why it mattered that religious practices were present and why it was significant that leaders and the groups they served so often took adversarial positions toward one another.

Democracy's strength depends on the rule of law, the Constitution, freedom of speech and assembly, fair elections, and the nation's system of government checks and balances. These principles and institutions have served democracy well. The multilayered complexity of these arrangements, frustrating as it often is, safeguards American democracy. When democracy is threatened, Americans historically have trusted the laws, the lawmakers, the courts, and the press to protect it. Today, no less than in the past, democracy's resilience depends on responsive representative institutions, fair elections, active civic participation, freedom of expression, and adherence to constitutional norms. Unless these institutions and norms are respected, democratic governance is weakened.

Religious advocacy is not the answer to the political challenges confronting the United States at this critical juncture in its history, any more than religious conviction is their cause. But religious organizations are so thoroughly intertwined with our national traditions and the foundations of our democracy that they too must be scrutinized. Whether we are among those who think democracy was founded on religious principles or are convinced that reasonable people would be better off putting religious convictions aside, the reality is that millions of Americans practice religion in one form or another. They enact it in churches, synagogues, mosques, ashrams, and temples, coming together in hundreds of thousands of places of worship large and small. Additionally, many Americans who do not identify with any religion hold considered opinions about how religion should or should not be practiced. And, although religious faith for many is a matter of the heart, it is also demonstrably influential in public affairs. Faith perspectives inform whom people trust, the issues they care about, and in many cases how they vote.

One might think that everything possible to say about religion's place in the life of our nation has already been said. Histories about it abound, polls measure it, and ethicists ask whether it could be practiced better than it is. We know that religious beliefs have inspired both good and ill. Religiously inspired activism has both mobilized social reform and resisted it. We also know that religious practices in the United States have always been diverse and that they are now more diverse than they have ever been. Diversity is one of religious practices' most salient features. Indeed, it is impossible to understand American religion without closely considering its diversity. The best descriptions of American religion emphasize this diversity. And yet, although many arguments have celebrated (or deplored) religious diversity, much confusion remains.

The reasons for this confusion are not new. A century ago, when organized religion in the United States was less diverse than it is today, it was taken for granted that Protestants, Catholics, Jews, and the leaders of other denominational and interfaith groups would speak to the issues of the day. Yet by the middle of the twentieth century, a prevailing view among academics was that religious beliefs and values were either a kind of implicit cultural subfloor that quietly supported the basic democratic norms on which everyone agreed, or were so weakened by secularization that they served mainly as a palliative in personal life. When religious activism appeared to have reentered public life in the 1980s, its association with the antiabortion, antigay "Christian Right" concentrated interest in the twin questions of how such political engagement was possible and what could be done about it. Specifically, how was it conceivable that traditionalists of this sort had become so politically active almost overnight? And how could those who disagreed with them counter their influence? These were interesting questions and they deserved to be studied, but they have not served us well in the long run. The very nature of the questions scholars asked about the Christian Right limited, rather than illuminated, the larger question of religious diversity's relation to democracy. Indeed, those questions implied that division is usually a problem rather than contemplating what it may contribute.

In the breach, two ways of thinking about religious diversity and democracy have taken hold, neither of which provides a satisfactory answer to the broad question of how diverse religious practices might contribute to democracy. On the one hand, much of the commentary focuses on organized religion but neglects the importance of its diversity. Such arguments include the view that religious commitment benefits democracy because this commitment generally undergirds a shared belief in justice, equality, human rights, and compassion; and that it encourages people to engage in civic activities—or that it is bad because it breeds intolerance, promotes irrationality, and inhibits the reasoned give-and-take democracy requires. "Religion" in these discussions usually means Christianity or, if not that, then Judeo-Christian or Abrahamic religion or some kind of organized religion, neglecting the fact that institutional religion in the United States takes many forms—some of which are highly individualized—and this diversity figures importantly in how people practice their various faiths. On the other hand, some discussions focus on diversity without paying much attention to religion per se. In these discussions, diversity—meaning differences of race, ethnicity, gender, and sexual orientation—is variously conceived as being good for democracy because it generates new ideas and sparks economic innovation, or else it is a problem that must be resolved for democracy to survive. Religious observance in its many varieties sometimes comes up as one of the many real but problematic diversities with which democratic governance has to contend. Whether it contributes is harder to say.

Examining what religiously oriented individuals and organizations have actually done puts the lie to these ways of thinking. Religious conviction hasn't contributed to American democracy simply by providing a sacred umbrella under which to huddle with our fragile unifying beliefs. Religious claims certainly haven't been sidelined or excluded from public life. They haven't been reanimated only by the Christian Right. Nor have they been a positive influence on democracy only in those historical instances in which activists advocated for abolition and civil rights. And religious identities haven't contributed only by influencing elections or giving candidates and public officials a tool kit of sacred idioms with which to speak.

Investigating what has actually been done shows that religiously oriented citizens have played an active role when important national issues were being debated. They have acted because of their diversity, putting that diversity into practice by vigorously proposing and defending alternative ideas, mobilizing constituents to be engaged in civic activities, and checking one another through criticism and dissent. Over the past century, religious groups and their leaders have contributed to American democracy in these ways, not in spite of their diversity but because of it. People have been propelled into action because they vehemently disagreed with one another. They were forced to contend with their disagreements, seeking and sometimes finding common ground, but in the process posing the hard questions about who we want to be, what our values should be, and how to get along with those who see things differently.

"Religion" is often conceptualized as a system of beliefs that uniquely speaks of humans' relation to the sacred. However, for present purposes—without denying the value of that general idea—I want to think of it in a different way. Drawing on what we know from studies of how religion is practiced in ordinary life, we can conceptualize religious practices in terms of *action, conviction,* and *contention,* meaning that they are something people do because they are convinced that what they are doing is right, and they hold these convictions in contention with behavior considered less desirable and indeed wrong. Thought of in these terms, religious practices amount to a way of engaging with the world.

They consist not only of participating in sacred rites but also of taking action in the affairs of one's community and nation.

Religious practices, so considered, connect to democracy in ways best suggested in what Belgian political theorist Chantal Mouffe terms agonistic pluralism. Democracy, she argues, is fundamentally messy, divided, and of necessity representative of diverse interests and values that can never be fully reconciled. While it may be conceived of as an ideal, democracy must be understood concretely as the political practices in which groups contend with one another. For this reason, she says, democracy cannot be understood sufficiently as a set of procedures through which people deliberate in the hope of arriving at a rationally articulated consensus. It consists instead of people mixing it up, arguing, debating, mobilizing, and negotiating with those with whom they disagree and yet treating them as adversaries rather than as enemies. What distinguishes an effective democracy is thus not consensus on deeply held shared convictions but a willingness to abide by norms of respect and civility and truthfulness, thereby making it possible for people who disagree to nevertheless live and work together.[1]

Democracy is weakened by conditions that impede these processes of contentious disputation. Authoritarianism under which agreement is coerced or inspired from fear and resentment is the most serious threat to democracy. It cuts off the free expression of dissent and the give-and-take from which innovative ideas originate. Hegemonic subscription to a dominant taken-for-granted ideology, religion, or set of economic principles is a second threat. That, too, cuts off debate. Apathy and disenfranchisement, both of which enable rules to be set by the few against the interests of the many, constitute a third threat. Extremism that radically interdicts the civil back-and-forth of adversarial constituencies is a fourth. Democracy is endangered in each of these circumstances less by disagreements—even by heated contention about rights, representation, and the meanings of democracy—than by too much agreement with prevailing hierarchies of power.

Hegemonic, authoritarian religious practices undercut democracy in all these ways. Yet the reality of religious diversity is that in countries that have experience with democracy it limits these dangerous tendencies even as they persist. Religious convictions threaten democracy mainly when adherents claim to have superior unquestionable knowledge from on high that derives from a particular source and yet applies to everyone in ways that define the common good. But under conditions of religious diversity, those arguments are subject to the criticism, debate, challenge, refutation, and revision that are essential to the health of a democracy. When diversity yields claims and counterclaims, even in instances when it generates factions and conflict, it is beneficial for democracy because it reduces the chance that any one majoritarian religion will command the bully pulpit that facilitates its hegemonic authority. Diversity's further contribution lies in bringing alternative ideas about the common good to the table, even ones that challenge received wisdom about the meanings of democracy, framing them less as incommensurable truths than as practical strategies of action. Democracy is strengthened by contention of this kind mobilizing civic participation, posing hard questions, and giving expression to dissent.[2]

Thinking of religious practices as groups of citizens acting and contending on the basis of their convictions necessitates acknowledging just how diverse American religion truly is. To be sure, many people look to religion for quiet solace, personal inspiration, and peace of mind in the midst of a world seemingly divided about everything else. Religion provides hope that everyone can live together in harmony. But religion is a source of disharmony, too, as it of necessity reflects its differing traditions and locations. It is the diversity of belief and practice that matters, not simply an underlying consensus. As Michael Kazin observes, "To take one's religion seriously almost requires a certain amount of conflict with those who seriously disagree."[3]

Diversity is the source of checks and balances, of skepticism toward moral hubris, and of dissent and counterdissent that propels religious organizations (and their opponents) to propose and aggressively defend their ideas about how Americans should live and be governed. Diversity among religious organizations provides the space in which unpopular perspectives can be kept alive and innovative ideas can incubate. By participating in diverse religious organizations, groups with diverse interests and needs can feel they have a voice. At its best, this diverse participation invigorates democracy the way James Bryce anticipated more than a century ago when he wrote of groups that "rouse attention, excite discussion, formulate principles, submit plans, [and] embolden and stimulate their members."[4]

Despite all these benefits, religious diversity also extracts costs, especially the divisiveness that gets in the way of religious organizations having a stronger hand in public affairs when they fail to work together. Another cost is the faith-based prejudice, discrimination, and antidemocratic extremism that have been so much a part of American religion throughout its history. Even the time and energy expended on conflict management can be considered a cost. The freedom of religion that American democracy seeks to guarantee creates the space in which inefficient as well as unpalatable expressions of faith can thrive. These costs have often compelled observers to view the nation's religious diversity as a problem—a troublesome reality with which democracy has had to contend rather than anything from which to benefit. From that perspective, the good thing about religion in America is that separation of church and state has kept it as far from the public square as possible—a fact that would surely please James Madison and Thomas Jefferson alike. And yet, religious diversity early in the nation's history was the reality that propelled the founders to bring church-state separation into being. Religious diversity has continued to be the guardian both of freedom to practice religion and of protection from religion.

Against the view that conflict among religious groups is simply a problem for democracy, a long tradition in the social sciences has recognized the "integrative" role of institutionalized conflicts. "Integrative" means that contending groups provide regular channels through which constituencies express their various values and interests. Their participation confers a sense of inclusion, of being heard and of possibly making a difference, that contributes to the legitimacy of the arrangements that make this participation possible. Playing by the rules in this respect reinforces the legitimacy of the rules. In addition, the conflicting interests and perspectives of different religious groups have often mitigated the severity of divisions based on social class, race, and region and have contributed to the formation of crosscutting alliances.[5]

The crucial aspect of this argument is the phrase "institutionalized conflicts." Religious conflicts in the United States take shape within a framework of institutions that consists, in the first place, of constitutional separation of church and state, which itself is subject to continuous testing and modification and yet sets boundaries on how religious groups exercise influence. Religious conflicts are further constrained by laws and regulations that protect against violence, hate crimes, and seizures of property. Traditions and norms also play an important role. These include the knowledge that past religious conflicts often resulted in violence and that democracy developed as a direct response to that history. Religious conflict is also constrained by norms of decorum and tolerance of diversity.[6]

To say that religious diversity is good for democracy is not to suggest a priori that a particular mix of contending religious traditions is optimal. How much or how little power one or another religious group should have is what religious leaders themselves argue about. The reality is that the United States has been religiously diverse from the start, and although concerns have always been expressed about the hegemonic aspirations of some and the rights of others, the constitutional protections of religious freedom and of separation of church and state provide the ground rules under which these interactions occur. These protections are never fully and finally adjudicated to everyone's satisfaction, which is one of the reasons why contention among religious groups is a constant forum for democratic deliberation. And the reality of these firm but evolving constitutional guarantees against religious establishment means that the question of religious diversity's contributions to democracy cannot be satisfactorily addressed simply in contrast to the default possibility of a single established theocracy. To argue only that religious diversity is better for democracy than a theocracy would miss the point. That view can be taken and still assert nothing about whether American religion in all its diversity mostly helps democracy or hurts it.

Religious diversity does mean that some organizations are necessarily more powerful and represent larger or more influential constituencies than others. Indeed, minority religions are of particular relevance to the practice of democracy. Under the American system, democracy's role includes upholding the rights and freedoms of minority religious groups. That in turn gives the leaders of minority religions an added incentive to advocate for democracy. The case can also be made that greater diversity overall increases the opportunities for leaders of minority religions to form coalitions and thereby increase their chances of winning arguments about democracy's protection of religious freedom.

It has been minority religions with which dissent has most often been associated. By virtue of being minority groups, religious minorities see things differently than majority religions do, especially because they have an enhanced stake in seeking acceptance for their distinct perspectives and interests. The dissenters best known in US history have been Puritans, Anabaptists, Quakers, and abolitionists, and, more recently, conscientious objectors, Jehovah's Witnesses, immigrants' rights activists, and antiracist advocacy groups. But dissent has not been limited to these groups; it has also been present in the larger, more established traditions. The past century has witnessed disagreements within every branch of American religion that manifest dissenting attitudes toward majorities, toward the practices of contending faith traditions and groups, and toward government. We have also seen the presence of religious dissent in organizations, movements, and individuals calling for elected officials to do a better job of upholding racial justice, protecting religious freedom, and checking government expansion.

Diversity of religious belief and practice must be understood, too, as the diversity represented in contention *against* religion. The story of religion's contribution to American democracy cannot be told without recognizing the critical influence of organizations that resisted what they saw as intolerance, indifference, hypocrisy, and subservience on the part of established religion. These voices of skepticism were part of the contention from the start and have remained so. Typically they have organized to prevent religious thinking from having too much of a role in public affairs, offering an alternative platform from which to speak.

The crucial episodes I examine in the following chapters deal with perennial issues that democratic governance in the United States has had to address. Resisting autocracy, protecting freedom of conscience, guaranteeing liberty of assembly, upholding the dignity of persons, making room for inclusion, addressing economic inequality, and protecting the health and wellness of the population are all challenges that we as a nation confront continually. From looking at specific instances, it becomes possible to see concretely how religion in its diversity and because of this diversity has contributed.

The threat of autocracy—of a leader or party that disregards the basic tenets of democratic governance—is one that must be vigilantly guarded against. Other than during war, when democracy faces an external threat, few times have seemed as endangering to American democracy as the 1930s. Although many considered the New Deal necessary, others saw its expansion of the federal government as a threat to democracy. Religious organizations actively debated the New Deal and the changes it implied. Some groups regarded it as no threat to democracy at all; others found it deeply disturbing; still others convened forums in which its strengths and weaknesses were discussed. The role religious groups played in the debate illustrates the significance of religious diversity. Although the nation was profoundly concerned with economic recovery, religious diversity brought into the public arena valuable perspectives about freedom, values, and moral responsibility.

The pacifist movements that emerged during World War I—and that continued to argue for peace and against rearmament through the 1920s and 1930s—reveal a different role of religious diversity than the one demonstrated in debating the New Deal. Religious organizations representing different traditions worked together to promote pacifism. Despite their theological differences, their cooperation declared that they all considered pacifism important. Conscientious objection took pacifism a step further. It posed the difficult question of how someone who refused to participate in war should be treated. During World War I, members of "historic peace churches" (Mennonites, Brethren, and Quakers) were generally granted an exemption of some kind, such as noncombatant service, because of their membership in those denominations. But by 1940, the courts recognized that conscientious objectors represented a wider variety of religious organizations and traditions. This recognition of diversity necessitated shifting the criterion for exemption from membership to claims made on behalf of individuals' own private beliefs. The story of how this happened is an illustration of religious diversity contributing to the clarification of freedom of conscience.

Like freedom of conscience, understandings of freedom of assembly were also sharpened by debates involving religious diversity. After World War II, America's reputation as a "nation of joiners" grew as more of the population moved to the suburbs, had children, and set records for membership in religious and community organizations. Commentators interpreted this enthusiasm for joining as an expression of Americans' desire for community. Participating in community organizations benefited American democracy, too, as Alexis de Tocqueville had argued years earlier. Community organizations were local, reflecting the diverse interests of their members and giving citizens a voice in public affairs. But members were not entirely at liberty to do and say whatever they wanted. Despite a constitutional guarantee of freedom to peaceably assemble, groups were subject to trespass and vagrancy laws, licensing ordinances, and restrictive covenants. Many of these laws and regulations had been advanced earlier in the century in support of Jim Crow segregation. In the 1950s similar laws and regulations were applied to civil rights organizations. With an interest of their own in freedom of assembly, religious groups were actively involved in litigating these laws and regulations. The groups took differing sides, arguing about different interpretations of "assembly," "speech," and "freedom," as well as about taxation and privacy. By the late 1960s, these discussions prepared the way for a significant enlargement of organizations engaged in political activism, protests, and efforts to promote new ideas about religion and democracy.

Another key issue in the defense of American democracy is embracing and upholding the dignity of the individual—which, among other things, has been especially debated in discussions of welfare policy. The late twentieth-century debate about welfare that consumed such a great deal of political energy arose on the heels of the civil rights movement in the 1960s and extended into the 1990s and early 2000s. The debate divided along partisan lines between advocates of private charity and advocates of government programs. Religious groups' arguments often separated along these lines as well. However, the religious community also contributed a wider variety of perspectives. Black churches, urban ministries, interfaith coalitions, and advocacy groups were often in the best position to work out creative solutions that combined private and public resources. When government-funded faith-based initiatives were introduced, these ministries and coalitions were able to contribute valuable perspectives on the essential questions of how best to serve the common good while also protecting the dignity of the individual.

Against the backdrop of the debates to which differing religious perspectives have contributed, a counternarrative best described as ethnoreligious nationalism—or simply as White Christian nationalism—also exists. Its argument is that whatever diversity exists within White Christian America, that diversity is inconsequential, at least among "true Christians," and is pitted against a heterodox bundle of threats that include African Americans, persons of no faith, Muslims, and immigrants.[7] Religious diversity challenges this nationalistic notion. Many religious groups take issue with it, arguing that nationalism is contrary to democracy. These groups argue for greater understanding of other traditions, an emphasis on rights, and respect for diversity. The arguments focus on race and ethnicity, gender, and sexual orientation. In recent decades they have also focused on immigrant rights. The arguments are contentious, prompting counterarguments and propelling civic engagement. They bring divergent views to bear on some of the most important questions about American democracy: Who counts as citizens and what are their rights?

Although the debates in which religious diversity has participated have dealt with inequality in other ways, these discussions have also contributed directly to questions raised by the widening gap between the very rich and the rest of the American population. One strand of the debate stresses individual freedom, which means limiting the role of government intervention in the economy and looking to private philanthropy for remediation of the wealth gap. Some religious groups have found their voice in advocating for these views. A different approach has called attention to the social responsibilities of corporations. Drawing on the *Rerum Novarum* papal encyclical of 1891 and the Social Gospel of early twentieth-century Protestants, some religious groups have advocated for corporate social responsibility. Other religious groups have developed wealth ministries and faith-friendly leadership programs. And still others have been active supporters of community organizing and the living wage movement. Through their diverging perspectives, they have informed deliberations about public policy, arguing that it should take account not only of economic considerations but also of moral responsibilities.

Then, too, no democracy is free from periodic crises that come from unexpected sources—such as a global pandemic. Along with every other US institution, religious organizations were caught largely unprepared by the coronavirus that swept across the nation in early 2020. Most followed the shifting guidelines from public health officials as the virus spread. They canceled worship services, shut down in-person meetings, and crafted ways to offer services and hold meetings online. A few leaders resisted. They interpreted the closure directives as government interfering with religious freedom, and some preached that God would protect them from the virus. The pandemic also revived debates about vaccinations. These debates reflected deeper tensions between some religious groups' teachings and their attitudes toward science and scientific medicine. Some of the groups were deeply skeptical of science and even more suspicious when government was the source of scientific information. Yet these debates were not the whole story. Many religious groups redoubled their efforts to facilitate health and wellness, including blood drives, wellness fairs, mental health initiatives, and parish nursing ministries, and many advocated for expanded health insurance programs and medical research. Relative to the contribution of other institutions, especially government and science, that of religious groups was small. Nevertheless, it was another instance in which religion's diversity reached diverse sectors of the population, illustrating that democracy requires both doing one's part and determining what that part should be.

Taking a historical view illuminates continuity but also brings into sharp relief a disturbing trend. Although religious diversity has in many ways increased, the vitality of its diverse expression has diminished in proportion to its alignment with partisan politics. Divisions between religious liberals and conservatives that corresponded with divisions between Democrats and Republicans were already present a century ago, but that alignment has become tighter in recent decades. The result has been a shift in the basis on which claims by religious authorities are made and a decrease in the capacity of religious organizations to facilitate discussions of varying perspectives toward government policies. Instead of constructive proposals being offered that bring groups with diverging views together, party loyalties dictate religious perspectives as well. Reference need only be made to discussions of healthcare, gun control, and racial equality to see how difficult it has become for religious groups to avoid political partisanship.

The partisanship along which religious diversity has become aligned has made it especially difficult to fully appreciate the contributions of recently arrived immigrant groups with diverse religious convictions of their own. Instead of accepting Muslims, Sikhs, Buddhists, and Hindus as epistemic communities with different styles of practice, a large swath of the Christian population has taken to denying its own internal diversities and treating the rest of the population as if it were alien. The alternative response of pretending that religious diversity is nonexistent except in superficial ways, while assuming that everyone is united by secular values, is little better.

My emphasis on the diversity of American religious beliefs and practices is meant as a challenge to the partisan way of thinking that afflicts some of the otherwise most reasoned discourse about how democracy is currently threatened and what to do about it. Implicit in many of these discussions is the assumption that religious practice is essentially a unitary phenomenon that is traditional, sentimental, authoritarian, fundamentally autocratic, and most evident in conservative movements. To conceive of religious practice in these terms is to implicitly argue that only liberalism, whether secular or religious, can protect us from the threat religious convictions usually pose to democracy. This view suggests that liberalism counters the potentially undemocratic conservatizing tendencies inherent in religious convictions and that championing liberalism as an alternative to these convictions is the best way forward. However, such a view ignores the essential fact of American religious diversity. It misses the point that religious groups— even in their conservative manifestations—are always divided and are constrained by these divisions. In treating American religion as if it were alien to democracy, this interpretation of liberalism results in heated responses defending religion by extolling its democratic virtues, a view that is also deficient and sometimes equally dangerous. Defending religious groups on the grounds that their values are consistent with democracy is too easy. It foregrounds the good and opens the way to labeling any other religious or secular tradition with which one disagrees as an impediment of democracy. Both views, in representing religious practices simplistically, ignore how internally divisive and conflicted those practices are. Thus both views fail to appreciate how much the arguments advanced in the name of religion are shaped by that diversity.

If democracy is understood to be the practice through which contention is negotiated, religion's diverse, competing, dissenting, and sometimes divisive claims are best understood as part of the practice through which democracy reinvents itself. Religious organizations' role in this context is manifestly different from that of legislative bodies, the courts, political parties, science, and the press, partly because it sometimes speaks with divine authority, but also because it brings to the table alternative epistemic claims, visions, and possibilities that are rooted in moral precepts. Religious practices' influence in a democracy lies not in coercion but in articulating claims and counterclaims about what is right and good. Democracy benefits when these claims are voiced from diverse quarters, sometimes in harmony and sometimes in sharp dis-agreement. The benefit is present even when claims are asserted dog-matically because religious diversity ensures that rebuttals and alterna-tive claims are also voiced. We are protected from a religious establishment not only by the First Amendment but also by the disunity of religion itself. This disunity powerfully deters religious groups from speaking with one voice. At the same time, disunity facilitates the vigor-ous questioning of entrenched assumptions and the airing of alternative visions of the good.

1

Against Tyranny

RELIGIOUS ADVOCACY IN THE
NEW DEAL ERA

TYRANNY THREATENS DEMOCRACY from without when a hostile
power attacks. Tyranny threatens from within when too much power
accedes to persons and agencies in command of the central government. The United States has experienced both, the former on December 7, 1941; the latter from concerns—some more warranted than
others—about subversive activities, overreach of the federal government, and chief executives who flagrantly disrespect the rule of law. The
threat from within is harder to measure and for this reason is more often
subject to partisan debate. The debate itself, as well as the policies that
follow from it, contributes to clarifying—and sometimes redefining—
what democracy is.

This chapter takes as a case in point the controversy generated by the
New Deal—a controversy that has been alluded to ever since in arguments about the scope of government authority. The debate that sur-
rounded the specific proposals put forth by the Roosevelt administration dealt with the power of the federal government and the question
of whether that power was being expanded in conformity with democratic principles or was threatening democracy. The debate illustrates
how religious diversity contributes when concerns about dramatic
shifts in the character of democracy are at issue. I begin by considering
how religious leaders in the 1920s regarded disunity as a weakness they

wanted to overcome in order to have a greater impact on public policy, then discuss how the Roosevelt administration attempted to cultivate support from religious organizations, and finally show how religious diversity prompted resistance to the New Deal and what lessons that resistance holds for us today.

The Appeal for Unity

In 1922, H. Richard Niebuhr, the younger brother of theologian Reinhold Niebuhr, published a book that was to become the touchstone for inquiries about religion in the United States for the next fifty years. *The Social Sources of Denominationalism* provided an incisive analysis of America's leading religious organizations. Identifying diversity as the most salient feature of US Protestantism, Niebuhr argued that the reason Protestants were divided into so many denominations was their roots in different nationalities, different regions, different social classes, and different races. Denominational differences, he said, were at heart not about theological disagreements. They were fundamentally the consequence of divergent social conditions.

Had that been all, Niebuhr's book would likely have been ignored like most other attempts to show that ideas were nothing more than a reflection of circumstances. Niebuhr's approach included enough Marxism to warrant the dismissal it received in some quarters. Niebuhr, though, was intent on making a larger point. If denominational differences were merely a reflection of circumstances, he argued, church leaders should work to overcome them. The trouble with division was that it prevented people of faith from engaging effectively with challenging social issues. Worse, it was an ethical failure. Divisiveness, he argued, was condemned by the gospel. People of faith should work to replace it with an inner unity, a spirit of harmony.[1]

A long and varied perspective on American religion favors consensus over dissensus and unity over disunity. Acknowledging that reality falls short of this ideal, the ideal is for people to get along better, hash out their differences, learn to be tolerant, and seek common ground in shared beliefs or an implicit agreement about moral principles. It may be that they do this by participating in interfaith organizations or simply by recognizing that they share basic human values. To the extent that believers can do this, they contribute to the common good. And to the extent that they fall short, the results are troubling: ineffective divisiveness in addressing social problems, and at the margins intolerance, bigotry, and discrimination.

Granted, much can be said for this view. Why not seek common ground? Why not forge interdenominational alliances that effect mergers across historic lines of division? Why not look for the basic values on which people of all faiths and people unaffiliated with any faith can agree? Nothing is lost in these efforts and much is gained. Why not identify and decry division whenever it raises its ugly head?

The ideal of consensus, though, must take account of the world in which we live. The same writers who argue so fervently for consensus embrace diversity up to a point and beyond that understand that the world is deeply divided. In Niebuhr's day it was divided between Christians and Jews, Protestants and Catholics, fundamentalists and modernists, and Black Christians and White Christians. Within each of the major faiths, schisms were periodic occurrences, and when organizations managed to avoid schisms, annual meetings of clergy and lay leaders were occasions for engaging in heated discussions of doctrine, morality, and church governance. As much as Niebuhr's call for unity was hailed by leaders at the top of several large denominations, it was deplored by leaders of other denominations who considered theological differences worth defending.

What Niebuhr understood, even though he hoped for unity, was that religion's disunity was also a strength. Denominational divisions existed because they articulated with the varied social reality that was America. The fifteen million Roman Catholics worshipped in parishes that bore the marks of Irish, Italian, German, and Polish immigration. Baptists whose regional and racial divisions dated to the 1840s numbered six million. The nation's two million Lutherans were organized into Norwegian, Swedish, Danish, Finnish, German, and Icelandic as well as multiethnic synods. Methodists divided themselves into seventeen varieties and Mennonites into sixteen. Further diversity was evident in hundreds of Jewish congregations, Buddhist temples, Spiritualist groups, and Theosophist organizations. In all, the nation's religious adherents were scattered among more than two hundred "denominations."[2]

The various sects and churches and synagogues and temples distinguished themselves theologically and in styles of worship, but they also expressed the varied experiences that had brought people to America and that continued to differentiate the population in terms of race, ethnicity, region, and social class. The differences reinforced these distinctive identities, accentuating valued traditions and giving them a voice, often in explicit rivalry with other traditions. And in contending for their convictions, their adherents also gave expression to what they thought America should be, which, as Niebuhr observed, meant contending for differing ideas about the state, its policies, and religion's relationship to the state.

When Niebuhr contemplated the divisions among Protestants, the disagreements that transcended styles of worship and that animated debates about the public life of the nation included Prohibition, evolution, women's suffrage, race relations, and the differing economic interests of city dwellers and rural inhabitants. Especially the advocacy generated by various temperance proposals, followed by Al Smith's candidacy as the first Roman Catholic to run for the presidency a few years later in 1928, brought religious leaders into the fray of partisan politics in ways that later critics would see as violations of strict separation of church and state. Whereas Catholics generally opposed Prohibition and favored Smith, Protestants supported Prohibition and feared that a Smith presidency would result in the repeal of Prohibition and give the Vatican a powerful voice in American politics. The two sides were mobilized to influence the election, and the issues seemed important enough that clergy gave up their reluctance to express themselves politically. In many communities, Protestants and Catholics were so deeply divided that they could cooperate on hardly anything.

The stock market crash of 1929 and the dramatic rise in unemployment that followed redirected the nation's leadership, including its religious leaders' attention, toward the economy. The political capital the

Republican Party acquired in winning the presidency and both houses of Congress in 1928 evaporated. Franklin Delano Roosevelt's decisive victory in 1932 set the stage for a decade of sweeping reforms. It was in interaction with these reforms that religious leaders repeatedly demonstrated the complexities of church-state relationships. The relationships were by no means limited to judicial interpretations of the Constitution. Religious organizations mobilized to express views about concrete actions they thought the federal government should take or avoid taking. They convened meetings, voted on resolutions they wanted sent to the administration, applauded some of the administration's policies, and condemned others. However much the programs that were put into effect were later hailed as having preserved democracy, leaders at the time faced an uncertain future in which the shape of democracy itself was at issue. What faith communities did to make their values known— and how diversity shaped their actions—is well worth understanding these many decades later.

The New Deal

At its annual convention in Cleveland on May 23, 1934, leaders of the Presbyterian Church in the United States of America listened as the evening's speaker encouraged them to devote their full-hearted support to the New Deal. "The moral aspirations of the church should reinforce the political efforts now being made to establish a new social order," the speaker asserted. The new order, "certain as it is to be realized in the end," he promised, will with the churches' help "be accomplished much more quickly and with infinitely less disturbance."[3]

The speaker was Harold L. Ickes, the one-time Chicago journalist and Bull Moose Republican whom Roosevelt had selected in 1933 to serve as secretary of the interior and who subsequently headed the Public Works Administration. Ickes, whom his biographer described as a "righteous pilgrim," was not only a skilled orator but also a trusted administrator who sought to embrace the Christian values instilled by his devoutly Presbyterian mother.[4] During a private meeting with Roosevelt a few days before his lecture to the assembled Presbyterians, the president assured Ickes it would be okay to cancel the trip, given Ickes's heavy travel schedule promoting the New Deal in addition to directing the Interior Department. No, Ickes said, doing so might lose the Presbyterian vote, to which Roosevelt responded, only half in jest, that they might lose it even if Ickes did make the trip.[5]

Roosevelt knew that the New Deal's success depended on support from the nation's congregations. Some sixty million Americans— approximately half of all men, women, and children—were members of local congregations. And besides the numbers, the president's need of religious leaders' support for the massive reforms he wanted gave those leaders an opportunity to speak in hope of being heard. Since taking office and even before as governor of New York, Roosevelt had cultivated the clergy in efforts to reform government and expand programs benefiting the poor. Ickes was an ideal spokesperson for these efforts. He believed the nation's Christians should lend themselves enthusiastically to the administration's reforms because the New Deal's objectives and those of Christianity were identical. "Christ wanted men and women to live upright lives," Ickes told the crowd in Cleveland, "but he also wanted them to have for each other understanding and good will and mutual helpfulness. He wished them to be good neighbors."

This was a message that progressive clergy were already embracing. Close to home, New York clergy hailed Roosevelt's ideas and prayed for him as they anticipated a new order in economic affairs. One likened him to a new messiah. The same was true in scattered locations across the country. At the First Congregational Church in Portland, Oregon, for example, Reverend Raymond B. Walker—a prominent spokesperson for the principles of progressive Christianity being taught in Protestant seminaries—said the nation might be in turmoil, but hearts were beating with hope because righteousness would ultimately prevail. Walker was persuaded that with scientific study, diligence, and toilsome adjustments a new order was slowly being created. The churches' role was thus to inspire people to go forth as happy warriors in the cause of moral ideals.[6]

The notion that good-hearted Christians would facilitate the moral uplift of America while Washington went about the task of creating a new social order, though, was insufficiently cognizant of the threat that many observers saw in Roosevelt's centralization of power. Critics worried that what was happening in the United States paralleled events taking place in Germany as well as events that had already resulted in the communists' assumption of power in Russia. Americans, they feared, were responding to the economic uncertainty sweeping the nation by seeking the security of totalitarian leadership. With Europe much in mind, writers wondered whether American democracy was being replaced with dictatorial power, soon to echo the Germans' cry of "Heil Hitler!" with "Heil Roosevelt!"[7]

Roosevelt's four terms in office have been regarded as one of the nation's most significant times of crisis. Democracy was threatened by the faltering economy to such an extent that many believed something like central planning or socialism was the only way to save it, while others worried that any such measures would weaken free markets and lead to either chaos or economic collapse. The rise of communism in Russia and fascism in Germany served as frightening examples of what could happen. Others worried that the US government was becoming autocratic. The arguments religious leaders advanced reflected these diverse views, not only as the opinions of individuals but also as resolutions formally adopted, as statements publicized in the nation's leading newspapers, in sermons, and in editorials expressing alternative arguments in widely circulated religious periodicals. The ways in which religious organizations mobilized constituents on different sides of the issues were fractious, to be sure, but at the same time contributed positively to the debate about what democracy was and how it could best be preserved.

The main lines of religious argumentation that developed in those years have continued to the present. Faith communities that focus on helping the poor through organized publicly funded programs and that worry about the corrupting influences of free market capitalism have mostly supported the kinds of government intervention in the economy that happened under the New Deal. In general, the impression that the New Deal did more to save democracy than to endanger it has made it possible for faith communities at this end of the spectrum to focus on how well or how poorly government programs were serving the needy and contributing to justice, equality, and equal rights as core principles of democracy. At the other end of the spectrum, religious leaders in the 1930s worried that the totalitarianism they associated with Roosevelt's administration posed a threat particularly to believers. They feared it set rulers above God, diminished the authority of the church, and destroyed believers' freedom to worship according to the dictates of their conscience.

How religious leaders addressed the threat of totalitarianism they saw in the 1930s is a valuable place to consider how religious diversity contributes to democracy. Because religion was diversely expressed and organized, it tackled the question of how best to safeguard democracy from multiple angles, ranging from strongly affirming the New Deal to warning of its dangers. In between these extremes, religious organizations served as venues for disagreements to be hashed out and for deliberations to be held with experts from labor, business, and universities. Frequently, the venues were clergy councils and board meetings. Just as frequently, the venues were church basements and fellowship halls where a speaker supporting the administration would be given the floor one week and a speaker with opposing views would come the following week.

Faith Communities' Diverse Responses

Ambivalence and indeed outright opposition to something like the authoritarian state the New Deal would be seen to represent was already an important theme in American politics in the years immediately preceding it. The 1928 presidential campaign between Herbert Hoover and Al Smith generated fear among Protestant leaders that the Democrats' Catholic nominee would introduce authoritarian rules from the Vatican that would dramatically compromise religious freedom. Dallas's Reverend Dr. George Washington Truett, who pastored the nation's largest Southern Baptist congregation, was among the most outspoken leaders warning of threats to religious freedom. In a 1920 address delivered from the steps of the US Capitol, Truett contrasted the biblical principle of "liberty" with the "ghastly tyranny" of "autocracy," referencing the difference not only in Baptist and Catholic theology but also in the recent clash of civilizations resulting in the Great War. "Autocracy dared in the morning of the twentieth century to crawl out of its ugly lair and proposed to substitute the law of the jungles for the law of human brotherhood," he declared. "For all time to come the hearts of men will stand aghast upon every thought of this incomparable death drama, and at the same time they will renew the vow that the few shall not presumptuously tyrannize over the many."[8]

Hoover's loss in 1932 cast him as a leading critic of FDR's emergency measures, which many saw as a dangerous expansion of federal government power. Hoover was a Quaker whose faith quietly stressed the inner guidance of the conscience by the Holy Spirit. This was hardly a religion of rugged individualism, despite sometimes being interpreted as precisely that, but it was an understanding of democracy that stressed individual freedom, personal responsibility, and charitable efforts rather than government programs.[9] In a 1933 letter to journalist Henry L. Stoddard, Hoover expressed concern that the nation's "moral anchors" of prudence, thrift, honesty, and frankness were being lost. "We are in the new era—the era of a new deal where white rabbits please and thrill the audience," he wrote.[10] *The Challenge to Liberty*, which Hoover published the following year, spelled out the contrast between small government liberalism and big government socialism. The latter consisted of expansive government administration and intervention in the economy, interference with the operations of farming and transportation, and a compromise of the Constitution and free press. It sounded very much like the New Deal.[11]

Pastors mostly expressed cautious optimism that Roosevelt's economic reforms would bring relief to the poor and jobless. At its 1932 national meeting, the Presbyterians' Committee on Social and Industrial Relations presented the results of a far-reaching report calling for denomination-wide discussions about unemployment and economic planning. Some of the Presbyterian leaders argued that states should be doing more to underwrite unemployment benefits, some thought the federal government should do more, some urged the church to be cautious about endorsing any such proposals, and others saw an opportunity to condemn capitalistic individualism entirely and to envision a new social order.[12] That summer at a meeting in Boston, speakers representing local Protestant, Unitarian, Jewish, and Catholic organizations repudiated individualism, agreed that charity was not enough, and called for new ideas for economic reform.[13] A few months earlier, the Federal Council of Churches had teamed with the Department of Social Action of the National Catholic Welfare Conference and the Social Justice Commission of the Central Conference of American Rabbis on a joint statement calling for appropriations from the federal government for public works and a program of unemployment insurance. Over the next few years, the signatories continued working on unemployment policies and supported the development of the National Labor Relations Act.[14]

Leaders who worried about the administration's centralization of power, though, cautioned that government expansion was inimical to both democracy and religious freedom. A 1933 editorial in the *Witness*, national weekly of the Protestant Episcopal Church, for example, warned of "fascism in the present set-up, with the possibility that we shall see a super-State created that will level down American life rather than raise it to the heights of which it is capable." Clergy should avoid "allowing the State to gobble up the church to use for its own purposes," the essay advised, citing government propaganda during the Great War as an example.[15] Similarly, a group of Presbyterian clergy strongly opposed the Committee on Social and Industrial Relations' recommendations. Other clergy worried that Roosevelt's dictatorial agenda aimed to redistribute wealth; they worried even more that some of their own number seemed to favor the administration's centralization of power. Another concern—warranted, as later information would show—was that government relief spending would lead to lower church charitable activity.[16]

Concern of this kind was sufficient that in December 1933, leaders who supported Roosevelt organized a conference in New York City on the "Religious Implications of the National Recovery Act," to which spokespersons for the administration as well as seminary professors and denominational officials were invited. Among the luminaries were National Industrial Recovery Act administration member William E. Sweet of Colorado, Roosevelt adviser and Columbia University president Adolf A. Berle Jr., and League for Industrial Democracy executive director Harry W. Laidler, as well as *Witness* editor and Church League for Industrial Democracy executive secretary Dr. William B. Spofford. Speakers emphasized the severity of the economic challenges facing the nation and reminded the conferees of their commitment to the churches' "social creed" of advocacy for fair competition, economic redistribution, a living wage, and restrictions on child labor. The same week, Roosevelt addressed the annual convention of the Federal Council of Churches, calling on the twenty-five denominations represented to stand with him in the struggle to uphold spiritual and social values.[17] Earlier that fall, the president had met with 3,600 delegates to the annual meeting of the National Conference of Catholic Charities, reassuring them that government efforts to rehabilitate the economy would not undermine the church's nongovernment service programs.

The administration's hope was for churches not only to align themselves with specific policies but to envision the New Deal as a spiritual awakening. The churches' task was ideological or, as they were encouraged to think, theological. The New Deal would bring to pass something akin to a new millennium. In a 1934 essay, Secretary of Agriculture Henry A. Wallace envisioned the New Deal being accompanied by a social transformation as profound as the Protestant Reformation: the human heart would be changed, the spiritual vacuum would be filled, self-interest and greed would be replaced by community-mindedness, people would "join together in a modern adaptation of the theocracy of old."[18] Embracing Wallace's vision, a Methodist bishop in Detroit declared, "We shall move into a new social order, essentially Christian at the core, or we shall slump back into paganism and night."[19]

But it was a challenge to persuade other religious leaders that the New Deal was a good idea. The churches were either "silent or critical" of the plan, a spokesperson for the New Deal told a crowd at the University of Virginia in 1934. The Jesuit Philosophical Society, meeting in Washington that year, predicted the New Deal would be ineffective.

At a meeting the following year, the Methodist Federation for Social Service charged the administration with having neglected the "forgotten man." The money changers were back in the temple, the group declared, top heavy with bureaucrats wasting the public's money. In Philadelphia that spring, an Episcopal leader denounced the New Deal as a program "conceived in a lunatic asylum" and "administered by lunatics." Another leader called it "hot tamale stuff that impedes recovery."[20] A meeting of the American Unitarian Association expressed greater support for government action but insisted that fundamental guarantees of free speech, free press, and freedom of assembly not be compromised.[21] Mormon leaders registered concern about federal relief transgressing the church's charitable functions. The New Deal, they feared, was government regimentation similar to the dictatorial assaults on religion occurring in Europe.[22] In Chicago, Dr. Lacy K. Williams, who headed the nation's largest African American Baptist denomination and cochaired the Baptist World Alliance with Dallas's George Washington Truett, was also skeptical, calling the New Deal an "insidious mixture of communism and socialism" leading to a godless society. "The press, public education, a free and untrammeled ballot as well as a free church," he asserted," should be "the basis of an abiding democracy of the type which all Americans, of no matter what racial strain, seek and must preserve."[23]

When the White House solicited input from the clergy in late summer 1935, many of the letters expressed practical concerns, such as whether the textile industry would be protected, how farmers would be affected, and what specifically would be done to regulate public utilities. Clergy were interested in how Social Security would be administered, whether they would be included, and what would be done to regulate liquor.[24] These were the issues that Catholic leaders discussed when they met in Los Angeles that spring and that Methodists discussed in Atlanta and that National Baptists discussed in Chicago: how employers and workers would be affected, what was happening to agriculture, and how clergy could better meet the needs of the unemployed. In addition, religious leaders voiced concerns about the centralization of power itself. Centralization struck clergy as implying regulation, bureaucracy, a dampening of individuality, and a peril to the Constitution.

They worried that Roosevelt's plans were inimical to the God-given right to own private property. Too much power, some said, was like too much liquor: it addled the brain.[25]

The most supportive groups were clergy and lay leaders working on labor issues—groups such as the National Religion and Labor Foundation, the Fellowship of Socialist Christians, the United Christian Council for Democracy, and the American Association for Economic Freedom. Supportive groups also included departments within denominations such as the Presbyterian Committee on Social and Industrial Relations and the Social Service Commission of the Episcopal Diocese of New York. Many of these groups had been working with labor leaders for better wages and protection against unemployment and now saw the New Deal as a step in the right direction. They also recognized that an economic reform of this magnitude carried implications for their particular constituencies. It wasn't only that democracy was being threatened or strengthened. It was rather that the opportunities and constraints in the lives of individual citizens were being changed. For example, Jewish leaders pondered how standardized working hours would affect the Sabbath. Christian leaders challenged workers to stick with the church instead of deciding that labor unions and government were their best sources of support. And in the ethnically and racially divided working-class neighborhoods of Detroit, Pittsburgh, Chicago, and other cities with high unemployment, it was not uncommon for pastors and priests to be engaged in labor organizing, working among the particular groups of Poles, Italians, Hungarians, African Americans, and others with whom they were most closely associated.[26]

The political dynamics of the era were sufficiently complicated, of course, that religious leaders' positions reflected opinions on multiple issues rather than only on the role of government in reforming the economy. Corruption and racketeering were concerns that prompted even Roosevelt's supporters to qualify their support. In 1930, for example, during his tenure as New York governor, Roosevelt had faced criticism from the powerful City Affairs Committee of New York under the direction of a distinguished panel of educators, attorneys, and clergy that included philosopher John Dewey, socialists Norman Thomas and Heywood Broun, writer Paul Blanchard, Methodist bishop Francis J. McConnell, Madison Avenue Community Church pastor John Haynes Holmes, and Free Synagogue rabbi Stephen S. Wise. By 1931 Holmes and Wise had mobilized a large coalition of the city's clergy, including Episcopalians, Presbyterians, Lutherans, Congregationalists, and Unitarians as well as the Anti-Saloon League and other Prohibition advocates and socialists, to draft charges against Mayor Jimmy Walker and to call on Roosevelt to launch a formal investigation. In one of his rare instances of criticizing clergy, Roosevelt accused Holmes and Wise of grandstanding and stood behind the mayor until Walker resigned. Holmes and Wise became supporters of the New Deal but increasingly turned their attention to issues it did not address to their satisfaction, including racial equality and civil liberties and assisting in founding the NAACP and ACLU.[27]

Holmes and Wise's collaboration was interesting less because one was Christian and the other Jewish than because it was one of the many ways in which religious leaders organized to bring diverse perspectives to bear on the most important issues of the day. Many of these organizations came into existence during or immediately before and after World War I, reflecting the diverse paths that brought individuals into positions of local or national leadership. For Holmes and Wise, it was serving large, well-financed New York congregations largely independent of denominational constraints and serving on civic committees. For National Religion and Labor Foundation executive director Jerome Davis, it was heading YMCA work in Russia during the war, where he acquired sympathies for socialism, subsequently holding a faculty position at Yale Divinity School and using his credentials to attract cooperation from Reinhold Niebuhr, Jane Addams, and Norman Thomas. Methodist Federation for Social Service chair Harry F. Ward was one of the Federal Council of Churches' leaders, authoring its Social Creed, serving on the faculty at Union Theological Seminary, and in 1934 founding the American League Against War and Fascism. Others, notably Sherwood Eddy and Reinhold Niebuhr, cooperated in

organizations ranging from youth ministries to experiments in cooperative farming, and still others, such as the leaders of Catholic Charities
and the Federation of Jewish Charities, drew on networks of social service agencies to provide information about numbers of families in need
and how government programs were helping. The positions these
organizations took and the networks they forged represented the various connections of religious leadership at the top with both national
and international interests.[28]

The convening power nationally prominent religious leaders enjoyed
was matched locally by clergy who organized forums to discuss the New
Deal's implications. Many of these meetings were neither supportive
nor critical of the New Deal but simply concerned with understanding
its implications. To that end, the gatherings included business owners,
labor leaders, public officials, professors, clergy, and interested laypeople as well as spokespersons for government programs. For example, an
African Methodist Episcopal Zion church convened a meeting in Yonkers in 1936 at which 150 attendees heard addresses by the pastor, a
judge, a local political candidate, and a New Deal commissioner. Similar
forums were organized by the African Methodist Episcopal Speaker's
Club in Atlanta, Greater New York Conference of Presbyterians, Boston
Baptist Social Union, Church League for Industrial Democracy in Baltimore, St. James Congregational Church Forum in Cleveland, and
California Universalist Convention in Los Angeles. These meetings
provided participants with opportunities to discuss the New Deal's impact on their communities and to debate whether they thought it was
going too far or not far enough and what else might be done to promote
economic recovery.[29]

Besides discussing ideas, religious organizations initiated a variety of
service activities. One emphasis, illustrated by the National Religion
and Labor Foundation, the Methodist Social Service Committee, and
the Council for Social Action in the Congregational and Christian
Churches, expanded churches' support of labor organizations.[30] Another focus was the consumers' cooperative movement, which by 1935
included more than six thousand local organizations through which

farmers sold grain and purchased supplies and independent oil companies produced fuel. The cooperative movement received support from church-sponsored seminars and investment and through organizations such as the Christian Cooperative Fellowship in the Midwest and the Delta Cooperative in the South.[31] Yet another focus was the formation of citywide and statewide social welfare agencies such as the Virginia Conference on Church Social Work, organized in 1937 on the model of smaller programs in Norfolk and Richmond.[32] As with other initiatives, the clergy and lay leaders who endorsed these various programs had to defend their views against adversaries who accused them of promoting socialism and deviating from the churches' spiritual ministries.[33]

Congregations' programs nearly always emphasized relief—food, shelter, clothing, job placement, financial advice, and counseling—for families affected by the economic crisis. The severity and scale of the crisis went beyond the means of all but the best-funded deacons' funds and parish relief committees, sometimes undermining the authority of church leaders and causing resentment among needy parishioners.[34] Nevertheless, congregations innovated as best they could. Whereas the New Deal programs had far more financial resources on which to draw, congregations had the advantage of being able to adapt in varied ways to local situations. For example, a study of Los Angeles congregations in 1935 found at least six distinct strategies for providing relief: serving large numbers of individuals and families directly in multiple ways that included food and shelter as well as cash, focusing on a particular need or clientele such as single mothers or the homeless, referring prospective clients to public agencies, partnering with nearby congregations, partnering with secular agencies, and raising money or hosting informational meetings. The strategies congregations adopted depended on the resources they could mobilize and the specific needs in their respective communities. One of the most active congregations was the Angelus Temple, founded in 1923 by Pentecostal evangelist Aimee Semple McPherson, which in 1936 alone through its Commissary Department supplied bread, vegetables, canned goods, and cash assistance to more than ten thousand families. In contrast, First Christian Church, a downtown congregation with fewer members and resources, worked cooperatively with a neighboring Methodist congregation to sponsor educational lectures on social issues by city and county officials and representatives of social work agencies.[35]

By 1936 the New Deal programs gained modestly greater acceptance among grassroots clergy, owing partly to Roosevelt's Good Neighbor League under the direction of Reverend Dr. Stanley High and subsequently under the supervision of Reverend Charles Stelzle. High was a Methodist from Nebraska who served as a flier in World War I, worked for the Methodist Board of Foreign Missions after the war, edited the nondenominational *Christian Herald*, lectured on behalf of Prohibition, and supported Hoover in 1932 before joining Roosevelt's team and becoming one of the president's inner circle. Stelzle was a Presbyterian who had grown up in tenement quarters on New York City's Lower East Side, worked during his childhood at a sweatshop and later as a machinist, held office in the YMCA, pastored a large congregation in St. Louis, and worked with the Anti-Saloon League before turning his attention to labor organizing and establishing the Presbyterian Department of Church and Labor.[36] The Good Neighbor League promoted the administration's policies through lectures at churches and essays published in church periodicals. Roosevelt hoped the effort would generate strong networks of local support, an aspiration that achieved some success in reaching clergy. However, many religious leaders remained unconvinced. For example, at a patriotic service in honor of Abraham Lincoln, Reverend Dr. Norman Vincent Peale of New York's Marble Collegiate Church asserted, "The New Deal is the worst blight social progress has ever experienced. What this country needs is less intelligentsia and more commonsensia."[37] Equally critical, Yale Divinity School dean emeritus Charles R. Brown published a scathing attack in which he wrote: "With a playboy in the White House, a mere opportunist who caters to popular feeling and whose chief desire is to make himself agreeable, who openly disregards his promises, who acts as the wind blows and who does not know what to do, thoughtful people of the North, South, East and West are considering the importance of having a more desirable type to control the economic order."[38]

Brown's remarks articulated what worried many of Roosevelt's critics. The president's wealthy background and upscale mannerisms contrasted sharply with the down-to-earth, homespun, commonsense values on which people in small rural congregations sought to conduct their lives. When people complained about the New Deal being dictatorial, they meant not only that Washington was telling them what to do but also that Roosevelt's authoritarian style was distant, arrogant, aristocratic, and untrustworthy. He was too wealthy, too brash, too flashy, and too eager to organize life under bureaucratic rules. They might vote for him because they were down and out and hoping for a better day, but government run by a man like that was fundamentally at odds with how they looked at human nature. And that was troubling well beyond the cultural differences it implied because the New Deal, as they saw it, represented nothing less than a threat to American democracy. "It was a new deal that put Russia where she is today [and] a new deal that put Germany where she is today," a Methodist layman wrote to a small midwestern newspaper in 1936. "It might be a new deal that takes your right to vote away from you. They have taken everything else away from us so let's think twice before we vote."[39]

It especially rankled church leaders already skeptical of the administration's plans when it became known that the Good Neighbor League was being run from Washington as a concerted effort to unite Protestant, Catholic, and Jewish organizations in support of Roosevelt's policies. Presbyterian leader Reverend Dr. Hugh T. Kerr of Pittsburgh was among several prominent clergy who accused the league of underhanded intervention in church affairs. "Curtailment of religious freedom," fellow Presbyterian Dr. John McDowell of New York declared, "may be all right for Russia, Germany, and Italy, but it is all wrong in America."[40] African American clergy whom the league had courted expressed skepticism as well. At a meeting in Harlem, two hundred African American clergy unanimously adopted resolutions criticizing the league's "hypocritical bid" for the Negro vote.[41] On a larger scale an unscientific poll conducted by the Literary Digest among some twenty thousand clergy across the nation representing predominantly White denominations found that 70 percent did not favor the New Deal.[42] Lay members were more evenly divided, but except among Roman Catholics they too were concerned. An early Gallup Poll estimated that 78 percent of Catholics were for Roosevelt, but only 46 percent of Baptists, 43 percent of Methodists, and 37 percent of Presbyterians and Episcopalians.[43]

The high percentage of Catholics who supported Roosevelt in 1936, Gallup noted, nevertheless represented an eight-point decline from four years earlier, prompting analysts to suggest that criticism within the church was having an effect. The most vocal critic was Father Charles Coughlin, whose weekly radio broadcasts reached hundreds of thousands of listeners. Coughlin's isolationism and anti-Semitism led to the cancellation of his radio program in 1939, but during most of the decade he received thousands of letters from loyal supporters and generous coverage in newspapers, especially those owned by William Randolph Hearst, who supported 1936 Republican presidential candidate Alf Landon. Whether listeners were persuaded that Roosevelt was sympathetic to communism or doing too little to support the church in other countries, Roosevelt's supporters worried that the criticisms were having an effect. "Sunday after Sunday, special sermons were preached in all the churches, directly against communism and indirectly, in most cases, against Roosevelt," an essayist observed in 1937. "Boys and girls in Catholic schools came home to tell their parents how the priests and nuns were against Roosevelt."[44]

But clergy organizations for the most part directed criticism less at Roosevelt than at his policies. "There has been set up what is called a planned economy," a gathering of Methodists stated. "What the individual needs today isn't a planned economy, but a planned regeneration." The Southern Baptist Convention decreed that the nation's supreme need in the face of depressed economic conditions was simply "to return to God in humble confession of sin." One of its leaders added, "Like the prodigal son, the New Deal has wasted its substance in riotous living." He could see no benefit coming from the "idiocies" of the administration's various programs.[45]

Criticisms of the New Deal

The arguments that went beyond name-calling criticized the administration's programs on several grounds. The fear of dictatorial power that worried critics was heightened by Roosevelt's personal visibility in championing government change and thus in bringing comparisons with Stalin and Hitler to mind. Totalitarianism European-style necessarily evoked fear that religious freedom would die—a special concern of Jews and other religious minorities. "Beware of a totalitarian government concentrated in Washington," Chicago attorney Salmon Oliver Levinson wrote in an essay titled "To My American Fellow Jews." "For in this concentration are the seeds of autocratic and bureaucratic power, the power to suppress, persecute, and ostracize minorities. And we Jews are now the most vulnerable of all minorities."[46]

The related concern was that Roosevelt's centralization of power would be used to effect a permanent transformation in the basic principles on which the society had functioned though most of its history. It was perhaps inevitable that programs advanced not only as emergency measures but as heralds of a new social order were met with skepticism. The claim from clergy supporting the New Deal that it would fulfill Christ's demands for an equitable distribution of wealth straightforwardly contradicted the way many Christians understood the Bible. To some, it seemed too optimistic and to others too easy. It ran against the grain of an American spirit conditioned to hardship, struggle, and discipline. It depended too much on esoteric ideas about monetary policies and not enough on old-fashioned ingenuity and sacrifice.

Reverend Dr. Carl Christian Hein was one of many prominent denominational leaders who feared the unsettling effects of the New Deal. Hein was a German immigrant who had come to the United States as a fifteen-year-old and settled in Columbus, Ohio, where he graduated from college and seminary. After ministering to congregations in Wisconsin and Michigan, he returned to Ohio and from 1930 until his death in 1937 was president of the American Lutheran Church and in that capacity was a frequent speaker at church conferences. The denomination, with congregations scattered from New York across the

Midwest to Iowa and in Texas and California, included some five hundred thousand members. At a district conference in 1935, Hein addressed the concerns about communism, rumors of war, and the economy that reflected the views of many in his denomination, arguing that current legislation inimical to God's laws "can only bring chaos" to the nation. "The corruption in the heart of humanity can be eradicated only by the application of the principles of Christianity," he declared. "Conditions will be righted only when men's hearts shall have changed." America had fought to defeat dictators and make the world safe for democracy, but he worried now that the New Deal was leading the nation into folly.[47]

Criticism of the New Deal reflected the view that local control of the kind present in families, churches, and communities would be replaced by government codes, rules, and regulations. "Regimentation," Henry Steele Commager wrote in 1934, was the threat people perceived endangering their liberties and constitutional rights. This was the fear that later generations would interpret as the imposition from industrialization, urbanization, and the growth of large bureaucracies on individuals' freedom to make choices in their daily lives. It was big government telling people what to do, what to eat, how to raise their children, and, if they were farmers, what they could grow. That was clearly a concern to Americans in the 1930s who had been used to the idea—if not the reality—of living in a nation of few government constraints. It was not the only concern, though.[48] Another concern was that central planning would result in chaos. The economic theory underpinning this argument was the view that markets provided the best guarantee of societal well-being, at least in the long run, and that government intervention in markets was destined to fail. The theological argument was nearly the same. Unregulated markets were consistent with divine laws. Human efforts to plan the kind of programs the New Deal represented were inevitably flawed by human frailty. Greed, shortsightedness, limited information, and limited intelligence would create insuperable difficulties. Even worse, a meeting of New England Methodists concluded, the New Deal would dampen public morale and impair confidence in social institutions.[49]

True reform, critics charged, depended on personal regeneration rather than government programs. One of the outspoken Catholic critics of the New Deal was Father John D. McCarthy of St. Patrick's Cathedral in New York City. McCarthy likened the era Western civilization was currently experiencing to dusk, when the sky is still luminous but darkness is soon to fall. Without moral regeneration, all the government programs in the world could do nothing. "No effective government or social sanction has been found," he contended, "to curb the nasty salacious writers, editors, publishers and producers who with sex obscenities, suggestions, nudities, lewdities and, God save us, science, debauch the immortal souls of men." The New Deal might succeed, he thought, but it was only a symptom of deeper malaise.[50]

The theology beneath remarks like McCarthy's ran deeper than sentiments based only on current affairs. It was the same commonsense outlook that had always asserted the value of people eschewing evil and pursuing the good. Ida Tarbell of muckraking fame, nearing her eightieth birthday, expressed it well in 1937 when she told a reporter, "I fear these are bad new days; nothing but laws, laws, laws. As if we could make people do right by laws! We are trying to bring about things legally that can only be brought about ethically." She thought maybe she was old-fashioned, but she was proud to say, "I still believe in my Bible. If in the past more people had accepted its spirit, we should not have had the bad old days; if more people will believe in it, we shall have good new ones."[51]

Historian Alison Collis Greene examined hundreds of letters to the White House from clergy located mostly in the South and concluded that apprehension about the New Deal was widespread. Theological and ethical concerns like McCarthy's and Tarbell's prevailed. But the clergy also perceived a threat to the churches' authority. The administration's programs seemed to be run at the top by Roosevelt's cronies who had little understanding of local affairs and at the bottom by men and women with no interest in incorporating the churches into their affairs. "It seemed clearer than ever to the New Deal's opponents," Greene wrote, "that the expanded federal state encroached dangerously on the churches' moral authority at both the local and legislative levels. A larger and more powerful state, they feared, meant a smaller and less powerful church."[52]

By 1938, the prospect of Roosevelt running for a third term, coming on the heels of the president's widely criticized effort to expand the Supreme Court, stoked additional concerns about tyranny emanating from Washington. The concerns varied, some of them driven by personal dislike of Roosevelt, but many of them reflecting the view that too much power over too long a period was being held by too few people at the top. When journalist Joseph Leib—a Roosevelt supporter—sent letters to eighty prominent church leaders around the country, not one favored the president having another term. Opposition included the president of the Federal Council of Churches; several Episcopal, Methodist, and Catholic bishops; and the pastors of regionally dispersed Presbyterian, Baptist, and United Brethren in Christ congregations.[53] Catholic leaders were especially worried that Roosevelt's expanding power might include a takeover of parochial schools.[54]

Organized Opposition to the New Deal

In addition to the opposition expressed in sermons and at church gatherings, several well-organized special interest groups emerged. One was the American Liberty League, which began in 1934 and soon claimed to have 150,000 members (a number that historians believe was exaggerated). The league described the New Deal as radical alien collectivism, an Americanized copy of Old World dictatorship, and a threat to both the US Constitution and the American way of life. It harked back to the "Red Scare" of the 1920s, likening the New Deal to the godless Soviet Union and asserting that it desecrated America's sacred ideals. The league's leadership was composed of business owners, lawyers, Republican officeholders, conservative Democrats, and a few clergy. Although its criticisms of the New Deal were not based primarily on religious arguments, it included religious freedom among the principles it said were threatened by Roosevelt's policies.[55]

In 1936 the league sponsored a prime-time radio broadcast by former New York governor and 1928 Democratic presidential candidate

Al Smith in which Smith lambasted the New Deal and challenged fellow Democrats to turn Roosevelt into a one-term president. Major newspapers printed the entire speech and smaller newspapers across the country repeated its central themes. The New Deal, Smith charged, had not reduced the cost of federal government but created new departments; it had increased the national debt, helped the rich and harmed the poor, abridged the rights of states, centralized relief programs, and violated the Constitution. The National Industrial Recovery Act, he said, was a "vast octopus set up by government." Its leaders had "stolen the livery of the church to do the work of the devil." Elected officials, Smith declared, should remember placing their hands on the Bible and swearing an oath not only to the Constitution but also to God. He challenged them to recall the story of the prodigal son. "Stop wasting your substance in a foreign land and come back to your Father's house."[56]

The league achieved limited success, despite producing large numbers of pamphlets and sponsoring dozens of lectures. Its failure owed much to Roosevelt's allies accusing it of being in the pocket of big business—an accusation based on the league's extensive support from the DuPonts—and thus tarnishing its appeal to ordinary voters.[57] Its opposition to Prohibition and its lack of clear religious leadership and language also kept it from reaching the nation's churchgoers.[58] However, as law scholar Jared Goldstein has shown, the league articulated a kind of "constitutional nationalism" that emphasized strict adherence to an original interpretation of the Constitution as an almost sacred principle of American identity, and any deviation from that standard, such as the New Deal, as an existential threat to the American way of life. The league's short-term effect in asserting the priority of judicial interpretation of the Constitution was to temper Roosevelt's attacks on the US Supreme Court; its longer-term impact was evident in similar ideas being expressed among conservative Republicans through the rest of the century.[59]

The group that did better at organizing grassroots opposition was the Spiritual Mobilization movement, which started in 1935 under the direction of Reverend James W. Fifield Jr., pastor of a thriving Congregational church in residential Los Angeles. Fifield forged a national network of clergy on the model of the Moral Rearmament movement and quietly cultivated the support of the National Association of Manufacturers and wealthy business leaders such as Armstrong Cork president H. W. Prentis Jr. and Sun Oil president J. Howard Pew. Like the American Liberty League, Spiritual Mobilization championed individualism, property rights, and (to a greater extent than the league) the positive power of believing in Christ.[60] These views when applied to economic policies were directly opposed to the arguments being advanced by progressive religious leaders about social justice and redistributive programs. Reinhold Niebuhr passionately denounced Fifield, writing: "He claims that his movement is purely religious and not political because he never explicitly identifies the 'pagan statism' which he regards as the enemy of religious freedom." To Niebuhr it was clear that Fifield's objections were leveled specifically at the New Deal. "His millionaire supporters are under no illusion about this," Niebuhr complained. "They give him all the money he needs to make this supposedly religious, but actually political, attack upon their foes."[61] Historian Kevin M. Kruse argues that Fifield's organization became the progenitor of a popular brand of Christian libertarianism that continued to promote small government ideas under the guise of Christian economics and receive support from business elites well into the 1950s.[62]

A third organization that mobilized against the New Deal called itself the America Forward Movement for Religion and Americanism. In 1936, a month before the fall presidential campaign began in earnest, America Forward organized the National Conference of Clergymen and Laymen, a three-day assembly at Asheville, North Carolina, attended by more than a thousand church leaders concerned that New Deal supporters in their denominations were leading the churches toward a communist takeover. Speakers railed against atheism, radicalism, the Federal Council of Churches, social action meetings on college campuses, and faculty at seminaries they said were encouraging attacks on the social order. The principal organizer was Reverend Ralph E. Nollner, a Southern Methodist pastor from Houston who earlier in the year had launched an anticommunist movement called the League of

Ten Million that spread the movement's message through his magazine, the *Christian American*, and in coming months organized "Americanist" meetings in New York City, Chicago, Indianapolis, and other locations across the South and Midwest.[63] The Asheville conclave illustrated two contending aspects of small-government advocacy that would be present in every subsequent effort to mobilize Christian sentiment against perceptions of government expansion. The first was an inevitable ambiguity of purpose and political orientation as advocacy drew from various constituencies and sought to merge these groups to form larger coalitions. The second was a tendency amid these ambiguities for identities to form along preexisting theological divides.

America Forward, like the Liberty League, drew support from Democratic leaders who had been opposed to Roosevelt's nomination in 1932, Republicans who hoped to regain power in 1936, industrialists, Prohibitionists, and progressives who by and large favored the New Deal but thought it should be implemented differently. The ambiguities associated with the movement's aims were abundantly evident in its selection of keynote speaker Retired Admiral Richmond Pearson Hobson for the Asheville conference. Hobson had achieved fame during the Spanish-American War, served as a Democratic representative from Alabama, and was a former member of the Anti-Saloon League and champion of national Prohibition, founder of the World Narcotic Defense Association, and organizer of the Constitutional Democracy Association, which he started in 1935. He was also an advocate for women's suffrage, railroad regulation, and federal support for education and highway construction. Hobson could hardly be considered an opponent of government expansion in toto, but he could appeal in varying ways to clergy disturbed at the recent repeal of Prohibition, lay leaders worried about Roosevelt's centralization of power, and patriots of all kinds wanting a strong military to fight communism and fascism.[64] The difficulty of holding together these various constituencies came to the fore before the conference ended when more than a hundred clergy walked out, insisting that Christianity should be more clearly emphasized, Jewish delegates expelled, and clearer statements about communism embraced. Among the dissidents was Kansas fundamentalist Reverend

Gerald R. Winrod, whose radio broadcasts mobilized anticommunist sentiment well into the 1950s.[65]

The tendency to divide along deeper theological lines ran through and simplified these competing orientations. Since its inception in 1911 the Federal Council of Churches had been a lightning rod for theological divisions. Modernists in mostly northern mainline Protestant denominations favored its ecumenical work, while fundamentalists as well as moderate clergy in southern and midwestern denominations opposed it. In addition to supporting the Federal Council of Churches, modernists generally were receptive to historical criticism that interpreted the Bible with reference to the periods and perspectives of its authors, while fundamentalists believed the Bible to be timeless and inerrant in all things. The two also differed in understandings of the direction of civilization, the former asserting that progress was dominant, and the latter arguing that conditions would worsen until the second coming of Jesus.

Partisan Divisions

Theological divisions that mapped as clearly onto regional differences as these did naturally fractured along political lines as well. Republican presidential candidate Alf Landon's 1936 presidential campaign, despite its weak showing, garnered support from scattered Protestant clergy in historically Republican states across the Midwest and West. Democratic opposition to Roosevelt was led by Georgia governor Eugene Talmadge, whose "Jeffersonian Democrats" worked against Roosevelt's reelection in 1936 with financial support from seventy-five-year-old Texas oil and lumber magnate John Henry Kirby. Kirby's political activities included founding the Southern Committee to Uphold the Constitution, and his assistant, Vance Muse, was known to have distributed photos of Eleanor Roosevelt in mixed-race company in efforts to damage the president's chances among White voters. The principal argument Jeffersonian Democrats advanced on behalf of small government appealed to the Constitution, which placed power not in the hands of the federal government but in the will of the people. Government that interfered with property rights and related financial decisions was thus in their view anathema.

Government abridgment of constitutional liberty resonated deeply with decades-old sectional grievances. "Many of those heroes of ours died for states' rights but the principle did not die," Kirby declared to an audience in Macon in 1936. "Though secession came to an end at Appomattox the liberty of the people to enjoy their constitutional blessings and safeguards was not yielded and will never be yielded. It is the eternal faith of our republic and will live on as long as our republic lives."[66]

It was difficult to see that programs designed to help the nation's economy recover directly threatened the churches, especially when New Deal proponents noted that churches, just like families, might be eligible for loans to repair houses of worship. In one instance, though, critics seized on evidence that the federal government had no respect for religion. That was the Tennessee Valley Authority, a surprising focus, except that the TVA was apparently operating without regard for the spiritual needs of the people it employed. The problem was that the TVA had created Norris, Tennessee, a town of three thousand people, to build the Norris dam but had not provided them with a place of worship. This, despite providing at taxpayers' expense a recreation hall, vocational school, and even a troop of "garden missionaries from Washington" to help the locals raise vegetables. Hearing the story, Senator Talmadge turned it to his advantage in attacking the New Deal. "They won't allow a church built in the town," he inveighed in speeches. "You preachers check up on that. The reason is the church is at cross purposes with communism."[67]

Southern Democrats' resistance to the New Deal further occasioned the return of a Christian-based populism that would surface repeatedly in small-government appeals. A reporter for the *New York Herald Tribune* who attended the Jeffersonian Democrats' convention at which Kirby spoke in 1936 wrote that the "spellbinders of Southern swamps and hills, the evangelistic rabble-rousers of remote plantations and the politicians of small-town life of the South sweated forth a fiery call for revolt." The meeting harked back to Huey Long, the Ku Klux Klan, and memories of the Civil War. "An old farmer, mustached, chin-whiskered, in soiled brown shirt and trousers and no socks . . . started an impromptu speech: 'God pity them and forgive them.' He meant the 'brain trusters' and 'wreckers' at Washington."

The most outspoken member of the clergy at the gathering was Reverend Gerald L. K. Smith, a Disciples of Christ minister from Wisconsin who pastored churches in the Midwest before moving to Louisiana in 1928. Smith impressed the reporter as the star of the show. "Yes, we said, 'give us meat and bread,'" Smith declared, "but we did not ask for Harvard Venetian Frankfurters served up on White House toast." Roosevelt and his "commissars," Smith said, were turning the Negroes toward communism and undermining the Bible. "I still have my God, my Bible, my Constitution and my America," he declared, but they were being threatened by the federal government. "What shall we do? Give me the flag, the Bible, the Constitution. We will build bonfires under that flag, we will march under it, we will restore the Constitution."[68]

North Carolina senator Josiah Bailey was one of the southern Democrats' most fervent New Deal critics. Initially supportive of the administration's emergency recovery efforts, he was increasingly distrustful of Roosevelt's expanding power. The grandson and son of Baptist preachers and the former editor of a Baptist periodical, Bailey issued a statement in 1935 reflecting, he said, his religious convictions: "Being a Baptist, I am liberal, and believe in liberty. Being a Democrat, I am a liberal and believe in liberty. Once we abandon the voluntary principles, we run squarely into Communism. . . . There can be no half-way control."[69] In 1937 Bailey authored an unsuccessful bipartisan "conservative manifesto" aimed at slowing the New Deal and came under attack by the NAACP for opposing civil rights and antilynching legislation. Arguing to solve "economic, social, and racial questions in the Southern way," he opposed northern politicians' hand in current affairs. "We fought one battle for white supremacy," he declared, "and we are ready to fight another, if necessary. If this means that we must do without federal aid, we will do without it."[70]

The most significant theological reflection about the dangers of New Deal–style government stemmed from influential conservative

Protestant leaders who had distanced themselves from the Social Gospel and from historical criticism and who embraced a premillennial form of apocalyptic thinking. Premillennial theology anticipated the imminent second coming of Christ and taught that the end times prior to the second advent would be fraught with increasing evil. It was this interpretation of history that cast the New Deal in particularly ominous terms. The New Deal in this view was not only a passing tyranny that might be remedied by legislation. It was indicative of the end times, as was the rise of Stalin, Hitler, and Mussolini.

Historian Matthew Avery Sutton, who has traced the political thinking of conservative Protestant leaders during this period better than anyone, argues that they consistently regarded Roosevelt as an Antichrist or at least as a harbinger of the end times. Remarks to this effect were evident in the sermons and writings of the most influential conservative Protestant leaders of the 1930s. Among them were Texas megachurch pastor J. Frank Norris, Los Angeles radio preacher Charles E. Fuller, Boston's Park Street Church pastor Harold J. Ockenga (future president of Fuller Seminary), Wheaton College president J. Oliver Buswell, future Billy Graham father-in-law and southern Presbyterian pastor Nelson Bell, Dallas Theological Seminary founder Lewis Sperry Chafer, *Sword of the Lord* publisher John R. Rice, and the editors of such popular magazines as *Moody Monthly* and the *Sunday School Times*. In the economic turmoil of the Depression and in Roosevelt's rise to power they saw the fulfillment of biblical prophecy leading to a dictatorship replacing democracy.[71] The best hedge against government tyranny was not to retreat in anticipation of Jesus's return but to work hard at keeping the church strong and to be vigilant as citizens. Small government let Christians do the Lord's work, which was the only sure way to combat ideas and policies contrary to the Word of God. This was a case that made sense to the many conservative Protestant Christians who would become known as evangelicals in the 1940s and who would become a powerful organized force for social and fiscal conservatism in the 1980s and beyond.[72]

The fact that these conservative Protestants became increasingly powerful in the last quarter of the twentieth century has reinforced the impression that White Protestant hegemony exerted its power and suc-cessfully resisted any groups challenging its privileged position, espe-cially Catholics, Jews, African Americans, and feminists. This view makes a great deal of sense when studies consistently demonstrate the anti-Catholicism, anti-Semitism, racism, and genderism that prevailed. Yet this view underestimates the religious diversity that did exist in the 1930s. Although the White Protestantism that prevailed was a dominant cultural influence, it was not unified. It was sufficiently fragmented and sufficiently limited that it provided spaces in which innovative and in-deed unpopular ideas were debated. When the focus of so much atten-tion was on the economy and on whether the New Deal was good or bad for American democracy, the venues in which religious deliberation occurred were frequently the places in which back-burner and marginal-ized issues were kept alive.

Racial equality was one of these issues. Historians have argued that the administration's dependence on the support of White southern Democrats kept it from effectively addressing segregation and voter suppression. White Protestant and Catholic leaders in the North fo-cused mostly on other issues, too, but one of the side benefits of these religious organizations being as diverse as they were was that church meetings served as forums in which racial issues were discussed and clergy could testify at hearings on these issues. Across the South, as lynching continued and White legislators, many of whom were active churchgoers, refused to back antilynching bills, antilynching advocacy grew in scattered congregations among pastors linked through com-missions on interracial cooperation and among churchwomen who had campaigned earlier in the century for women's suffrage. By 1933, when Franklin Roosevelt declared his support for antilynching legisla-tion at a meeting of church leaders in Cleveland, the Association of Southern Women for the Prevention of Lynching had branches in thir-teen states. In addition, the strongest voices for racial equality were from African American leaders, increasingly expressed through the legal work of the NAACP but also from powerful Black clergy, such as Chicago's Dr. Williams, New York's Reverend Adam Clayton Powell, and scholars such as W.E.B. DuBois and Benjamin Mays who wrote about racial segregation in religion and challenged clergy to address economic issues.[73]

In Retrospect

To many twenty-first-century writers who recall the New Deal era as one of the brightest episodes in democratic administration, the rancorous criticism levied by small-government religious leaders is difficult to appreciate. Many accounts ignore it or treat it as backwater populism. The criticism in fact did little to impede the implementation of New Deal policies. It did contribute, however, to the debate about what democracy should be, how it should be practiced, and what it implied for American values and for religion. The criticism was internally divided, stemming from the different regional, ethnic, and racial identities that Niebuhr described and, beyond that, reflecting debates within the hierarchies of major denominations. Spokespersons contended with one another, whether in opposition to the New Deal or in support of it, in ways that called on constituents to consider alternatives and policy modifications and to think about how the New Deal was affecting their relationships as citizens to the federal government. Vying for influence prompted religious leaders at times to challenge other leaders directly and at other times to join forces across religious lines.

Denominational and interdenominational organizations supplied the mechanisms through which people with differing views convened to discuss their differences. At one extreme, clergy felt strongly that the supreme danger facing the nation was the subversion of democracy from centralized government, while at the other extreme clergy argued that unbridled economic individualism posed the greatest threat. From the view that disagreement of this sort among church leaders was counterproductive, the debates were regrettable; yet, in real time, the discussion was an example of religious diversity providing an opportunity for healthy debate about pressing social issues. In addition to in-house discussions within congregations, many religious organizations convened meetings at which ideas were solicited from business and labor leaders as well as from educators and clergy. These were organized by citywide clergy associations, civic groups, denominational committees and church councils, and by the leaders of religiously affiliated colleges and universities.

Diversity was an important reality in the in-house discussions that religious organizations convened, the multisectoral consultations they organized, and the interfaith statements they issued. To be sure, demagogues used religious appeals that went profoundly against democracy, but they were roundly opposed by other religious leaders. Diversity favored that kind of open contention. It also influenced how religious leaders presented their arguments. Contrary to the notion that religion is guided by a unique institutional logic based on divine revelation, the arguments that religious organizations advanced usually demonstrated other claims, especially generic arguments about human values, needs, care, love, and assistance. Equally common were pragmatic arguments based on leaders' personal experience and their consultations with experts in business and academia. Central planning could work, it was argued, because it worked in industry. Engineering the economy was no different from engineering technological innovation. And, against these ideas, critics warned that central planning would either lead to chaos or result in tyranny.

For all the ways in which it amplified public debate, religion's influence on those discussions was of course limited. Roosevelt chafed at critics accusing him of dictatorial ambition but easily deflected these accusations with strategic programming and persuasive rhetoric. The religious leaders who opposed Roosevelt were ineffective in keeping him from winning reelection. Much of their opposition was voiced through elite organizations that had only weak connections with the average parishioner. The statements that included criticisms of the New Deal were scattered thematically, ranging from practical concerns to naive views about economics and from ideas about private charity to guidance for believers' spiritual lives. The most pointed statements about tyranny and totalitarianism were directed toward Europe rather than America, and the ones that warned of internal dangers to democracy rarely dealt specifically with how those threats might be thwarted.

The New Deal era, then, is one in which religious diversity contributed to varied opinions being expressed and varied constituencies having forums in which to articulate their views. The economic crisis motivated faith communities and their leaders to speak out, doing what they could to connect moral concerns with social issues, and mobilize social service programs as well as forums for further discussion. The programs and forums were guided by religious convictions, differed according to varied traditions and interests, and gave constituencies an opportunity to register their concerns about government overreach. All of that contributed. But it could not have happened without the institutional safeguards that protected democratic governance and the public officials who respected these safeguards.

In 1939 Columbia University historian Allan Nevins, whose biography of Grover Cleveland had won the Pulitzer Prize in 1933 and who would go on to write a celebrated eight-volume history of the Civil War, summed up the 1930s in a lengthy essay published in the *New York Times*. Nevins was critical of the New Deal, writing that parts of it were a complete failure, other parts were only a temporary palliative, and still others were succeeding only at an exorbitant increase in the national debt. How the economy would fare was still in doubt. He was convinced, though, that an important cultural shift was taking place. Through the strenuous effort of the nation's leaders and its citizens, democracy was being strengthened and its resilience vindicated. Not only was it strengthened, Nevins believed; its meaning was changing. The idea that democracy meant a kind of rugged individualism in which individuals were free to do whatever they chose to do was no longer as compelling or as easily taken for granted as it once was. An awareness was growing, he believed, that democracy meant interdependence among the nation's various interest groups and regions, that it was fragile, and that it required effort to keep it strong against tyranny.[74]

Nevins did not examine the grassroots organizations that had contributed to this realization. Had he done so, he undoubtedly would have emphasized business, labor unions, and civic groups but could not have missed the role of religious organizations. Despite religion's focus on personal salvation and, as such, its contributions to American individualism, the evidence demonstrates that this was not the whole story. Indeed, the debates in which religious leaders engaged criticized individualism consistently, calling for greater attention to neighborliness and an ethic of care, and they tried in the vocabularies they knew best to address questions about how powerful the central government should be, how to hold it accountable, and what the responsibilities of citizens should be when faced with the extraordinary circumstances in which they lived. Even seemingly individualistic arguments about morality and spiritual renewal dealt with balancing the roles of government with those of families and communities. These were the arguments that contributed to a deeper public consciousness of democracy and that served in significant ways to prepare the nation for the wartime challenges that lay ahead.

2

Liberty of Conscience

PACIFISM, WAR, AND
CONSCIENTIOUS OBJECTION

THROUGHOUT OUR NATION'S HISTORY, liberty of conscience has meant the political freedom to think, believe, and worship in ways that deviated from established—official—religions. It was the right to be a Quaker or Baptist or Muslim or Jew and it was the right to dissent from any religion. Freedom of conscience was the constitutional right to think or worship privately as one wished and the liberty to speak, assemble, and worship publicly without fear of suppression or intimidation. Over the years, the meaning of conscience and its relationship to religion and democracy have evolved. In this chapter I trace one of the most important aspects of that evolution.

From 1941 to 1945, when the United States mobilized its vast resources to combat totalitarianism, the contentious divisions that had characterized the nation's religious organizations during the 1930s ceded to the demand for national unity. It was imprudent for religious leaders to say anything that seemed unpatriotic. This was especially true for groups that had been pilloried during World War I as conscientious objectors, communists, and anarchists, or on suspicion of being German sympathizers. Whatever religious leaders may have thought about Roosevelt's economic policies, it was now time to demonstrate loyalty to the administration's efforts to protect the nation militarily and to advance freedom abroad.[1]

If religion's chief contribution to American democracy in these years was to support the war effort, its diversity nevertheless continued in quieter ways to provoke questions about what democracy was and to mobilize arguments and counterarguments about how best to keep it strong. By 1938, religious organizations were mobilized in support of or in opposition to Roosevelt running for a third term. Support and opposition to various proposals to end lynching and combat racial discrimination divided faith communities. They debated each step of the president's plans to arm the nation and send armaments to Europe. They were becoming aware that Jews were being persecuted and killed. And religious organizations were beginning to anticipate the international roles they would be asked to play in aiding refugees. These policies and proposals were all situated within the context of questions about how best to preserve and protect democracy—the cherished but also precarious system of government that guaranteed, in Horace Kallen's words that year, "freedom and equality to all human individuals and groups, regardless of their birth, their race, their faith, their sex, their social status or their political affiliation."[2]

The freedom that religious diversity played the most interesting role in upholding in these years was freedom of conscience. The idea that democracy depended on citizens being free to think, speak, and worship according to the dictates of conscience was of course present from the nation's earliest days. Freedom of conscience implied that citizens could speak in ways that ran against popular opinion and that at times violated the law. However, adjudication was necessary to specify the conditions under which democracy did in fact protect this most fundamental liberty, especially when patriotism was at issue. As the nation headed toward war, the question that brought freedom of conscience to the forefront of public deliberation was whether it could be a legitimate reason to resist military conscription. Religion was an integral feature of these discussions, providing as it had in previous years through membership in pacifist denominations a reason for some to resist, but then, as religious diversity came to be increasingly acknowledged, shifting emphasis toward the moral authority of individuals themselves. The outcome of these deliberations was a more personal or individuated understanding of conscience that would have a profound impact on subsequent interpretations of the democratic protection of human rights.

Advocacy for Peace

During the 1930s, many of the nation's religious leaders advocated that democracy was best served when religion emphasized peace and when religious leaders did what they could to work for peace. These views had become priorities between 1914 and 1918 and were strengthened by the hope at the end of the Great War that diplomacy underwritten by the League of Nations could prevail. They were grounded in biblical teachings about loving one's neighbor, living in harmony, and being peacemakers. They were also refracted through different theological, ethnic, and political lenses, and with contrasting views toward the Soviet Union, Germany, and the League of Nations. Although religious leaders agreed that peace was preferable to war, they and the organizations they represented formulated diverse arguments about what should be done to preserve democracy.

The Church Peace Union, founded in 1914 with an endowment of \$2 million from Andrew Carnegie, was one of several antiwar organizations oriented specifically toward religious communities. With representatives from more than thirty denominations, its aim was to organize international peace conferences among clergy, sponsor lectures and publications, and produce material to be taught in local congregations. In the 1930s, it advocated for arms reductions and debated symbolic measures of opposing war such as refusing to authorize clergy to serve as chaplains. Another group was the Fellowship of Reconciliation, an interfaith peace and justice organization founded in 1915, which by the 1930s embraced far-reaching social reform as the best means of resisting war. Other peace organizations included the American Union Against Militarism, National Council for Prevention of War, World Peace Foundation, Woman's Peace Party, and World Alliance for International Friendship through the Churches. The leaders of these organizations included clergy, attorneys, public officials, and academics, all of whom lectured widely at churches and to student groups.[3]

Multipurpose ecumenical organizations, denominational agencies, and local congregations also advocated for peace. Christian Endeavor, the evangelical youth organization founded in 1881, for example, held a meeting in Kansas City in 1929 at which its twelve thousand delegates pledged their support of the multilateral Kellogg-Briand Pact, which sought to eliminate war as an instrument of national policy. The same year, ecumenical meetings supporting the agreement were held in Nashville and then the following year in Washington, DC, and the year after that in Chicago. In 1933, church leaders organized a community-wide peace rally in Hartford, and in Boston churches hosted an interracial rally for peace. Also in 1933 the Southern Baptist Convention formally endorsed Roosevelt's appeals for peace, the Catholic Association for International Peace held two days of meetings in Washington, DC, and Methodist leaders met in Chicago to discuss how to bring the peace movement to the "man on the street." That fall, the Federal Council of Churches called for a reduction of armaments, a nonaggression pact, greater international economic cooperation, and strict international control of weapons manufacture. In all, some fourteen Protestant denominations—Baptists, Congregationalists, Methodists, Presbyterians, and others—were on record as having church-wide programs of education for peace.[4]

An unrepresentative survey of Protestant clergy reported that three-quarters wanted the church to oppose all future wars, and a slight majority were opposed even to wars of defense.[5] Commentators voiced considerable uncertainty, though, that religious advocacy for peace was effective or, for that matter, the best way to proceed. Surveying the situation in 1933, Stanley High acknowledged that church support had probably facilitated passage of the Kellogg-Briand Pact and was still shaping public opinion against war, but he doubted that much else had been accomplished. Preachers who espoused pacifism, he said, were arousing less enthusiasm among the laity than prohibitionists had. Pacifism, moreover, was generating resistance from critics who considered it weak, cowardly, or communist inspired.[6] These were issues, though, that clergy and laity deliberated with one another at regional and national meetings, rather than simply airing them through the media. A meeting of the New England Methodist Episcopal Conference in 1935 was typical. Strong arguments for and against pacifism resulted in a middle-ground statement that stopped short of political activism but encouraged pacifist teaching. "The agencies of the church should be used in teaching that Christians cannot legitimately engage in war," the body asserted. "Conscience is a reliable guide only when it is enlightened and sensitive."[7]

Differences of opinion were evident within as well as between local congregations. At the National City Christian Church, a historic congregation near the White House, for example, the board refused to approve a series of peace resolutions adopted by the church's youth society condemning compulsory military training and calling for a Sunday school course on peace. In Hartford, Connecticut, the First Congregational Church polled its 83 members, finding that 37 opposed compulsory military training and 46 favored it. In Atlanta, National Baptist Convention pastor J. Raymond Henderson, one of the city's leading African American clergy, mused about the division in his congregation: "It matters not how upright a preacher may be, it is a near axiom that whenever his deacon or trustee board turns against him, he had better begin packing."[8]

The difficulties in promoting peace were compounded when religious leaders sought, as they often did, to accommodate the varying interests of international constituencies. The Baptist World Alliance was a case in point. Founded in 1905 principally among Baptists in Great Britain and the United States, the alliance hosted an international convention every five years to discuss common issues and promote networking among clergy. By the 1930s, it included representatives from Germany and held its 1934 convention in Berlin. It was thus in the unusual position of representing the differing interests of clergy whose countries would within a few years be at war. In 1934 it affirmed that war was contrary to Christian teachings and that nations, following the principles of the League of Nations, should surrender some of their

sovereignty in the interest of establishing an international authority—
an idea unappealing to the German delegation, which pressed for stronger condemnation of the Soviet Union.[9]

Further difficulties were evident when peace organizations attempted
to address specific international agreements amid rapidly changing circumstances. The World Disarmament Conference, to which sixty countries sent delegates in 1932 and which convened again in February 1933,
illustrated these difficulties. The Church Peace Union and World Alliance for International Friendship supported the disarmament proposals
and continued to do so even after Hitler assumed power in March 1933
and Germany withdrew from the conference that fall. A year later, the
Church Peace Union issued an Armistice Day manifesto in the name of
Catholic, Jewish, and Protestant leaders proclaiming that war should
never again be waged in the name of religion and condemning "with
swift heat all boorishness in reference to our international neighbors."
As practical measures, the manifesto urged the cessation of all prepara-
tions for war, drastic reductions of military and naval budgets, and the
end of military training.[10] But these were decisions well outside the
realm and expertise of church leaders, many of whom felt it more
important to counsel the hearts of believers than to demand sweeping
social and economic change. It was easy for critics to ridicule the in-
effectiveness of such statements, as one did in observing that the Federal Council of Churches spoke for only a handful of leaders rather than
millions of members, and as another critic did in mocking peace statements endorsed by show of hands "with pianissimo organ accompani-
ment in darkened churches."[11]

Dissent against the administration's buildup of armaments shifted
into high gear during Roosevelt's second term in office. The National
Peace Conference, representing approximately forty educational and
religious organizations, urged Roosevelt to organize meetings aimed at
international disarmament. In New York City, Protestant leaders Harry
Emerson Fosdick and Samuel Shoemaker lent their voices to the effort.
World Peaceways, founded by National Council of Jewish Women executive secretary Estelle M. Sternberger, used magazine advertising and
radio programming to combat prowar sentiment in hope of establishing

a cabinet-level secretary of peace.[12] Catholics, Methodists, and Southern Baptists formed regional disarmament committees, and the Churchmen's Campaign for Peace through Mediation, organized by the interdenominational Ministers' No War Committee, held mass meetings in Cincinnati, Cleveland, Detroit, Los Angeles, Milwaukee, Nashville, and several other cities to push Congress toward challenging the president's emergency powers. By May 1941, the Churchmen's Campaign claimed to have enlisted the support of more than two thousand clergy from twenty-eight denominations.[13]

Pacifism as a theologically informed perspective on war was thus debated at three levels: at the level of the nation's priorities, where the question was whether national policy could reasonably be based on nonresistance and nonviolence; at the level of religious communities, where doctrines pertaining to formal stances toward war could be formulated; and at the level of the individual pastor or layperson, where matters of conscience were paramount. Religious organizations' attempts to influence national policy through peace rallies and statements about disarmament and neutrality were limited, increasingly so as conditions in Europe made it more evident that the United States would become involved. Where churches had a more influential role to play was in teachings about conscientious objection.

Conscientious Objection

During World War I, Mennonites, Quakers, and Brethren—the groups known as historic peace churches—had opposed military service on grounds formalized in church teachings. In recognition of these teachings, section 7, subdivision 4 of the 1917 Selective Service Act exempted from military service any member, ordained minister, or seminary student of a "well-recognized religious sect or organization [whose] existing creed or principles forbid its members to participate in war." Conscientious objectors who were members in good standing of these denominations could apply for exemption, and many of them did. Estimates of the numbers are imprecise but suggest that out of 2.8 million inductions, roughly 4,000 were conscientious objectors, the majority of whom were Mennonites.[14]

Although they were officially exempt from both combatant and noncombatant service, many conscientious objectors experienced intimidation at the hands of home guard militias and neighbors. Henry Cooprider, a twenty-one-year-old Mennonite who lived on a farm in Kansas at the start of World War I, was an example. When his father refused to purchase war bonds, a mob tarred and feathered Henry's brother. Soon after, Henry was drafted and declared himself a conscientious objector. In an interview years later, he recalled what happened. He and the other conscientious objectors were taken to an army base where they were placed in a stockade, given worn-out clothing, and subjected to days of "cuss words" and shaming. "We were called every name there is that would be degrading. If it was possible to run down the idea of living a Christian life, they did everything possible along that line." Several times they lined the men up and said they would be shot unless they changed their minds. Those who refused to participate even in noncombatant activities received prison sentences of up to twenty-five years.[15]

Members of the historic peace churches held differing opinions about what exactly conscientious objection implied. Mennonites and Brethren tended toward nonresistance as a lifestyle of defenseless love in the face of evil and modeled on Jesus's teachings and example. Nonresistance was in this sense deeply personal but also supported by the community of like-minded believers whose orientation tended away from conflict and wider societal engagement. Quakers, in contrast, were more socially activist, which prompted an interpretation of nonviolence as a potentially transforming public witness for peace.[16]

Mennonites, Quakers, and Brethren were not the only denominations that taught nonviolence or that included members who were convinced that war was wrong. Among those who applied for conscientious exemption were Christadelphians, German Baptists, Methodists, Unitarians, Seventh-day Adventists, and members of Pentecostal and Holiness congregations. Some who claimed exemption on biblical grounds were not members of congregations; others were socialists and representatives of pacifist organizations such as the Fellowship of Reconciliation, the American Union Against Militarism, and the No-Conscription League. Was it constitutional, therefore, to grant exemption on the basis of membership in particular religious organizations? Or, given the diversity of religious and nonreligious interests at issue, was it necessary to establish more inclusive grounds for freedom of conscience?[17] This was not the first time these questions had been raised.

Few of the cases that had gone to trial during World War I were as widely discussed as Emma Goldman's. Born the daughter of an impoverished Orthodox Jewish family in Russia in 1869 and emigrating to the United States in 1885, Goldman became a controversial social activist and writer who lectured to large audiences on behalf of free speech, anarchism, and birth control and spoke frequently against militarism and war. In 1916, as the United States moved toward entering the war, Goldman and fellow Russian-born antiwar activist Alexander Berkman founded the No-Conscription League, lecturing and distributing information on its behalf. In 1917 the two were arrested, convicted of conspiracy against the selective draft law of New York City, fined $10,000, and sentenced to two years' imprisonment. Goldman and Berkman appealed to the US Supreme Court, which affirmed the lower court's decision. On December 21, 1919, Goldman and Berkman were deported to Russia under the newly expanded Anarchist Exclusion Act.[18]

The Goldman case brought religious diversity directly to bear on liberty of conscience. Henry Weinberger, the attorney for Goldman and Berkman, presented a statement to the Supreme Court that included a lengthy review of arguments grounding freedom of conscience in the history of Western religion. Weinberger's principal arguments could be summarized as follows: first, the exercise of freedom of conscience was the mark of the free individual who, like a "disciple of Jesus" or any "lonely thinker," contributed to the evolution of democracy; second, the "truly conscientious objector" was a pioneer like martyrs of the faith such as Jan Hus, John Wycliffe, and Ulrich Zwingli; third, the Protestant Reformation led by these martyrs had been "a great uprising of the human spirit" waged against the church's control of body and conscience; and fourth, freedom of conscience was now endangered chiefly by the state. Weinberger further argued that the Selective Service Act's exemption from military service of members of a "well-recognized religious sect or organization [whose] existing creed or principles forbid its members to participate in war" was a violation of Goldman and Berkman's rights under the First Amendment. This was, Weinberger said, an exercise in religious establishment: "For the first time in our national history the nation holds an inquisition into a man's faith or his mode of worship or the church he attends, and imposes duties or grants exemptions accordingly."[19]

Weinberger's argument was an expansive interpretation of religious diversity. It was by no means the first, but it was a defense of freedom of conscience that included those who were not religious. Goldman had repudiated her parents' Judaism after moving to the United States and over the years had lectured favorably about atheism and against Christianity's state-like repression of independent thought. Yet, as Weinberger did, she saw in certain religious figures admirable examples of free expression. In a speech to the jury during her trial, for example, she argued that freedom, joy, beauty, and progress demanded recognition of the "complexity of the human soul." If she and Berkman were criminals, she said, then "we are criminals even like Jesus, Socrates, Galileo, Bruno, John Brown and scores of others."[20] Historian David Waldstreicher, who carefully examined Goldman's lectures and writing about religion throughout her life, concluded that in "a universe of competing redemptive creeds" she was a "maverick who invented her own religion."[21]

Schenck v. United States was the other World War I era case that directed attention to freedom of conscience. The case went to the US Supreme Court when Charles Schenck and Elizabeth Baer appealed a US District Court conviction in the Eastern District of Pennsylvania. Schenck was the executive secretary of the Philadelphia chapter of the Socialist Party, and Baer (a doctor) took minutes at the meetings. With other members of the chapter, they printed and distributed thousands of copies of a leaflet that challenged the constitutionality of conscription and called on citizens to petition representatives for its repeal. The

leaflet asserted the constitutional principle "that freedom of the individual and personal liberty are the most sacred things in life." The conviction, which carried prison sentences of six months and three months,
respectively, was based on the 1917 Espionage Act. The Supreme Court
upheld the conviction on grounds that freedom of speech could be
abridged when the nation was at war. In the majority opinion, Associate
Justice Oliver Wendell Holmes Jr. famously declared, "Free speech
would not protect a man in falsely shouting fire in a theatre and causing
a panic."[22] But six months later in *Abrams v. United States* the court
limited the concept of "present danger" to an "immediate evil," with
Holmes writing that "we should be eternally vigilant against attempts
to check the expression of opinions that we loathe."[23]

Schenck and Abrams were landmark cases bearing on freedom of
speech more than only on conscientious objection. They upheld the
principle that freedom of conscience includes the right to express one's
opinions freely. Unlike the Goldman case, they did not include arguments about religion, but ideas about religion and diversity were part
of the backstory. In *The Great Dissent: How Oliver Wendell Holmes
Changed His Mind—and Changed the History of Free Speech in America*,
legal scholar Thomas Healy argues that during the summer between
Schenck and Abrams, Holmes was wrestling with thoughts about freedom of expression, writing in a letter to Harold Laski about the Catholic
Church killing heretics and Puritans whipping Quakers and, at Laski's
urging, rereading John Stuart Mill's *On Liberty*.[24]

In 1940, the questions that conscientious objection had posed during
World War I came to the surface again as the US Senate and House of
Representatives held hearings over the Selective Service Act, which became law as the nation's first-ever peacetime universal draft registration
and conscription measure. At Senate and House hearings in July and
August speakers representing the military, veterans, state governments,
local citizens, farmers, youth, socialists, labor, pacifists, the NAACP, and
religious organizations offered testimony for and against the measure.
Religious speakers included Baptists, Brethren, Congregationalists, Disciples of Christ, Episcopalians, Methodists, Quakers, Roman Catholics,
and Seventh-day Adventists, as well as nondenominational clergy and

the Federal Council of Churches. They presented proposals about conscientious objection and cast them in terms of upholding democracy—and their statements reflected a range of views.

One line of argument expressed the same concern that critics had advanced about the New Deal: it saw in peacetime conscription an impending dictatorship. A speaker representing the Society of Friends, for example, asserted that in a true democracy "the individual citizen has the greatest opportunity for spiritual, intellectual and physical development," but the present "war system" that seeks "military victory at whatever cost" was leading the nation toward dictatorship.[25] This was an argument the peace group representatives shared. As Women's International League for Peace and Freedom representative Catherine FitzGibbon asserted, "Is there not something totalitarian and dangerous in the spy-hunt conducted by self-appointed groups throughout the country, groups like the Ku Klux Klan? Now, add to those unhappy tendencies in this country a peacetime universal compulsory service and the totalitarian pattern is practically complete. Then indeed, the democratic way will have perished from the earth."[26]

Democracy on this account squared readily with narratives about America being founded by free citizens fleeing authoritarian governments. For Quakers, it spoke to centuries of religious persecution in Europe. It was easily disconnected from religious connotations, though, except in references to religious freedom, and thus was a weapon deployable against any kind of conscription. As a spokesperson for the Committee on Militarism in Education argued, "The essential idea underlying military conscription is the major premise of every dictatorship and all totalitarianism. It is the assumption that the individual citizen is but a pawn in the hands of unlimited state power." Indeed, it was in effect "a seizure of a man's body, time, and service by force" and therefore was "abhorrent to free men."[27] Almost of necessity, this view also implied that a democracy could defend itself only by raising a volunteer army—the feasibility of which was roundly criticized by proponents of military preparedness.

The Quaker argument differed in two important respects. First, it presented its views about pacifism as an ideal but one that was acknowledged to be held by a minority, which meant that it explicitly accepted that American democracy consisted of diverse, conflicting views. Second, it couched its idealistic minority position in terms of a higher authority than democracy, specifically in the teaching and practice of Jesus as understood by persons with deeply held conscientious convictions. The point of resisting conscription, as far as democracy was concerned, was less to uphold democracy than to qualify its authority, suggesting that it could not be upheld by coercion and could be strengthened only by a deepening inner conviction of self-discipline and sacrificial resolve. It was the Quaker position to willingly die for America but not to kill for any reason.

The argument that fit best with the positions taken by Baptist, Episcopal, Methodist, and Presbyterian groups was that conscription, if necessary at all, was the prudent option insofar as it seemed evident that war was coming and that preparation beyond that of a voluntary army was necessary. Therefore, if democracy had to be defended this way, provision should be made for those—surely a small number but present in all denominations—whose conscientious objections did not permit them to participate in military action. This was the *realist* position taken most prominently by Reinhold Niebuhr, who argued that true pacifism was impractical, given the threats posed by the broken world in which the nations lived.[28]

Each of the major denominations nevertheless did debate how best to accommodate conscientious objection. Methodists voted to support individual members who applied for exemption from selective service as conscientious objectors but cautioned that the church did not condone the violation of any law and urged conscientious objectors to find positive ways to demonstrate support for America. Episcopalians provided assistance in registering conscientious objectors. Congregationalists, Disciples of Christ, and Baptists (Northern) passed supportive resolutions declaring themselves believers in the supremacy of conscience. Universalists arranged financial support. Reform rabbis declared, against some opposition, that conscientious objection to military service was consistent with Judaism. Lutherans approved a proposal recognizing it but also declared the Christian citizen's duty to obey and support lawful government. Presbyterians asked local presbyteries to consider supporting conscientious objection but tabled a proposal urging Congress to lend its support: "The church must stand for liberty of conscience," the statement declared. Catholics affirmed the church's teachings about "just war" and at the same time supported conscientious objectors in specific instances.[29] In short, the various groups agreed that something should be done to acknowledge the right of conscientious objection, but they disagreed about *what* should be done.

The American Civil Liberties Union was the organization through which a solution was found. The ACLU had several advantages in rendering credible arguments. Having been founded in 1920, the union had leadership combining legal expertise with a variety of experience and affiliations that contributed to its legitimacy for participating in this particular debate. Among its founders and directors was Roger N. Baldwin, a conscientious objector in the previous war; Reverend John Haynes Holmes, also a long-term pacifist; FDR associate Harold Ickes; Crystal Eastman and her brother Max Eastman, whose parents had both been Congregationalist ministers; labor leader Elizabeth Gurley Flynn; and settlement house icon Jane Addams, among others. At the 1940 congressional hearings, University of North Carolina history professor Howard Beale, who was a friend and close associate of Baldwin, methodically presented the case for administering a program for several categories of conscientious objectors, modeling the proposal on the successful British National Service (Armed Forces) Act of 1939. Assuring the congressional committee that the ACLU did not share the totalitarian beliefs of communists and Nazis whose liberties of speech and assembly the organization had nevertheless defended, Beale described himself as "a simple believer in the validity even in time of crises of the teachings of Jesus and the political faith of Thomas Jefferson." Beale's sole aim in appearing at the hearing, he said, was to speak for the protection of liberty of conscience.

Beale proposed that the provision for conscientious objectors be broadened beyond the 1917 protection based on membership in the historic peace churches. The revised provision, he argued, should include protection for "conscientious objectors of all other religious denominations and for conscientious objectors on nonreligious grounds who, by established membership in organizations of fellowship, such as the Fellowship of Reconciliation, or the War Resistors League, can establish the sincerity of their objections." And rather than specifying the organizations that qualified, Beale suggested simply that any person "who is conscientiously opposed to participation in war in any form" should qualify for consideration. The proposal further stipulated that hearings would be required, at which evidence and testimony would be given, and that persons deemed exempt from military service would be placed into several categories of exemption.

What exactly conscience was and how it related to religion were defined broadly in Beale's arguments. Conscience was personal, it had to be sincere, and individuals were supposed to be free to follow its dictates even when others disagreed. It was a matter of conviction rather than only an opinion. And it could perhaps be informed by something similar to religion that might not be called religion. Under question at the congressional hearing, Beale gave examples of people whose convictions were guided by humanitarianism as well as those whose conscience was informed by Jesus. Beale thought ways could be found to test the genuineness of a person's conscience. But was it an inner voice, an intuition, a warmhearted whispering from above, a religious belief, or what? Others who testified at the hearing suggested substituting words such as "moral assent" or "ethical or philosophical," deleting references to religious belief entirely, or leaving it to the Justice Department to decide.

The Selective Training and Service Act, instituted on September 16, 1940, followed Beale's proposal with the exception of placing the authority for conscientious objection reviews in the hands of local boards rather than in the Justice Department. The measure did not require that conscientious objectors belong to a religious or pacifist organization but stated that nothing in it "shall be construed to require any person to be subject to combatant training and service in the land or naval forces of the United States who, by reason of religious training and belief, is conscientiously opposed to participation in war in any form." Approximately seventy thousand registrants claimed exemption under these terms, of which the Selective Service boards honored about half. Most were members of the historic peace churches, but hundreds were Catholics or belonged to mainstream Protestant denominations, and dozens were Jews, Christian Scientists, Unitarians, members of small denominations, or members of interfaith organizations such as the Fellowship of Reconciliation and War Resisters League. In all, more than three hundred different organizations were represented. In addition, more than six hundred applicants indicated no religious membership or affiliation.[30]

In 1943 US circuit judge August Hand in *United States v. Kauten* rendered an interpretation that attempted to resolve the lack of clarity in the Selective Service Act. Conscience and religion, whether people called them that or not, were universal, he argued, and amounted to pretty much the same thing. "Religious belief," he wrote, "arises from a sense of the inadequacy of reason as a means of relating the individual to his fellow men and to his universe—a sense common to men in the most primitive and in the most highly civilized societies"—a conviction that wasn't necessarily illogical but somehow went beyond logic. "It is a belief finding expression in a conscience which categorically requires the believer to disregard elementary self-interest," he explained. Moreover, it can be regarded as "a response of the individual to an inward mentor, call it conscience or God, that is for many persons at the present time the equivalent of what has always been thought a religious impulse."[31]

In practice the local Selective Service boards continued to rely heavily on religious affiliation in adjudicating conscientious objection cases. Members of peace churches, supportive denominations, and pacifist organizations were able to bring documents and invite witnesses to testify on their behalf. Still, it was understood that conscience was a matter of *personal* conviction. It could not be demonstrated on the basis of religious teachings and moral principles alone. It had to be a moral conviction that was evident in how a person spoke and acted.[32] In England, where conscientious objection was also widely discussed, philosopher Gilbert Ryle compiled a simple list of criteria for assessing the depths of conscience. The public tests of a conscientious conviction,

Ryle said, were (1) that it be uttered "regularly, relevantly and without hesitation"; (2) that other things said regularly, relevantly, and unhesitatingly "presuppose it"; (3) that a person is "ready or eager to try to persuade other people of it and to dissuade them of what is inconsistent with it"; (4) that the person "regularly and readily behaves in accordance with it on occasions when it is relevant"; and (5) that the person "feels guilty" and "resolves to reform" when not behaving in accordance with it. On these criteria, conscience was like other rules to which one conformed (such as prudence and etiquette), Ryle argued, but differed in extending beyond specific roles and situations. It was a matter of character deeply ingrained in a person's habits and outlook on life.[33] A report from the US Department of Justice acknowledged the "extreme difficulty" involved when "each particular case required exploration of the subjective conscience of the registrant."[34]

In 1946, as the Truman administration considered granting amnesty for certain categories of conscientious objectors, the question of what exactly counted as "religious training and belief" continued to be deliberated in the courts. Judge Hand's 1943 definition seemed to many critics to define religion too broadly. In *Berman v. United States* Associate Justice Harold M. Stephens of the US Court of Appeals for the District of Columbia addressed the issue at length. Stephens had been raised in Utah and during his years practicing law in the state was known as a critic of the Mormon Church's role in business and politics, but in representing the American College of Surgeons he became impressed with the Catholic-run hospitals he visited and the nuns and priests he met. In his early forties he became a member of the Catholic Church, reportedly telling a friend, "I cannot content myself with the present relativist theories; I believe that there are absolutes in the field of morals and conduct." Whether his personal convictions had an influence or not, his decision in Berman argued that conscientious objection status should be granted only to persons who believed in God or a supreme being or power. The dictionary and the *Encyclopedia of Social Science*, he said, made it clear that religion always implied a conviction in the existence of a supreme being.[35]

Stephens's decision, though, included an argument that would increasingly trouble the discussion of conscience and religion in the years ahead. "All the discoveries of science and the deepest reach of minds do not fill a life or satisfy the soul hunger to understand the daily joys and sadnesses and disappointments of life or to understand the ultimate purpose of creation," he wrote. "Faith in a Supreme Power above and beyond the law of all creation mollifies our fears and satisfies our longings." That was the function religion played in grounding a person's conscience deeply enough to guide moral decisions. But could not that function be derived differently for different individuals? In a dissenting opinion in the case, Judge William Denman asserted as much, noting the differences between Christianity and Buddhism and how Berman's conscience had been shaped by moral philosophy.[36]

The wider implication of the debate about pacifism and conscientious objection was to focus a vital question about the practicalities of democracy on freedom of conscience. Unlike in the previous war, when membership in special recognized religious sects was the basis for granting someone an exemption from military service, it was now up to particular individuals to demonstrate that their convictions were deeply held, consistent, sincere, and sufficiently similar to traditional religion to be counted as such. Nothing about this was entirely new. Respect for freedom of conscience had always been a feature of American democracy. But now its importance was reasserted. It was the result of the various religious, pacifist, and nonpacifist groups arguing about what they thought democracy should be. In emphasizing the individual as the primary subject in the matter, liberty of conscience permitted individuals from different faiths and with humanitarian orientations to each articulate their arguments in their own ways. This was by no means a perfect solution since the decisions ultimately rested in the hands of local boards. The deliberations nevertheless affirmed that freedom of conscience was something more than freedom to pursue self-interested aspirations. Democracy was supposed to guarantee even the freedom to dissent from what everyone else believed, as long as the dissent kept within certain bounds.

Constraints on Conscience

Religion figured as importantly in debating the constraints on conscience as it did freedom of conscience. The debate about conscientious
objection put the burden of conscience squarely on the shoulders of the
individual, requiring it to be defended on the basis of personal convictions rather than on grounds of membership in a particular denomination. However, it was rare that an individual would come to those convictions without the input and support of trusted others. Conscientious
objectors participated in formal and informal social networks that provided opportunities to discuss their convictions. Campus ministries,
the YMCA and YWCA, pacifist groups such as the Fellowship of Reconciliation, local chapters of the Society of Friends, and meetings in
local churches all served in this capacity. During the war these organizations played an important role in supporting the work of noncombatants. At the start of the war approximately two thousand men from
ninety-two religious denominations were noncombatants. They were
located in former Civilian Conservation Corps camps and in repur-
posed school buildings, assigned to forestry and agricultural projects
and at hospitals and mental health facilities under the authorization of
the Selective Service director. The camps were organized by Mennonites, Brethren, Quakers, and Catholics, coordinated by the National
Service Board for Religious Objectors, and supported by the World
Peace Commission of the Methodist Church, the Disciples of Christ,
the Commission on the Conscientious Objector of the Federal Council
of Churches, and the Catholic League of Conscientious Noncombatants. By 1944 fifty-eight Civilian Public Service camps with approximately 6,600 noncombatants were in existence. Another 12,000 conscientious objectors, many of whom were Seventh-day Adventists, were
engaged in special services including medical work, and approximately
1,500 conscientious objectors were in prison.[37]

Conscientious objection required conscience to be constrained by
an unwavering commitment to God, Jesus, the Bible, some other supreme deity, or an equally central conviction of supreme importance. It
was an obligation to principle. But those who opposed conscientious

objection and those who emphasized participation in the military defense of the country also regarded conscience as a duty. The differences hinged on what the individual's responsibility to society was understood to be. Freedom of conscience was constrained by its relationship to society, leaving it less in the hands of the individual and more in the social conditions making it possible. Democracy rather than freedom of conscience was the prior in the relationship of the two. Without democracy, freedom of conscience was impossible. The highest calling of a person of conscience was thus to defend democracy. Whereas the argument for conscientious objection allowed for diversity in how a person's conscience dictated responsibilities toward military service, the counterargument conceived of 100 percent national unity in matters of conscience. This argument was also cast in religious terms.

One of the more interesting arguments came not from a member of the clergy but from Rutgers University president Robert C. Clothier. Clothier had attended the Haverford School, which at the time was affiliated with the Society of Friends, and had served in an administrative position at the school for six years during the 1920s, but if he was ever sympathetic to pacifism, he was an outspoken critic of it by the time he assumed the presidency of Rutgers in 1932. "It sounds well to say that there will be no war if our men refuse to fight," he said in his 1934 baccalaureate sermon, "but unfortunately it does not work out that way. For when a country declares war, forces are unleashed which leave the individual no freedom of action."[38] In a letter to a conscientious objector in 1942, Clothier elaborated: "Every man who is unwilling to exert his own efforts to win this war is tacitly aligning himself with the enemy, with the champions of that barbarism" that threatened to "wipe out Christianity and civilization." It was unconscionable, he said, not to "help those who are risking their lives for the very things for which our Saviour stood."[39]

Whether conscience should be understood in terms of variation among individuals or in terms of a national consensus also became the central issue at the Methodist General Conference in 1944. Those who took the former position emphasized the rights of individuals to act as they saw fit and argued that the church "should honor conscientious decision, whether it leads to participation in or abstention from war." Those who held the alternative view argued that the church should side with the nation rather than the individual and thus declare itself fully in support of the war effort. "God himself has a stake in this struggle," one spokesperson argued, which necessitated "the use of military forces to resist an aggression which would overthrow every right which is held sacred by civilized men."[40]

Catholic teachings that emphasized the justness or unjustness of war recognized the necessity of evaluating varying circumstances. In doing so, Catholic teachings put the burden of conscientious objection on the individual parishioner—always in consultation with the church—to demonstrate that the state was wrongly preparing for war or defending itself militarily. This teaching in effect asked the conscientious objector to assert that the nation's policies based on knowledge beyond that of the ordinary citizen or the church were wrong. "The presumption certainly must be that the government has fuller knowledge and can pass a better judgment upon the nation's danger and needs than can the private citizen," Catholic scholar John K. Ryan observed.[41]

The argument for a nationally unified conscience was also cast as a criticism of religious diversity. During the 1940 debate about selective service, one of the outspoken critics of exemption on the basis of conscientious objection was Reverend Meredith Ashby Jones. Jones was a prominent Southern Baptist minister in Atlanta known for progressive views on interracial cooperation and interfaith activities. But his progressive views did not include supporting conscientious objection. "We need only think of the countless religious groups with their vast varieties of interpretations of the 'will of god,'" he wrote, "to see what a 'confusion worse confounded' it would make of society." It would "mean nothing less than anarchy" for individuals to resist authority on the basis of conscience. Rather than deferring to individual moral judgments, the better way, he believed, was to submit to the government's authority and "seek through orderly processes" to influence the will of government.[42]

It was troubling to many, though, to think that 100 percent commitment to the war effort from 100 percent of the population was the

grounds on which democracy should be defended. "Uniformity of opinion is an evil," Bertrand Russell wrote in the *American Scholar* in 1943.
Russell did not agree with those who refused to participate in the war
as conscientious objectors, but he welcomed the diversity they represented. "It may well be desirable that a few should hold a certain opinion," he wrote, "even if it would be disastrous if many held it."[43] The US
Supreme Court took a similar position that year in a case involving
Jehovah's Witnesses. Two years earlier the court had ruled that patriotic
uniformity was so important to the war effort that Jehovah's Witness
children should be compelled to salute the flag. But in 1943 the court
reversed itself on grounds that individual rights should prevail. "To enforce those rights today is not to choose weak government over strong
government," Judge Robert Jackson wrote. "It is only to adhere as a
means of strength to individual freedom of mind in preference to officially disciplined uniformity for which history indicates a disappointing
and disastrous end."[44]

Implicit in these arguments was an acknowledgment that conscience
had to take account of social circumstances. However deeply grounded
they might be in biblical teachings, these ideals were contingent on the
realities of the situation. Were it not enough to see that Jesus himself
was a realist, then it surely was necessary to recognize the grave condition of the world at war. A notable example of someone making this
argument was Union Theological Seminary dean Henry Van Dusen,
who had maintained close relations with the Fellowship of Reconciliation in the 1930s, served on the editorial board of its publication, *The
World Tomorrow*, and expressed appreciation for its pacifist ministry.
But in 1939 he distanced himself from pacifism and became a critic of
the isolationism he saw peace groups advocating. In 1940 Van Dusen
cofounded the interventionist Century Group and played an active role
in mobilizing support for intervention in the war in Europe among
prominent religious leaders. Given the "fluctuations and uncertainties"
of difficult times, he wrote later, "truth does eventually make itself
known to those who conscientiously fit themselves to receive and dis-
cern it."[45] Another example was *Christian Century* editor Charles Clayton Morrison, who had been one of the most vocal critics of emergency

armament measures in the 1930s and in 1940 was at odds with Van Dusen's interventionism. But in 1942, with America at war, Morrison described the situation as a "twilight zone of morality," a tragic reality from which there was no escape. The danger of totalitarianism was so great as to eliminate the right of the individual to choose how to respond. Duty to the nation in the defense of democracy had to be the determining priority. Freedom of conscience was no less important, in his view. It simply needed to be directed toward the good of the nation.[46]

In one of the more interesting cases of conscientious objection, freedom of conscience was defined as defying or moving past certain religious teachings. This was the case of Sergeant Alvin C. York, the decorated World War I hero whose one-man blitz in 1918 had scored 25 enemy killed, 182 captured, and 32 machine guns disabled and whose heroism made the 1941 film about his life the highest-grossing film of the year. When Sergeant York again registered for military service, the lead story line in much of the publicity described him as the "most famous conscientious objector in American history." The reason was that York had been raised in a small denomination in the Wesleyan-Holiness tradition that taught conscientious objection as part of its emphasis on Christian liberty. But York rejected those teachings when he was drafted, and the story of his reversal fit well with his courage in battle. It was a story of moral resolve, of choosing to follow one's conscience by *participating* in war. "I don't see how any man can be a real Christian conscientious objector in this war when it's Christianity and Christian liberties we're fightin' for," he told a reporter in 1942. "It's always been a Christian's business to fight sin and the devil, and surely Hitler is next on the list!"[47]

Besides the emphasis the war placed on moral conviction, it also prompted religious leaders to discuss with renewed energy the importance of *training* conscience. The idea of conscience as being supremely personal fit well with religious teachings about individual responsibility. It was the individual who needed to learn how to make difficult decisions. But moral principles had to be learned. The individual had to develop habits and dispositions. Whatever conscience was, these were the promptings that guided it. "Conscience is influenced by custom, tradition, training, and education," a 1942 study guide for youth published by Christian Endeavor advised. Conscience was like the control room on a battleship "to direct the fire power of its massive guns." It gave direction to one's life. Each life was different. "People do not all have the same conscience." But conscience had to be learned early in life, sharpened, and obeyed. The "home, school, and church" should cooperate in its training.[48]

Further Refinement

Freedom of conscience as it pertained to conscientious objection came before the courts again in the 1960s. In its 1948 revision of the Universal Military Training and Service Act, Congress provided for exemption from combatant training and service for any person "who, by reason of religious training and belief, is conscientiously opposed to participation in war in any form." But, as adopted from Judge Stephens's argument, religion was defined as "an individual's belief in a relation to a Supreme Being involving duties superior to those arising from any human relation." Religion specifically excluded "essentially political, sociological, or philosophical views or a merely personal moral code."[49] In a case that was to become a landmark, Daniel Seeger claimed exemption as a conscientious objector but was rejected because he denied believing in a Supreme Being. Seeger had been raised in a devout Roman Catholic family, attended parochial school, graduated from Queens College with a major in physics, and become active in the Morningside Heights Meeting of Friends at Columbia University.[50] His claim for exemption was based on "belief in and devotion to goodness and virtue for their own sakes, and a religious faith in a purely ethical creed." He cited Plato, Aristotle, Spinoza, Tolstoy, and others in defense of the intellectual and moral integrity of his beliefs. "It is our moral responsibility," he wrote, "to search for a way to maintain the recognition of the dignity and worth of the individual, the faith in reason, freedom, and individuality, and the opportunity to improve life for which democracy stands."[51]

When the case went to the US Supreme Court in 1964, the American Jewish Congress (AJC), Ethical Culture Society, and American

Humanist Association submitted amicus curiae briefs. Writing for the AJC, attorney Leo Pfeffer argued that limiting conscientious exemption to persons believing in a Supreme Being constituted preferential treatment of certain religions over others. It would in effect give preference to Christians, Jews, and Muslims over Buddhists, Taoists, Confucians, and members of any other nontheistic faiths. Although their numbers might be small, Pfeffer argued, the constitutional rights of these adherents of nontheistic religions should be upheld. Indeed, as Thomas Jefferson had asserted in 1786, religious freedom was "meant to comprehend, within the mantle of its protection, the Jew and the Gentile, the Christian and the Mohametan, the Hindu, the infidel of every denomination." It was not only unconstitutional for Congress to define religion by restricting it to belief in a Supreme Being, Pfeffer argued, it was also impractical. Religious diversity made it so. Were Congress, let alone local draft boards, given the task of determining what counted as belief in a Supreme Being, they would run into the timeworn divisions that had caused one group's God to be another's heresy. "One can imagine with amazement the theological disputations that might ensue." Nor would it be possible, Pfeffer thought, to find some other reasonable grounds on which to resolve the problem. He doubted that believers in God could be proven to be more honest and conscientious than nonbelievers.[52]

The appeals court had made much the same argument about religious diversity a year earlier in reversing Seeger's conviction. "We feel compelled to recognize that a requirement of belief in a Supreme Being," the court observed, "cannot embrace all those faiths which can validly claim to be called 'religious.' Thus it has been noted that, among other well-established religious sects, Buddhism, Taoism, Ethical Culture and Secular Humanism do not teach a belief in the existence of a Supreme Being." Elaborating, the court noted that America "has long prided itself on the enormous diversity of religious beliefs which have been able to find acceptance and toleration on these shores." It had been this historic diversity that encouraged the development of the First Amendment and that was now present as a "vast conglomeration of differing ideas and ideals." In the face of this diversity, the court concluded, it was now imperative to recognize that "a pervading commitment to a moral ideal is for many the equivalent of what was historically considered the response to divine commands."[53]

The Supreme Court upheld the lower court's decision in reversing Seeger's conviction. It also acknowledged the importance of religious diversity, noting the presence of more than 250 "sects" in the United States and many views about God. However, in an attempt to show that Congress had been correct all along in defining religion in terms of belief in a Supreme Being, the court argued that something like a Supreme Being was implied in all religions. It quoted extensively from theologian Paul Tillich, Bishop John A. T. Robinson, and several other sources suggesting that all religions did believe in a superordinate being or power, differing only in what they called it: ultimate concern, source of your being, what you take seriously without any reservation, Supreme Being, or God. Everyone, the court argued, whether living in primordial times or in advanced societies, has some mental picture of God even if they use other language to describe it. With that in mind, the court ruled that religious belief pertaining to questions of military exemption had to be "a sincere and meaningful belief occupying in the life of its possessor a place parallel to that filled by the God of those admittedly qualified for the exemption." It affirmed that exemption would not be granted to persons whose opposition to war was from "a merely personal moral code" or to those "who decide that war is wrong on the basis of essentially political, sociological or economic considerations." And it left to local boards and courts the decision of "whether the objector's beliefs are sincerely held and whether they are, in his own scheme of things, religious."[54]

Although the Seeger decision affirmed the value of taking an inclusive view of religion, it did more to underscore the individuality of conscience than to provide a satisfactory understanding of religion. Leaning as heavily as it did on Tillich, it said nothing about religions focusing on meditation, practice, ritual, and service as opposed to ultimate concern. It imagined religion as an underlying substratum of beliefs that surfaced in interchangeable mental pictures. It left unspecified the meaning of "occupying in the life of its possessor a place parallel to that filled" by a

Supreme Being, suggesting only that something deep or deeply fulfilling might qualify. It took for granted the idea that religion's "place" was to fill a psychological void by providing answers about the cosmos. The implicit understanding was that religion was all about meaning in life and had something to do with a sense of moral obligation, which arguably was a popular view at the time among certain theologians and social scientists. Yet it diminished the idea that a "personal moral code" would count while at the same time implying that whatever someone considered "religious" might indeed be religious.[55]

The view that everyone had a need for religion and therefore embraced some meaning-giving belief system that functioned like religion, even if it was called something else, was a gloss suggesting that religious diversity didn't matter after all, at least as far as the courts were concerned. But what about someone who explicitly challenged that view? That was the position taken by the petitioner in *Welsh v. United States*, which the US Supreme Court decided in the petitioner's favor in 1970. Elliott Welsh, whose case began in 1964 when he was twenty-three, claimed exemption from military service on grounds of conscientious objection, asserting that he could not affirm or deny belief in a Supreme Being and striking the words "my religious training" from the application form. The court determined that the language Congress had used in providing for exemption on the basis of religious training and belief did in fact "limit religion to its theistic sense" and confined it to "formal, organized worship or shared beliefs by a recognizable and cohesive group" and in so doing contravened the Establishment Clause of the First Amendment. Exemption should be neutral with respect to religion, it declared, including those "whose belief emanates from a purely moral, ethical, or philosophical source." Moreover, the decision implied the possibility for later cases to include arguments about ethical convictions deriving from specific historical and contextual considerations. Although affirming that conscientious objection should not be based on considerations only of "policy, pragmatism, or expediency," the case acknowledged that ethical convictions might include "strong beliefs about our domestic and foreign affairs."[56]

In July 1970, the Office of the Director of the Selective Service System issued a memorandum to local draft boards specifying the criteria to be used for persons seeking to be classified as conscientious objectors. The primary test was to be the sincerity with which the person's beliefs were held. The beliefs had to be strong enough to rule out being held simply as a matter of expediency. They could include "solely moral or ethical beliefs, even though the registrant may not characterize these beliefs as 'religious' in the traditional sense or may expressly characterize them as not 'religious.'" Moreover, the person "need not believe in a traditional 'God' or a 'Supreme Being' to be considered favorably." But beliefs should be held with the "strength of traditional religious conviction" and be of the kind that directed a person's life "in the way traditional religious convictions of equal strength, depth, and duration have directed the lives of those whose beliefs are clearly founded in traditional religious conviction." In short, traditional religion remained the standard by which convictions were to be judged, but what counted as traditional religion was left unspecified.[57]

The debate over conscientious objection, then, had shifted the ground on which claims could be made. The diversity of religious traditions that had associated exemption with membership in historic peace churches in 1917 was now broadened to provide for arguments to be made by individuals based on the deeply held moral convictions they derived from multiple sources, including philosophical and ethical as well as explicitly religious training and belief. The shift was consistent with greater acknowledgment of the ways in which questions of life, death, health, happiness, freedom, moral obligation, and meaning could be addressed. It was also congruent with the moral individuation that a diverse society composed of fluid geographic, occupational, interpersonal, and ethnic spaces appeared to require. Freedom of conscience was increasingly to be the practical grounds on which individuals claimed their rights and privileges as citizens.[58]

It was not surprising in a way that conscientious objection gravitated from a consideration of church membership toward an emphasis on the authority of the individual. All the major traditions taught individual moral responsibility. That conscientious objection should be acknowledged as a decision based on moral conviction was something on which all or nearly all could agree. But another dynamic was present as well. Diversity, whether in the marketplace or in religion, exposes individuals to multiple options from which they may choose and in so doing fosters a kind of individuality. It is the individual, then, whose identity is strengthened as the person who has the authority to choose. Moreover, the grounds on which moral convictions are chosen are harder to defend on the basis of objective teachings, leaving convictions to be subjectively defended as felt obligations.[59]

By the end of the twentieth century, study after study demonstrated that religion was one of the ways in which Americans asserted their unique personal identities. Their views were diverse because they had been raised in more than one tradition, mingled with schoolmates from other traditions, left home, moved from place to place, read and listened to what they wanted, and formed their opinions about faith as much in resistance to organized religion as in conformity with it. Moreover, the choices people made varied widely, ranging from fundamentalist Christianity to progressive Judaism and from orthodox Catholicism to New Age metaphysical practices.[60] It was not that community attachments were breaking down but that they were becoming increasingly porous and thus necessitating greater acknowledgment of the unique paths through which personal convictions were formed. Nor was it the case that convictions were necessarily shallow or fluid; it was entirely possible for individuals to adopt deep convictions and to defend them as essential to their personal identities. Conscience was informed by religious diversity and diversity was in turn authorized by the ideal of conscience. What mattered was the depth of one's experience and how sincerely its meaning was held. The individual who freely decided what to think about religion was also free to hold diverse opinions about social and political issues and to know that others would disagree.

Although its meanings shifted decisively toward individual interpretation, freedom of conscience was never quite as exclusively decided by personal conviction as those interpretations may have suggested. Just as the courts held on to religious conceptions—however vague—of conscience, so religious organizations jealously guarded their conviction that their definitions of conscience should prevail. Over the course of the twentieth century and into the twenty-first century, religious and nonreligious organizations continued to advocate for varying interpretations of the rights and limitations implied by freedom of conscience, applying these varying interpretations to issues of civil liberties and freedom of religion.[61]

Democracy as we experience it today has been influenced by these developments in understandings of conscience. To some, this development appears as evidence of a society in which religion no longer has any bearing on moral guidance. It is better understood, though, as an outcome predicated on the fact that religion is diverse, and this diversity is shielded from infringement by an establishment of religion as much as from any corrosive tendencies of government and secularity. The individual whose rights are to be protected is a person whose conscience need not be validated by a group, tradition, or organization but by the depth of personal experience and sincerity of personal convictions. It is an understanding of individual freedom that sometimes extends the sovereignty of the individual to the point of embracing eccentric beliefs. However, the attendant freedom is accompanied by an obligation to give those beliefs reasonable accommodation under the law and to adjudicate when they must be restrained to uphold the rights and freedom of others. These considerations are the ones that continue to bear significantly on an ever-expanding array of debates about privacy, pluralism, and competing conceptions of morality.

3

Freedom of Assembly

CONFORMITY AND DISSENT IN THE 1950S

IN 1944 the distinguished Harvard historian Arthur Schlesinger published an essay tracing the significance of America's voluntary associations from the colonial era to the present. Writing as he was during the war, Schlesinger contrasted the freedom of association guaranteed in America with the suppression of civic, religious, and labor organizations by the Axis powers in Europe. He reminded readers of Alexis de Tocqueville's assertion that voluntary associations were the key to understanding the strength and survival of American democracy and, as later writers have done, acknowledged the dark side of associations as illustrated by the Ku Klux Klan, Bundism, and the Christian Front. If America was a nation of joiners, he thought, it was because the associations they joined were constantly diversifying, providing new opportunities to pursue distinct interests and ideas: "A process of splitting and splintering . . . has marked the course of practically every sort of association," he wrote. "The history of religious denominations teems with instances."[1]

Schlesinger's discussion signaled two aspects of voluntary associations that remained puzzling. If they were so important during the usual course of affairs, as they were when Tocqueville visited, could they buffer the society against tendencies toward nationalism and even totalitarianism? Tocqueville himself had hinted at the danger of popular opinion becoming so oriented toward a singular interest that local associations could no longer bring alternative perspectives to bear on national politics. And if voluntary associations were so effective at buttressing democracy, could they ever be sufficiently abrasive to challenge and extend common understandings of democracy by facilitating a "vigorous spirit of nonconformity"?[2]

What Schlesinger could not fully foresee in 1944 was that both of these questions would become important in the conduct of national affairs in the coming years. In the 1950s ample evidence demonstrated that voluntary associations were popular and growing. But commentators expressed concern that the culture was being driven by conformity—conformity to which membership in clubs and congregations and civic groups was contributing. Were such groups being affected so much by the media and by middle-class materialism and of course by the Cold War, critics asked, that they were making Americans more content to accept the status quo than they were to enliven public debate? And in the 1960s the question was whether voluntary associations of the kind Tocqueville and Schlesinger had written about were holding middle America together at all or were being displaced by dissidents, protestors, and street demonstrations.

In many accounts, the 1950s and 1960s could not have been more different from each other. The one was characterized in the person of Dwight Eisenhower, steady, staid, the wartime hero who as president was plainly reliable to a fault, and the other by John F. Kennedy, youthful, charismatic, visionary, spirited, and too soon gone. The temperament of the 1950s was driven by the fear of thermonuclear war but also by the baby boom and the Korean War and suburbanization, television, and religion. The temperament of the 1960s was guided by the civil rights movement and the war in Southeast Asia and turmoil on the nation's campuses. The associations that prevailed, stereotypically at least, in the 1950s were the Jaycees and Eastern Star and bowling leagues; in the 1960s, the NAACP, Southern Christian Leadership Conference, and Students for a Democratic Society. By the end of the decade, historian of American religion Sydney Ahlstrom could write, "Radical theology, powerful countercultural movements, a search for new lifestyles, serious dissatisfactions with traditional modes of religious expression, and widespread questioning of long-accepted views on the church, the university, and the state have put the 1960s into sharp contrast with the postwar period of affluence and religious revival."[3]

Religion's contribution to American democracy had always been as an enabler of voluntary association. Indeed, the origin of the reference to freedom of assembly in the First Amendment, alongside freedom of speech and freedom of religion, is thought to have been the trial of William Penn in 1670 for attempting to gather for worship at the Quaker meetinghouse in London in violation of the 1664 Conventicle Act, a case that was widely known in the American colonies.[4] As dissenters in the colonies sought to worship in places governed by established churches, freedom of assembly became as important as freedom of religion. The associations that impressed Tocqueville in the 1830s were intertwined with camp meetings, revivals, and temperance societies, loosely connected with one another through federations and circuit riders but mostly present as local societies in towns and villages.

A century later, congregations were still the most numerous of all voluntary associations but were increasingly linked with reading clubs, parent-teacher organizations, home demonstration units, and fraternal orders. In the 1950s, religion—now present in newly established suburban congregations—underwent what some considered a revival, evident in high rates of membership and attendance at religious organizations. Public commentary placed a great deal of emphasis on America as a God-fearing nation in contrast with godless communism. Religion was no less important in the 1960s, but its salience was questioned by the short-lived "death of God" impulse, by concerns about young adults' lack of adherence to creedal dicta, and by questions about whether religious commitment was truly a powerful voice for civil rights or an impediment.

Although it is true that religion in the 1950s was conformist, it was organized around diverse traditions and its growth was realized not only in membership but also in an expansion of the institutional forms it had been developing since the end of the nineteenth century. Its contribution to democracy was less a consensus around an Americanized ideal and more a convergence of perspectives about the strengths of

American democracy and the challenges facing it. The freedom of religion that Americans hailed in the 1950s was the same freedom that created spaces, starting in the 1950s and continuing in the 1960s, for a much wider variety of forms and ideas to take root. Moreover, what contributed to the strength of voluntary associations in both decades was the legal framework in which they existed.

If democracy is an agonistic endeavor, religion's contribution to that endeavor through its diverse and sometime perverse contentiousness was no less (or more) important in the 1950s than in the 1960s, only different. The 1950s were not as quiescent as they have often been regarded in retrospect. The 1960s were as disruptive as they are remembered to have been, but the dissent and counterdissent were the means through which an understanding of democracy that paid greater attention to human differences and rights was forged. In neither decade did religion function as an establishment or as a singular influence in public affairs. In both, it facilitated free assembly at the grassroots where serious convictions could grow.

A focus on freedom of assembly casts the issue of religious diversity in a different light from how its role was often conceived in the 1950s. Social observers in those years recognized that American religion was diverse, perhaps uniquely so. But the reason diversity was interesting was that the diverse groupings—Protestants, Catholics, Jews, and others—all seemed to be pointing in the same direction, producing harmony and tolerance, and thus reinforcing an underlying cultural consensus. This was quite different from the view that religion was fundamentally contentious. And yet, as historians have looked at the period, its contentiousness has come more clearly into view.

Postwar Democracy

Religion in America in the years immediately following World War II was surprisingly unchanged in theological content and even to some extent in personnel from its Depression-era predecessor. The anticommunism that critics used to attack the New Deal's expansion of federal power provided the starting point from which to launch new concerns about the spread of communism from the Soviet Union. Church leaders who were otherwise unified in supporting a strong US military, just as they had been during the war, took different sides on government programs affecting domestic life and, for that matter, differed on specific policies. Few disagreed that states should invest in expanding colleges and universities and that the federal government should assist veterans through the GI Bill. But the public was less sure that the US Department of Agriculture should continue regulating crops and even less willing to support federal intervention in matters of civil rights and school desegregation. Resistance to these forms of federal government expansion gained expression in arguments about states' rights and local self-determination. But those were not the only arguments, well mobilized and conflictual as they were. Faith was also expressed in quieter ways, largely among friends and neighbors participating in local congregations and drawing on familiar arguments about personal morality and individual responsibility. And these arguments were complicated by the nation's ascendant middle-class confidence in rationally organized, efficient governance as the necessary cudgel with which to combat Soviet aggression.

World War II marked such a massive upheaval in the nation's business arrangements, military expenditures and service, labor relations, and agriculture, and in the relationships of ordinary Americans to the federal government, that classifications of historical eras typically identify greater discontinuity than continuity between the postwar years and the prewar years. The invention and deployment of atomic weapons and the ensuing nuclear arms race between the United States and the Soviet Union further marked this distinction. From the late 1940s through the late 1980s, the Cold War provided a reality that no discussion of churches' relationships to the federal government could ignore. The threat of godless communism was a Cold War theme that nevertheless linked the postwar theologies of political concern with legacies of New Deal opposition. Roosevelt's opponents in the 1930s mentioned time and again the possibility that the New Deal was leading the nation toward Soviet-style communism.

An important aspect of the debate about strengthening American democracy also showed continuity with the prewar era. Although Eisenhower's election to the presidency in 1952 brought an end to the Democratic administration that had begun in 1932, and although Eisenhower's style was quite different from Roosevelt's, commentators expressed similar concerns about the expanding power of the federal government. Eisenhower's victory in 1952, winning 83 percent of the electoral college votes, was almost as large as Roosevelt's in 1932, which had captured 89 percent. Nothing compared with Roosevelt's massive 98 percent electoral college win in 1936, but Eisenhower's 86 percent win in 1956, with only the Deep South staying Democratic, was close. Unlike Roosevelt, whose Democratic party held both houses of Congress throughout his administration, Eisenhower had Republican party control of Congress during only his first two years of office. Nevertheless, religious leaders who otherwise favored Eisenhower, as well as Democrats, voiced worries—amplified by economic uncertainty and fears of atomic warfare—that democratic principles were being compromised by central government. Eisenhower's opponents played on these fears, suggesting that his instinct would be to rule the nation as he had the military.[5]

The debate about central government as a potential threat to democracy in the 1950s nevertheless differed from its counterpart in the 1930s. After more than a decade of getting used to government intervention in the economy, paying for and sometimes receiving Social Security benefits, serving in the military, and qualifying for veterans' benefits, families were used to being linked to the federal government in ways they had not been in 1932.[6] That meant it was unnecessary for Eisenhower, unlike it was for Roosevelt, to persuade a reluctant public that government should interfere in their lives. Although Eisenhower initiated large government initiatives such as the interstate highway system and furthered the development of nuclear weapons, the overall size of the federal government as measured by (inflation-adjusted) spending remained stable during his eight years in office. Moreover, the Soviet threat presented a compelling case for the United States to be strong at the top as well in terms of keeping the economy from faltering and continuing to build advanced weapons systems. The key was to be well organized and efficient, promoting industrial strength and technology while at the same time maintaining a traditional emphasis on freedom, individual initiative, and ingenuity.[7]

If democracy was to be all these things—if it was to be an alternative to communism that made full use of advanced technology and held true to the values it had cherished in the past—varying definitions of how democracy should be practiced were nevertheless present. Religious organizations, as they had done in the past, weighed in with competing ideas that reflected their differing traditions and social locations. Most of the views and activities that were mobilized around these views took shape between two extremes. On the one hand, it was conceivable to argue that something of value was being lost and that religion's role should be to keep people's minds focused on God. On the other hand, it could plausibly be argued that religion should encourage people to actively embrace the challenges of participating in the new, highly bureaucratized, urban, technologically advanced postwar world. Although democracy's strength did not depend on one or the other argument winning, the debate kept in play the questions that mattered.

The Upturn in Religion

A widespread view in the 1950s held that religion was one of the things that made America what it was, and that religion was thriving, which was a good thing, given the godlessness that was spreading throughout the communist world. Journalist George Cornell was one of the first to seize on the notion that Americans were turning to God in large numbers and that this vitality, inspired as it probably was by atomic-age anxieties, was a healthy development. In a series of articles published in 1951, Cornell argued that the old days of feuding among denominations were over and that the churches were working together as never before to promote unifying values. The new spirit, he thought, was evident in local interfaith councils, ecumenical meetings among Protestants, rising enrollment in interdenominational seminaries, and organizations promoting cooperation among Christians and Jews.[8]

By 1959 polling suggested that a religious revival was indeed occurring, at least if Americans were truthfully reporting how often they attended weekly worship services.[9] In addition, a remarkable 81 percent told pollsters they believed religion could solve all or most of today's problems, and 69 percent thought religion's influence was increasing.[10] But in the early 1950s, and even throughout the decade, the view that America was in a spiritual crisis was also widespread. "We do not have to read deeply in the philosophy and literature of today to sense the degree to which our age has come to seem a period of moral and spiritual chaos, of certainties abandoned, of creeds outworn, and of values devalued," sociologist Robert Nisbet wrote in 1953.[11] The worry was that Americans were inattentive to the dangers of communism abroad and the seductions of materialism at home. It appeared that confusion and indifference about moral principles were on the rise. The call was to strengthen democracy by revitalizing the nation's commitment to God.

Reason enough could be found for people to believe that religion was vital to keeping democracy strong. Just as Roosevelt had done before and during the war, Presidents Truman and Eisenhower after the war spoke frequently about the connections between religious faith and democratic values. At the Washington Hebrew Congregation in 1952, Truman celebrated the temple's prophetic role in arousing the conscience of free people toward righteousness. The following week at a Presbyterian church in Alexandria, Virginia, Truman elaborated, asserting that democracy is "built upon a spiritual basis—on a belief in God and an observance of moral principles" and that "religious faith is the strength of our nation." Campaigning against Truman that fall, Eisenhower invoked in his stump speeches the "power of moral and spiritual forces to bind us together" and called on voters to go forward "under God, firm in their faith, confident of their future, united in their purpose."[12]

In the struggle against communism, religion was America's spiritual weapon for strengthening the nation's commitment to democracy. In 1951, as American soldiers deployed to Korea, the Commission on

Religious Education of the National Conference of Christians and Jews distributed pamphlets to the chaplains serving the troops, providing them with reasons to be thankful for democracy and to fight for its preservation. "I am glad that I live in a land where I can believe in God and say so publicly without being looked upon as an enemy of the state," one of the pamphlets asserted. "I know that my wife will not be corrupted as in Communist states by the principle of free love which ridicules the ideas of fidelity; I know that when my wife bears me a child, it will be my child."[13]

In 1953, during the first weeks of Eisenhower's presidency, the inaugural National Prayer Breakfast took place with more than five hundred dignitaries taking part as speakers held the nation's basis of government to be under God.[14] Over the summer, the National Association of Evangelicals initiated a "March of Freedom," declaring, with Eisenhower's endorsement, that the freedom Americans cherish is from God and that only those who are obedient to God are assured of freedom.[15] That fall an interfaith committee of clergy and laypeople organized the Foundation for Religious Action in the Social and Civil Order to spearhead a "spiritual counteroffensive" against communism. The organization, with a distinguished advisory board including Billy Graham, Theodore Hesburgh, Herbert Hoover, Henry Luce, Norman Vincent Peale, Elton Trueblood, and the presidents of several corporations and universities, sought to unite "all people who believe in a Supreme Being into a movement having as the avowed aim and purpose the promotion of confidence of people everywhere in religious truth as the prime support of human freedom." To that end the organization pledged to revive an awareness of the spiritual foundations of democracy. It saw itself pitted against not only communism but also the secular forces in America and throughout the world bent on the destruction of religion. At its 1954 National Conference on the Spiritual Foundations of American Democracy, the speakers included Atomic Energy Commission chair Thomas Murray, Rabbi Will Herberg, Theodore Hesburgh, and brief luncheon remarks by President Eisenhower. Herberg's lecture on "The Biblical Basis of American Democracy" stressed biblical realism's acknowledgment of original sin and argued that without explicit recognition of "a majesty beyond itself," democracy would become despotic.[16]

Linking religion and democracy was a vehicle through which spokespersons from widely differing locations in the social landscape could assert their allegiance to the common good. J. C. Penney, whose 1,600 retail stores were doing an annual business of over a billion dollars, was widely quoted as affirming the belief that Christianity was fundamental to American democracy and that Americans should conduct themselves as true Christians, letting their light shine in everyday living and trusting in God.[17] Hotelier Conrad Hilton, who hosted the 1953 prayer breakfast, wrote newspaper columns asserting the nation's need for help from God and published a widely circulated portrait of Uncle Sam on his knees before God.[18] Purdue University president Frederick L. Hovde argued in a commencement address that the true basis of social order in a nation guaranteeing freedom to its citizens was its "Christian ethic."[19] Secretary of State John Foster Dulles, addressing the Council on Foreign Relations, observed that people everywhere want to "worship God in accordance with the dictates of their conscience" but are denied that freedom when countries promote an "atheistic creed."[20]

In the same vein as these prominent leaders, grassroots organizations advocated for a closer relationship of faith with patriotism. Spiritual Mobilization, the group founded in 1935 by Congregationalist pastor James Fifield, encouraged towns and cities to celebrate the Fourth of July as a national religious festival, observing the divine source of the nation's liberties. The General Federation of Women's Clubs launched an "Americanism" campaign that called on members to read their Bibles. "We must strengthen our religious way of life," the organization asserted, "because a true democracy cannot be maintained without a spiritual foundation."[21] In 1954 the Pledge of Allegiance was modified to include the words "under God." Two years later Congress adopted as the nation's official motto "In God We Trust," requiring its placement on all US currency.

Against the perils of the postwar era was the hope that consensus could be sustained around a common core of deeply held values. A renewed commitment to the principles of individual liberty and freedom of conscience was needed, but also adherence to a public conscience that manifested itself in old-fashioned neighborliness and patriotism and a commitment to the American way.[22] In many discussions the quest for common values edged toward something like an established religion, only one that was nonsectarian. At town hall meetings and political rallies speakers declared that American democracy was based on the "spiritual concept" that humans are created in the image of God and endowed by their creator with an innate desire for freedom. The nation's capacity to pursue truth, to speak freely, and to be confident of the results was grounded in religion. A central core in the Judeo-Christian tradition was presumed to be present to which all could pay heed.

If it was generally agreed that religion was good for democracy, the various faith communities approached the topic from differing perspectives. Catholic bishops at the 1952 board meeting of the National Catholic Welfare Conference issued a statement condemning the idea that religion could be treated as a "common factor" among various opinions and sentiments, declaring that faith could be "lived in its entirety only through the one true Church of Christ."[23] In Los Angeles the assembled Protestants celebrating Reformation Day heard that Martin Luther's Ninety-five Theses was the path to modern democracy.[24] At Wayne University in Detroit, Canon Howard Harper asserted that John Calvin was the originator of modern democracy.[25] At Temple Israel in New York, Rabbi William Rosenblum observed that a democracy should make "room for differences" in religious opinions and practices.[26]

In 1955 Will Herberg's widely read *Protestant-Catholic-Jew* argued that America's tripartite religion gave each of its traditions' adherents a location from which to express their common commitment to the American way of life, which could be defined in one word: democracy. Under the differences, Herberg believed, was a common faith, God centered, responsive to God's love, and self-transcendent in providing ground to the meaning of existence.[27] But when the US Senate Subcommittee on Constitutional Rights scheduled a hearing that same year to discuss freedom of speech, freedom of assembly, and freedom of religion, it called off the hearings on religion because Protestant, Catholic, and

Jewish leaders foresaw too much disagreement for the hearings to be constructive.[28]

Disagreements were also evident in the efforts of those who worked hardest to forge interfaith alliances. As historian Healan Gaston has shown, the Foundation for Religious Action in the Social and Civil Order's public face of agreement among Protestant, Catholic, and Jewish leaders masked deep misgivings among the leaders themselves as well as among critics. The Catholics involved wanted the organization to press for religious education in schools, about which Protestant leaders were at best divided and Jewish leaders were almost uniformly opposed. In addition, theologically conservative spokespersons who wanted membership in the organization limited to believers in God and who were as opposed to secularism in general as to communism in particular disagreed with leaders who felt that such exclusiveness would deter liberal Protestants and secular Jewish groups from joining.[29] Contention of this sort was often portrayed as weakness because it prevented religious organizations from speaking with one voice. Yet it was also indicative of organizations functioning as venues for policy discussions to take place.

The backdrop against which these disagreements took place included another concern: Was democracy being weakened by conformity? The concern about conformity was not only about religion and it did not discount the differences between Protestants and Catholics and between Christians and Jews. It was rather the sense that Americans—at least White middle-class Americans—were adhering to common values they did not quite recognize that were geared toward fitting in, following the crowd, and apathetically pursuing their self-interested material desires. It was suburban homogeneity, the "man in the gray flannel suit," mass production, the "lonely crowd." The concern was that this kind of conformity was a slippery slope trending toward the authoritarianism that had undermined democracy in Europe. Tocqueville had warned that democracy was subject to these tendencies, noting how public opinion was already lowering the standards with which Americans debated important issues of the day. What had been apparent in the 1830s now seemed more evident as growing numbers of Americans entertained themselves with television. Religion, for its part, might be growing, but critics wondered whether it was superficial, doing more to make people feel good about themselves than to deepen their convictions. God was being domesticated, one leader observed, such that attempts "to extend the scope of democracy or to work for peace outside narrow and officially approved limits are suspect."[30]

Nation of Joiners

This was the context in which the issues Schlesinger had posed about the United States as a nation of joiners came again to the fore in discussions about American democracy. Critics argued that participating in voluntary associations was itself a kind of conformity. A nation of joiners, they said, was a population of lonely people who wanted to fit in with their neighbors. Joining a lodge or attending a church was the thing to do. The topics might vary from one group to the next, but the norms of decorum were the same: congeniality, material comforts, quiescence about public affairs. When the General Federation of Women's Clubs encouraged its five million members to open meetings with prayer and Bible readings, for example, was that simply another manifestation of conformity to the spiritualized version of the American way? Were church groups contributing to a common personalized therapeutic faith despite their denominational differences? Hadn't Tocqueville anticipated this might be the case?

The better argument was the one that Tocqueville had also made: voluntary associations were the grassroots mechanisms through which a diverse population made its diverse interests known. In the 1830s they were associations of farmers and villagers and tradespeople. In the 1950s they were still organizations of farmers and villagers and tradespeople, only more of the tradespeople lived in cities. They were meeting in well-furnished suburban worship spaces as well as in town halls and village churches. And they had expanded their activities and influence through federations that linked them across regions and in the range of special interests to which they were devoted. Among the many local associations were women's clubs, fraternal orders, parent-teacher associations, and labor unions that spanned regions as well as local groups that met in homes, schools, and bowling alleys.

Whether America was truly a nation of joiners depended on how one considered the evidence. In 1958 a report by a pair of distinguished sociologists published in the *American Sociological Review* concluded that "the findings hardly warrant the impression that Americans are a nation of joiners." But this was an odd conclusion, given that the 1953 national survey on which the report was based had by the authors' admission not sufficiently probed respondents' recall, had apparently misled respondents into thinking that church membership didn't count, and yet found that a majority of respondents (53 percent) said at least one member of their family held membership in at least one voluntary association. The report also confirmed what journalists and later studies would show, which was that memberships were more common in cities and suburbs than in rural areas and in middle-class families with children.[31] When the authors revisited the topic several years later, they did conclude that voluntary association membership was growing: specifically, the proportion of families reporting at least one member belonging to a voluntary association grew between 1953 and 1958 from 53 percent to 62 percent, and the proportion of individuals reporting membership (excluding unions) between 1955 and 1962 increased from 36 percent to 43 percent.[32]

Had membership in religious congregations been included, the numbers would have been much higher. Data compiled by the National Council of Churches in 1951 and 1952 (although missing some denominations and based on estimates from others) suggested that at least 92 million Americans were members of religious organizations and that the number of local congregations exceeded 285,000. This was at a time when the total US population was 158 million, meaning that at least 58 percent were religiously affiliated. The large numbers composed the memberships of nearly 40,000 Methodist congregations, approximately 28,000 Southern Baptist congregations, 25,000 National (African American) Baptist churches, 15,000 Roman Catholic parishes, 13,000 Presbyterian churches, and 12,000 Lutheran churches.[33]

By 1960, total religious membership grew to 114 million, representing 64 percent of the population and supplying the adherents of approximately 318,000 local congregations. Baptist, Methodist, and Roman Catholic congregations were still the most numerous, present in nearly every state. Diversity was also well in evidence: 4,000 Jewish congregations, 4,000 Jehovah's Witnesses congregations, 3,500 Church of Jesus Christ of Latter-day Saints congregations, 3,000 Seventh-day Adventist congregations, nearly 400 Greek Orthodox churches, and 350 Russian Orthodox churches. Although many of these churches were small, the average congregation of some 350 members was large enough to host smaller study and discussion groups organized around gender, age, and local interests and to connect members with committees and boards outside the congregation.[34]

Political scientist Robert D. Putnam, writing some years later in *Bowling Alone*, argued that on the whole voluntary associations grew in membership and participation from the end of World War II to the late 1950s or early 1960s and then plateaued before declining through the end of the century. Putnam noted that parent-teacher association membership increased dramatically, which was understandable given the rising proportion of families with school-age children. Growth was also notable in voluntary associations that had begun earlier in the century and were now spreading into middle-class suburbs. These included scouting organizations, women's clubs, and Masonic lodges.[35]

Inquiries into the aims and activities of local groups, religious and otherwise, identified several prevailing characteristics. First, they were indeed local, even though many were linked through regional and national federations, holding their meetings at churches, schools, Masonic lodges, and community centers. Second, they hosted speakers and initiated discussions on a wide range of civic issues such as morality in government, communism, religious freedom, schools, conservation, mental health, voter registration, alcohol, television, birth control, and juvenile delinquency. Third, they included training in church and community leadership and provided opportunities for civic skills, such as public speaking and door-to-door canvassing, to be practiced. Fourth, they were often gender divided, with men belonging to organizations such as Rotary, Moose, Odd Fellows, Knights of Columbus, the National Council of Catholic Men, and Presbyterian Men, and women belonging to Ebell Society clubs, the League of Women Voters, Catholic Big Sisters, Hadassah, the National Council of Jewish Women, United Church Women, and the African Methodist Episcopal Women's Missionary Society. And fifth, they tended to be internally homogeneous— along racial, ethnic, religious, and political lines—in part because of affinity preferences among those who joined and because of holding meetings in churches, schools, and neighborhood centers that were homogeneous owing to decades of racial segregation and social class stratification.

Writing in 1954, sociologist Arnold Rose argued that one of the principal benefits of voluntary associations for democracy was serving as strategic mechanisms of adaptation to changing social conditions. "As soon as a felt need for some social change arises," he wrote, "one or more voluntary associations immediately spring up to try to secure the change." Their role thereby was to draw the government's attention to something new, assist in identifying a solution, and alert voters to the issue. It might take a while, Rose argued, but change was sure to occur through gradual steps along the way. Participants would be motivated by a sense of satisfaction from having done something worthwhile. And once the problem had been solved, the association having identified it would likely fade away.[36] Rose of course had in mind the kinds of associations that Americans joined in the early fifties: the person who joins a sports club, gains enjoyment from it, and puts pressure on the local government to provide parks and recreational facilities; the veteran who lobbies for veterans' benefits; the member of a fraternal organization or church or service club who performs good deeds in the community and thereby keeps the government from intruding; and the farmer or factory worker who pays attention to the special interests of farmers or factory workers. These were the mechanisms through which the middle class shaped society and through which incremental social reforms could take place.

Rose's argument accurately expressed the fact that voluntary associations were widespread and were indeed oriented toward a broad range of social concerns. It was important, Rose argued, that voluntary associations were in fact voluntary and thus capable of motivating individuals who would probably not be motivated if they were forced to participate in something they did not care about. It was significant that voluntary associations, unlike government programs and laws, could tailor their appeals to the varied interests of particular groups, cultivating distinctive religious, ethnic, regional, and avocational preferences. Moreover, it was true—and would likely be true in the future—that voluntary associations originated when people identified problems that were not currently being addressed. But was that all? If so, how was it possible to explain the transition from functional middle-class voluntary associations like sports clubs and fraternal organizations to the ones focusing on protest that would appear in greater numbers a few years later?

Freely to Assemble

A key to understanding the evolution in voluntary associations' adaptation to changing conditions was the First Amendment's protection of freedom to assemble. Joining a voluntary association implied the right to freely assemble, and this right could usually be taken for granted but in many instances had to be clarified and, in the process, redefined. Americans who joined voluntary associations in the 1950s largely took for granted that *wanting* to assemble was enough to ensure that they *could* assemble. If they were interested in forming a supper club or bowling league, they were fairly assured of being able to do so. The same was true in religion. Unlike in colonial Massachusetts and Virginia where religious establishment laws kept dissenters from assembling, it had long been possible for members of minority religions to hold meetings. Not only could they gather for worship and prayer but they were also protected, just as businesses and farmers were, by statutes that facilitated their purchase of land, sale of property, construction and maintenance of buildings, and solicitation of money.[37] In contrast to the nineteenth century when camp meeting revivalists needed the local sheriff to keep hucksters and prostitutes from setting up shop across the road, nearly all worshippers now had dedicated spaces of their own. What happened in these spaces, moreover, was protected in every state by laws prohibiting "disturbances"—variously defined as molesting the preacher, defacing the building, threatening someone on their way to or from a meeting, preventing someone from entering the building, shooting a gun near the meeting, throwing a jug through the window, "cracking nuts," or "behaving ridiculously."[38] The idea was to ensure not only that worshippers could assemble but that they could do so peaceably.

By the twentieth century, thanks to the expansion of family incomes, town planning, infrastructure, and zoning ordinances, plenty of churches, schools, lodges, club rooms, and town halls provided spaces in which to meet. It was nearly always possible within reasonable limits for uncontested accommodations to be arranged. And, although exceptions were rare, the instances in which freedom of assembly *was* contested demonstrated the importance of such physical accommodations. For example, when conflict at a Baptist church in Chicago broke out in 1952, one faction locked the church doors, forcing the other faction to meet on the church steps. Two years earlier a similar incident occurred when a White church sold its property to a Black church, whereupon the White parishioners locked the door and proceeded to block entry to the new owners. In 1954 a nonsectarian boys' club that had been headquartered for seventeen years at a Unitarian church in Washington, DC, refused to integrate its membership, whereupon the church used its control of the meeting space to pressure the club to integrate. When the club refused, the church asked it to leave.[39]

Some of these disputes illustrate the important extent to which freedom of assembly depended on specific interpretations of the law. In an influential 1954 case, trustees of the North Rocky Mount Missionary Baptist Church in North Carolina brought suit to retain ownership of the congregation's property when the pastor and a majority of the members decided to reorganize the church under the auspices of an independent Baptist denomination. The North Carolina Supreme Court ruled in favor of the trustees, even though they represented a minority of the membership, arguing that church buildings are not the property of a local congregation at a particular time because they have been constructed through the gifts and labor of people over time on the basis of convictions related to a denomination or faith tradition. In its ruling, the court admonished the litigants that the time had come to exercise the Christian graces of reconciliation, forbearance, and brotherly love. The case set precedent almost immediately for litigation on a national scale when opponents of the merger that was to create the United Church of Christ in 1957 challenged aspects of the proposal on similar grounds.[40]

Freedom of assembly in other cases involved disputes between congregations and municipal ordinances that governed where people could meet and what they could do. Pawtucket, Rhode Island, where Samuel Slater had established the nation's first textile mill in 1793, provided an interesting case. As a center of industry, the community was the location of periodic labor disputes during the nineteenth and early twentieth centuries. In 1916 when nine hundred machinists and five hundred silk weavers went on strike, the town passed an ordinance prohibiting anyone from making a political or religious speech in Slater Park. The law went unchallenged until 1950, when local members of the Jehovah's Witnesses invited a guest preacher to deliver a "Bible discourse" to their assembly in the park. Having received official permission, the group held meetings on two successive Sundays, but as the crowd swelled the speaker was arrested the following Sunday. The Rhode Island Supreme Court eventually upheld the conviction, but not without dissent from one of the justices and wide discussion among legal scholars as to its significance.[41]

The issues were complicated by the fact that the Pawtucket case involved a religious group, which posed the question of whether religious groups should be treated differently than nonreligious groups. Laws restricting freedom of assembly were deemed unconstitutional when particular religious groups were singled out but were allowed to stand when they appeared to have been applied reasonably and without prejudice, as the court did in Rhode Island. In contrast, Jehovah's Witnesses won a 1951 case in Maryland when the US Supreme Court determined that they had been denied the right to hold meetings in the park "for no apparent reason except the [town] council's dislike for appellants and disagreement with their views."[42] But in a case the same year the New Hampshire Supreme Court ruled against Jehovah's Witnesses on grounds that no groups had ever used the park in question "for religious meetings or sectarian purposes" and that "constitutional rights are not abridged if there are still adequate places of assembly for those who wish to hold public open air church meetings."[43] Taken together, the cases illustrated an important fact about religion's contribution to freedom of assembly: the contribution did not reside simply in the congregations happily meeting and forging civic bonds among their members; congregations were also active participants in the ongoing deliberations through which the meanings and limits of freedom of assembly were determined.

Because freedom of assembly so often implied a building in which to assemble, zoning was repeatedly the focus of litigation. In suburban Atlanta, for example, plans to construct a new Christian Church building ran into trouble when members of an existing Christian Church congregation testified to the municipal planning commission that the proposed church was too close to theirs. In Chicago the city's zoning board turned down an application in 1953—the first time it had done so since the city's zoning ordinance went into effect in 1923—when neighbors objected to a spiritualist church being built in the community. The board decided the proposed building was too small for a lot that could be put to better use, worried that the property would not be maintained to the standard of the expensive homes nearby, and figured the members probably wouldn't be living in the neighborhood. In another instance, the zoning board stipulated that off-street parking be provided even though the orthodox synagogue's members walked to services.[44] Other communities drew distinctions among kinds of religion, for instance allowing scouts and civic clubs to meet in churches but not at Jewish centers. In other cases churches and synagogues faced restrictions on the height, size, and architecture of buildings and the size and location of parking lots; some communities were allowed to construct buildings in lower-income neighborhoods but not in high-income developments. As in the cases about meetings and disturbances, the terms under which freedom of assembly operated had to be negotiated.

Assembling for Dissent

In 1958 restriction of freedom of assembly of a different sort came before the courts. Religious and other community groups had never been required to disclose the names of members. Some groups over the years, such as Masonic lodges, advertised themselves as "secret societies," and others, especially small sects, operated as closed membership groups that took pride in the privacy they guaranteed their members. Religious groups had long believed in protecting their members' identities even from proposals by the US Census Bureau to ask questions about religion on grounds that this information could result in government interference.[45] The associations whose members were most at risk were communist and anarchist groups, especially during the 1920s and 1930s, but cases involving these groups clarified the conditions under which freedom of assembly was protected. The landmark case involving freedom of assembly was *DeJonge v. Oregon* (1937), in which the US Supreme Court reversed the plaintiff's conviction in a lower court for having attended a meeting of the Communist Party. The ruling affirmed the value of free assembly to provide opportunities for free political discussion and declared that a person's liberty to participate should not be curtailed, even if the group advocated violence, unless the person specifically and personally acted to incite violence or overthrow the government.[46]

The case that came to the US Supreme Court in 1958 and 1959 grew out of the antisegregation bus boycott and protests of 1955 and 1956 in Montgomery, Alabama. Churches—including Mt. Zion Church, where an initial strategy meeting took place; Dexter Avenue Baptist Church, pastored by Reverend Martin Luther King Jr.; and Holt Street Baptist Church, where a mass meeting attended by an estimated five thousand persons was held—played a central role as places of assembly. To hinder the desegregation activities taking place, the state of Alabama passed laws preventing attorneys from bringing suits against segregation laws and requiring the NAACP to publish the names and addresses of its members. The NAACP resisted on grounds that members whose names and addresses were known were already being subjected to intimidation, such as losing their jobs and having their homes firebombed, and would be prey to future threats if membership information was published. In its decision the Supreme Court determined that Alabama had violated the right of due process guaranteed by the Fourteenth Amendment. The decision also held that freedom of assembly included freedom from such intimidation and to that end included the right to keep secret the names and addresses of members.[47]

The NAACP received support in the case from a study conducted by the American Jewish Congress's Commission on Law and Social Action. The commission's report, titled *Assault upon Freedom of Association: A Study of the Southern Attack on the National Association for the Advancement of Colored People*, described each of the southern states' attacks on the NAACP and defended freedom of association as an "indispensable part of the struggle to preserve democracy against totalitarianism" as well as a basic constitutional guarantee. The report included a foreword by National Council of Churches president Eugene Carson Blake and statements from Protestant and Catholic leaders as well as from social scientists and public officials. "The time has come for law-abiding citizens of the United States—whatever their opinion of the NAACP—to rally to its defense in those states where its very right to existence as an organization is being challenged not merely by private individuals but by government itself," wrote the director of the Social Action Department of the National Catholic Welfare Council.[48] In further support of the NAACP, a coalition of religious and secular organizations filed an amicus brief on behalf of the American Jewish Congress, American Baptist Convention's Commission on Christian Social Progress, American Friends Service Committee, Anti-Defamation League of B'nai B'rith, Board of Home Missions of the Congregational and Christian Churches, Council for Christian Social Action of the United Church of Christ, and United Synagogue of America, among others. "We as churches," a related statement issued by the Texas Church

Council declared, "recognize the grave threat to all associations and all liberties when the freedom of any voluntary association is assailed. The freedom of one is the freedom of all."[49]

The amicus brief, authored by attorney Leo Pfeffer, argued that private voluntary associations, whether religious, civic, educational, or recreational, are constitutionally protected from attempts by state or federal government to prohibit or inhibit their activities. Attempts such as those imposed by the state of Alabama, the brief asserted, "place in jeopardy the fundamental constitutional right of individuals to join together to form associations in order to express and advance their views." Citing Locke's arguments about religious association, it emphasized that "civilized society contemplates free and voluntary association" for the enjoyment of one another's company as one of the fundamental means through which the pursuit of happiness is achieved. As such, voluntary associations, it said, should be welcomed "as an indispensable aspect of a democratic pluralistic society." The brief's sponsorship by a variety of religious organizations was meant to signal agreement among them but also to underscore the importance of voluntary associations as sources of diverse values and perspectives. They represented the manifold interests on which a vibrant democracy depended.[50]

It followed that voluntary associations should compete freely with one another rather than command the state's power to get their way. The common interest had to be taken into account as well as the special interests of particular groups. In other decisions, the court ruled to restrict the Ku Klux Klan and the Communist Party, and in the case of religion, it supported chaplaincies in the military and tax exemption for religious organizations on grounds of contributions to the public interest but restricted public support for parochial schools. Religion, Pfeffer argued, had to be understood as more than the sincerely held convictions of individuals, important as those were. It had to be understood as structured, institutional interest groups that engaged in patterned activities to achieve their objectives.[51]

At the time of the ruling in *NAACP v. Alabama*, many religious organizations were engaged in civil rights advocacy. Between 1950 and 1954, the St. John African Methodist Episcopal Church in Topeka, Kansas, was the principal location in which Oliver Brown and several of the other plaintiffs met in the case that went to the US Supreme Court as *Brown v. Board of Education*. Congregations were also places in which protests took place. One example occurred later in the 1950s when the Student Nonviolent Coordinating Committee organized kneel-ins to challenge Jim Crow practices in White churches. Black students visited Sunday services at White churches and were variously denied admission, admitted to a restricted space for colored participants, or welcomed, all providing publicity about what churches were or were not doing to support racial integration. In other instances congregations passed resolutions protesting racial discrimination within their denominations and provided meeting space for speakers to be heard and for street protests and sit-ins to be planned. An early drugstore chain sit-in, for example, was organized and practiced in the basement of a Catholic church in Wichita, Kansas.[52]

The civil rights movement exemplified another important feature of freedom of assembly—assembling meant forging *networks* of associations. These networks tied people with common interests together, often reflecting particular religious traditions that in turn accorded with racial, ethnic, and regional differences. Many—such as the National Student Christian Movement among Protestants and the National Federation of Temple Sisterhoods among Jews—were networks that tied together local chapters within religious traditions. Others were issue oriented, based on existing ties but organized around particular events and activities. For example, on January 1, 1959, approximately 2,500 people calling themselves Pilgrims of Prayer for the Public Schools convened in Richmond, Virginia, where they listened as speakers denounced school segregation, and then marched nineteen blocks through the rain to deliver a statement to the governor. The event's success depended on a network of Black churches. The demonstration was led by Black clergy and their members from approximately three hundred congregations scattered across Virginia, the District of Columbia, and the Carolinas. The clergy knew and had previously interacted with and supported one another: they were members of the Virginia Baptist State Convention, which formed after the Civil War to start independent

Black churches led by Black clergy without input from White churches; many of the clergy were alumni of the Virginia Theological Seminary and College in Lynchburg; and many were interconnected through the Congress of Racial Equality and NAACP.[53]

But religious groups also mobilized citizens who favored segregation. To combat the Brown decision, White citizens circulated petitions at deacons' meetings and Bible study groups, hosted speakers at women's missionary societies, submitted petitions to mayors and governors, organized White citizens' councils, and launched special interest groups—such as the North Carolina Association for the Preservation of Segregation and the States Rights Association of South Carolina. Over the next decade White churchgoers variously resisted desegregation by refusing to welcome Black visitors, disaffiliating from denominations that formally advocated racial reconciliation, and quietly supporting police and public officials in the name of law and order.[54] Some of these efforts to resist desegregation included arguments based on Jim Crow restrictive housing covenants in which White residents claimed that their right of freedom of assembly would be infringed if their neighborhoods were racially mixed.[55] Southern writers also argued that freedom of association implied the right not to associate—an argument deployed in the early 1960s by opponents of school integration and by Barry Goldwater in his 1964 presidential campaign.[56]

The other key to understanding the continuity between freedom of assembly in the 1950s and its more conflictive counterpart in the 1960s was the diversity of organizational styles and aims to which freedom of religion contributed. The increase in religious service attendance that pollsters documented was only the surface manifestation of a larger post–World War II expansion in religion that included buildings, seminaries, private colleges, and specialized denominational boards and committees. Congregations and denominations became more diverse in the kinds of ministries they were able to support. Equally important, spaces were available in which activists and reformers were able to develop programs that were insulated from the usual constraints of congregational and denominational policies. Some were progressive, seeking to broaden the meanings of democracy and its implications, while others focused on resisting those endeavors. The process, which was characterized by conflicting views within and among groups that considered themselves religious and among those that did not, benefited from the resources and styles of meeting that prevailed among voluntary associations in the 1950s but further diversified those resources and styles as well.

For example, in 1948 a group of students from Union Seminary in New York City initiated an inner-city ministry called the East Harlem Protestant Parish. With support from the seminary and seven Protestant denominations, the organization deliberately ran programs that countered the direction of postwar trends in American religion. It eschewed suburbanization and investment in buildings, engaged in community activism, and worked across racial lines. Over the next two decades, it assisted in developing leadership in local churches, staged protest marches and meetings against police brutality, advised parishioners on union strikes, initiated drug treatment programs, and helped residents deal with housing, health, and employment issues. It struggled with financial shortages, internal conflicts, and fraught dealings with public officials, health professionals, and social workers, and from the start it was guided by the idea that religion should be a free expression of the dictates of conscience (one of its founders had spent time in prison as a conscientious objector). It also served as a model, replicated in Chicago, Cleveland, Detroit, San Francisco, and several other cities, of how organized religion could enable the creation of spaces for innovation. Although much of what it did was conventional, offering prayer, Bible study, and worship as other congregations did, it used its distinctive funding and location to represent the interests of its inner-city community.[57]

Campus religious organizations were another launching pad for innovative activities and groups. During the 1950s college enrollments grew from approximately 2.1 million to 4.1 million and by the end of the 1960s climbed to 8 million. And, while enrollments doubled in private institutions, they grew sixfold in public institutions, which challenged religious leaders to start new campus ministries and expand others that had begun on selected campuses early in the century. Mainline

Protestant denominations, Catholics, and Jewish organizations founded student groups and provided financial support to cover the cost of buildings or rental space, dinners and outings, and the salaries of full-time staff. One notable consequence was that campus clergy were insulated from the constraints to which clergy in congregations were subject and thus were freer to engage in civil rights and other protest activities.[58] Some of the most notable civil rights demonstrations were in fact an outgrowth of campus ministries. One example was the 1967 school desegregation protests in Houston that gained national attention and that grew out of a campus ministry at Texas Southern University headed by African American Baptist minister William Lawson.[59]

Many of the campus ministries, though, were focused apolitically on personal faith, and yet in the process they cultivated leadership skills and facilitated social networks that carried social and political implications. For example, Campus Crusade for Christ, founded in 1951 at UCLA by Bill Bright, a former confectionary company owner, organized chapters on forty campuses by 1959, spread to more than a hundred by 1963, and during the 1960s expanded into an international ministry with chapters in twenty-five countries. Geared toward athletes, business majors, and other campus leaders and increasingly dependent on wealthy donors, it maintained a relatively quiet but consistent anticommunist stance and by the early 1970s was identified with antiabortion and antigay efforts.[60]

Just as campus ministries did, specialized organizational niches with independent funding and insulated from the middle-of-the-road expectations of local congregations provided spaces in which activism challenging middle-class conventions could take place. Metropolitan congregations with endowments and relative autonomy from denominational administration provided some of the most important of these niches. One example was the Community Church of New York, which had supported Reverend John Haynes Holmes in cofounding the NAACP and ACLU and advocating for pacifism before World War II, and which continued to provide a platform for Holmes's advocacy of pacifism in the 1950s and served as a meeting space for Jewish and humanist groups as well as Unitarians in the 1960s. Another example was

San Francisco's Glide Memorial Methodist Church, where support from a generous endowment gave it the freedom to engage in civil rights activism, minister to the city's homosexual population, provide legal aid to persons arrested by the police, stage rock concerts, and host antiwar speakers.[61] In contrast, shoestring groups operated without such funding. For example, Koinonia Farm in Georgia, founded in 1942 as a self-supporting place for families to live as a Christian community—and to enact racial reconciliation—initiated the Fund for Humanity in the 1960s, which evolved into Habitat for Humanity International in the 1970s. Catholic monasteries provided another space for social activism, notably through the work of Dorothy Day, Thomas Merton, and Daniel Berrigan.

Although little was made of it at the time, religious publishing was another vehicle through which religious groups forged activist networks. Religious publishing in the form of denominational periodicals had grown steadily since the early 1800s and by the 1950s was expanding rapidly. After World War II the interest in national and international news that had been driven by the war gravitated toward a middle-class reading public eager to define itself as prosperous, up to date, and interested in the latest trends in fashion, appliances, automobiles, and leisure activities. *Life, Time,* and the *Reader's Digest* supplied information on all these topics—including religion. Religious publications such as *America, Christian Century, Christianity Today, Commonweal,* and the *National Catholic Reporter* attracted a growing middle-class audience as well. Less visibly, networks of reading clubs, book discussion groups, Bible studies, newsletters, and bookstores emerged with an audience that spanned the various smaller evangelical Protestant denominations. These networks, even though they were composed of readers from different denominations, forged common interests, exposed readers to common authors, and facilitated a growing awareness of common views about social and political issues.[62]

In a few cases, the networks that started in book discussion groups grew into national movements. One of the more successful of these movements was led by Lottie Beth Hobbs, a church secretary at a Church of Christ church in Houston who wrote books for women advocating traditional concepts of femininity and spirituality, gained a following through churchwomen's groups, and lectured about Christian schools and the dangers of communism. By the late 1960s Hobbs had founded a grassroots organization called Women Who Want to Be Women and in the early 1970s became one of the national leaders against the Equal Rights Amendment.[63] Another such movement was the American Public Relations Forum, a Southern California anticommunist Catholic group whose members formed a loose network of women who also participated in Spiritual Mobilization, Pro-America, and Freedom Clubs and discussed common concerns about schools, race relations, and legislation.[64]

Although most of the issues to which religious organizations contributed were domestic, international issues were also of interest. Especially in contrast with the international spread of communism, Christians and Jews saw themselves playing a role in the furtherance of democracy abroad. When the United Nations adopted the Universal Declaration of Human Rights in 1948, religious groups applauded its defense of liberty, freedom of religion and conscience, and freedom of peaceful association but also debated the particulars of how it should be interpreted. The Baptist World Alliance, representing Baptists in fifty-two countries, issued a manifesto encouraging nations to ratify the UN declaration. The manifesto charged that totalitarianism should be resisted not only when it appeared as communism but also whenever Roman Catholicism or other state religions discriminated against religious minorities. A spokesperson for the World Council of Churches cautioned that the declaration would be meaningless without specific laws and human rights committees being established. The National Council of Churches, meeting in 1952, affirmed its support of the declaration but urged that it be supplemented with economic aid and technical assistance to underdeveloped countries. Methodists also affirmed their support but rejected language criticizing free enterprise, asserting instead that democracy is ruled only by principles of liberty and justice. The Catholic Association for International Peace urged that the declaration be revised to reference God specifically as the source of inalienable and equal rights. Others, speaking as individual religious leaders, expressed concern that the declaration was inconsistent with certain aspects of national sovereignty expressed in the US Constitution.[65]

The steps religious groups took to further democracy included the resettlement of refugees and the transmission of international aid. When President Eisenhower established a Committee for Hungarian Refugee Relief in December 1956, almost all of the thirty-eight thousand refugees were resettled with the assistance of local religious congregations, in some instances against misgivings that the refugees might be communists. Congregations in New York, Wisconsin, Kansas, Maine, California, and dozens of other places helped refugees find housing and jobs, learn English, and enroll their children in school. Eisenhower praised the effort as a contribution to the fight against the "ultimate tyranny" of communism.[66] This resettlement work grew from earlier efforts that included direct assistance from US congregations to refugees in Europe during World War I initiated by the American Friends Service Committee, and relief work during World War II under Roosevelt's War Relief Control Board conducted by the National Catholic Welfare Conference, Lutheran World Relief, Church World Service, American Jewish Joint Distribution, and American Friends Service Committee. These and other organizations, including the United Methodist Committee on Relief and the National Association of Evangelicals' War Relief Commission, continued their work under the Truman, Eisenhower, Kennedy, and Johnson administrations. Coming at the work from their varying traditions, ethnicities, and styles of ministry, they exemplified the kind of organizational participation that political scientists Gabriel Almond and Sidney Verba, writing about voluntary associations and democracy in 1963, thought essential to greater pluralism.[67]

The vast variety of groups, movements, and advocacy organizations that populated the nation during the 1950s and 1960s, then, was further evidence of the "splitting and splintering" of America's voluntary associations that Arthur Schlesinger aptly described in 1944. The sundering of old ways and the formation of new endeavors were probably inevitable given the profound demographic, economic, technological, and cultural changes the nation was experiencing. But if all that creative adaptation was inevitable, it was also furthered by the fact that America was a nation of joiners, not simply because Americans liked joining, but because the right to freely assemble was something they were willing to defend. Joining was thus much more than simply participating in the neighborhood club or church of one's choice. Participating in a voluntary organization required advocating for the specific rights on which freedom of assembly depended, and negotiating about definitions of privacy, freedom of speech, property, and community safety. These definitions, even when they were determined by the courts, took account of differing contexts and therefore were unstable, which meant that democracy's role had to be understood as a continuing process of contestation and adjudication.

4

Human Dignity

WELFARE PROVISION, THE STATE,
AND CHARITABLE CHOICE

IT IS NOT MENTIONED EXPLICITLY in the US Constitution or the Declaration of Independence, but human dignity is one of the core values of our system of government. A well-functioning democracy, we believe, must institutionalize rules in the form of laws, norms in the form of social conventions, and habits in the form of taken-for-granted personal and group ways of behavior that in concert uphold dignity and defend persons from being subjected to indignities. Chief among these indignities are practices that prevent people from freely making choices in the pursuit of their interests and happiness. We hold dignity to be the source of unalienable rights and ultimately the standard against which we judge the laws and policies that govern us. Dignity pertains to all humans, not just to citizens or elites or those who have achieved exceptional merit. Dignity is thus expansive, and it is moral, a standard against which right and wrong are judged and to which people living in a democracy are expected to feel obligated.[1]

Human dignity is a prevailing emphasis in both religious and nonreligious traditions. The biblical tradition that informs American culture asserts that humans have superior worth because they are created in the image of God. Having eaten of the tree of the knowledge of good and evil, humans have the unique capacity to exercise free will in making moral choices.[2] An emphasis on human dignity is also grounded in arguments that do not refer to religion. One is that humans are a species above other species by virtue of our capacity for reasoning. Another is that humans are distinctive and thus worthy of dignity because we act freely and are capable of setting our own values. Yet another holds that dignity should be considered as a high universal value because it is in fact highly valued across numerous philosophical, religious, and cultural traditions. Other arguments are concerned less with defending why human dignity is important than with specifying what it might mean in practice and yet in broadly applicable terms. Notions of agency, capacity, and self-worth have become operative in these discussions, as has an emphasis on the recognition, respect, freedom of choice, and equality of opportunity on which dignity depends.[3]

Human dignity is an ideal topic for examining how religion contributes to democracy. Dignity is a value and is commonly understood as such, a value that implies something of worth that has to be protected, argued for, and defended rather than treated merely as a feature of the human condition that somehow sustains itself or that depends only on material prosperity and equitable market conditions. Dignity is the kind of value that proponents of religion say is furthered by religion's teachings about the divinely sourced worth of the individual. Assertions about the religious values underpinning conceptions of human dignity do not advance understanding of how religion contributes, though, unless attention is given to the concrete ways in which dignity has been defined and operationalized.

After World War II, the horror of mass slaughter and the unthinkable degradation of humanity that had been committed during the war, and during the one preceding it, prompted renewed emphasis on the conditions necessary for the protection of human dignity. In 1945 the preamble to the charter of the United Nations affirmed faith in the "dignity and worth of the human person." In championing the Universal Declaration of Human Rights, Eleanor Roosevelt associated rights and freedom with humans' dignity to "walk the earth with their heads high and look all men in the face." In 1950, while praising the UN's support in Korea, President Truman castigated the Soviet Union's evil, violent, and cynical attacks on decency, democracy, and human dignity. In 1953 the

US bishops serving as the administrative board of the National Catholic Welfare Conference issued a lengthy statement titled "The Dignity of Man," which asserted the superior worth of humanity and the natural dignity of every human being. In 1954, addressing an international conference organized by World Christian Endeavor, President Eisenhower argued that the dignity of man, which reflected the spiritual character of humanity, was the reason to work for free government.[4]

Although human dignity was a value about which there was widespread agreement, how it was interpreted varied. Jean-Paul Sartre, whose 1946 *Existentialism Is a Humanism* was both praised and criticized, argued that the best defense of human dignity lay in acknowledging humans' totally inescapable responsibility for their own choices and actions. The Catholic bishops' statement emphasized the divine grace from which human honor derived and against which violence, vice, injustice, oppression, and depersonalization were exhibiting a troubling increase. Political scientist Harold Lasswell equated it with democracy, arguing that dignity was best described as wide sharing of the decision-making process. Eleanor Roosevelt believed in the inherent dignity of all human beings as the common condition of humanity and thus in the universality of human rights. The various descriptions derived from Judeo-Christian thinking, Kantian idealism, and humanism. They also reflected postwar emphases on the dignity of work, human agency, education, self-actualization, and international development.[5]

The issue that illustrates almost more clearly than any other the competing moral claims the various faith communities advanced in the interest of upholding human dignity is poverty. Few issues during the last third of the twentieth century were as widely and consistently regarded as an assault on human dignity as poverty, and few were as deeply contested as the question of how programs directed at the alleviation of poverty should be conducted to minimize these violations. From Lyndon Johnson's War on Poverty through the Personal Responsibility and Work Opportunity legislation enacted during the Clinton administration, and from the Bush administration's Faith-Based and Community Initiatives through subsequent administrations' promotion of faith-based public assistance, religious organizations advocated directly—and were interlocutors in other deliberations—for competing views about how best to assist and at the same time uphold the dignity of the poor. In asserting alternative claims about dignity, religious organizations cast the issue of public welfare in moral terms and did so in ways reminiscent of the debates about centralized government in the 1930s. In the 1960s and increasingly during the last two decades of the century, moral claims were made, on the one hand, that assistance to the poor should be a matter of rights, publicly funded, systemic, and rationally evaluated, and on the other hand, that it should be administered through private or a combination of private and public funding, based on an ethic of compassion, and oriented toward the whole person, including spiritual needs and aspirations. The lines separating the two were not distinct; indeed, there were variations and mixed approaches as far as specific policies were concerned.

Within the larger, much-documented history of the debate about welfare policy, it is possible to identify a stream of arguments specifically about human dignity and oriented variously toward the morality of rights, equality, freedom, self-worth, responsibility, and thriving. The various religious and nonreligious groups that advocated on behalf of these issues contended vigorously, sometimes in collaboration and often in opposition to one another, for alternative perspectives. These arguments referred deeply and from diverging perspectives to democracy. They dealt with specific programs for income assistance, healthcare, and housing but they were also about human decency and dignity. They served in their own ways as reminders that democracy is supposed to be about more than partisanship and self-interest, even when partisanship and self-interest so often prevail.

A Time for Choosing

On January 14, 1982, President Reagan delivered a lunchtime address at the Waldorf Astoria Hotel in midtown Manhattan. Governor Hugh Carey, Senator Daniel Patrick Moynihan, Mayor Ed Koch, Cardinal Terence Cooke, and dozens of the city's business elite were there. David Rockefeller of Chase Manhattan Bank introduced Reagan. The nation had been in a recession since July and unemployment had risen to 7.5 percent. Moynihan, Cooke, and others in the room had been involved at various levels in federal antipoverty efforts since the 1960s. Reagan devoted more than half of the speech to the issue. Echoing the line from his inaugural address that "government is not the solution, government is the problem," he observed that the current ills were the fault of big government and needed a different approach. "The best view of big government is in a rearview mirror," he said. Big government was inimical to the "human spirit," to freedom, individual initiative, and personal responsibility. The future lay not in the America "bound by the Potomac" but in the one "beyond it." That was the America "whose rich tradition of generosity began with simple acts of neighbor caring for neighbor."[6]

Those who had followed his career since the 1960s knew these were themes Reagan had embraced for as long as he had been active in electoral politics. Reagan's small-town roots in rural Illinois forged a lasting affinity with the idea that small government is best. In the early 1960s Reagan cooperated with Edgar C. Bundy's Church League of America to produce a film about the welfare state in which he depicted state welfarism as a threat undermining the American traditions of individual liberty, local rule, and free enterprise. The thirty-minute film was distributed at one hundred dollars a copy to civic clubs, patriotic organizations, and churches, although no evidence indicates that the effort was widely successful.[7] Certainly its impact was far less significant than Reagan's 1964 nationally televised speech, "A Time for Choosing," which supported Barry Goldwater's presidential campaign and launched Reagan on his own path to the presidency.

"A Time for Choosing," which Reagan delivered to a studio audience in Los Angeles, followed the script his stump speeches for Goldwater used and was patterned after the Hoover Commission's tactic of highlighting outrageous examples of government waste, inefficiency, and indeed lack of common sense. "They've just declared Rice County, Kansas, a depressed area," Reagan said as an example of the Johnson administration's ludicrous efforts to address unemployment. "Rice County, Kansas, has two hundred oil wells, and the 14,000 people there have over 30 million dollars on deposit in personal savings in their banks. And when the government tells you you're depressed, lie down and be depressed." The more government spent on poverty, the worse poverty became, he argued. It was the same danger the nation faced from communism: an ideological war between the American tradition of individual freedom and the opposing trend toward totalitarianism. "The full power of centralized government—this was the very thing the Founding Fathers sought to minimize."

The speech resonated with a large swath of the American public who believed that democracy meant freedom and that freedom meant working together in local communities to get things done. It was consistent with Tocqueville's notion that voluntary associations protected Americans from an undemocratic centralization of government. Voluntary associations provided individuals with the means to articulate their diverse interests and express their ideas and grievances. Community groups facilitated deliberation, bonding, and trust, and, as Tocqueville also suggested, they got things done. When a neighbor fell sick or a barn needed to be raised, neighbors banded together. This was good for democracy because it kept power in the hands of local citizens rather than having it gravitate toward central authorities. And it was more efficient because it was attentive to the variation in local needs and opportunities. It did not preclude government from getting involved in solving problems, but it implied that local government was more effective when it worked in partnership with voluntary associations.

Reagan devoted much of the "Time for Choosing" speech to criticizing the welfare state, terming it the kind of centralized government that turned free men and women into "the masses," stripping businesspeople of incentives, threatening farmers' livelihoods, and substituting government planning for individual initiative. He cautioned that the nation was being "spiritually" and "morally" weakened as we traded "our freedom for the soup kitchen of the welfare state." Although he did not state it explicitly, it was clear that Reagan viewed the welfare state as dehumanizing. The most memorable part of the speech was the story of a woman in Los Angeles a judge had told Reagan about who came before the court seeking a divorce. The woman had six children and was pregnant with her seventh. Her husband was earning $250 a month. But if she did not have a husband, she was eligible for $330 a month from the Aid to Families with Dependent Children program. "Yet anytime you and I question the schemes of the do-gooders," Reagan observed, "we're denounced as being against their humanitarian goals."[8]

The story in miniature expressed competing views of human dignity. The view from the perspective of the welfare state was that the woman was a person of worth who unconditionally had a right to the assistance for which she was eligible under the Aid to Families with Dependent Children program. Whether the terms of the program were the best that could be provided was a matter for policy determination. She was not at fault for doing what she thought best. She was a free agent capable of making her own choices, limited as they were. From Reagan's perspective, dignity implied not only freedom but also moral responsibility. The welfare state was conducive to neither. It impinged on freedom and it undermined moral responsibility. Explicitly, public welfare programs were ill conceived; implicitly, the woman was at fault for having too many children and perhaps also for seeking a divorce. The persons in the story who exhibited dignity were the ones who understood better than the do-gooders what true humanitarianism was.

The story, the speech, and the wider divergence of perspectives about the intersections of welfare, dignity, and democracy were the context in which religious organizations and their spokespersons contributed to the debate. The perspective critical of the welfare state that Reagan represented gained traction among religious groups that had been critical of the New Deal or that felt that many in the liberal wing of the religious establishment had become soft on communism and weak on orthodox doctrine. The connection between communism in Europe and the welfare state in America that had been voiced since the 1930s suggested a threat to human dignity that people of faith should resist. "The conscience of the conservative," Barry Goldwater wrote in 1960, "is pricked by anyone who would debase the dignity of the individual human being. Today, therefore, he is at odds with dictators who rule by terror and equally with those gentler collectivists who ask our permission to play God with the human race."[9] As he campaigned for president in 1964,

Goldwater urged the churches to denounce communism and keep their focus on individual morality. In Los Angeles, Freedom Club's Reverend Dr. James W. Fifield Jr., who was leading the fight against the merger that would bring the United Church of Christ into being, affirmed his support of Goldwater, arguing that the welfare state was expensive, lacked morality, and preached negativism that the churches should reject. Christian Crusade evangelist Billy James Hargis was another critic of the welfare state, likening it to communism in its attack on individual initiative and individual responsibility.[10]

Separation of church and state figured into the churches' views as well. It was within the purview of congregations to preach repentance and salvation, to encourage "brotherly love," and to care for widows and orphans. Those were appropriate ways of assisting the needy and of respecting their dignity as brothers and sisters of faith. It was not appropriate, however, to post statements in the church bulletin about civil rights or the War on Poverty, let alone discuss candidates for public office from the pulpit. This was the view that many clergy and lay leaders embraced along with commentators who worried that the War on Poverty was politicizing religion. It was pleasing to hear exhortations "to take more seriously God's commandments to brotherly love," William F. Buckley wrote in 1964. But he thought the churches should heed Edmund Burke's warning: "No sound ought to be heard in the church but the healing voice of Christian charity. The cause of civil liberty and civil government gains as little as that of religion by this confusion of duties."[11]

Those who supported the War on Poverty, in contrast, viewed it as a measure that they should publicly embrace and as an opportunity to which their own programs could contribute. As the Johnson administration drew up its proposal to send to Congress, the National Catholic Welfare Conference immediately endorsed the plan. At a May 1964 meeting of the Council of Churches of Greater Washington, a network representing twenty-five Protestant denominations, Assistant Secretary of Labor Daniel Patrick Moynihan explained the War on Poverty, and the delegates voted to contact committee chairs and members of Congress to urge passage of the facilitating legislation. The following month in Atlanta, the Community Council on Social and Religious Reform pledged its aim of cooperating with newly authorized agencies to combat poverty and provide job training. Over the next year, the National Council of Churches and the Synagogue Council of America also went on record supporting the legislation.[12]

Some of the strongest statements were made by the National Conference of Catholic Bishops. In its 1966 "Pastoral Statement on Race Relations and Poverty," the conference asserted that laws and programs to address poverty should be based above all on a conviction in the common dignity of all: "We are all the children of God. We share the same rights before God and man. [We] desire that the doors of opportunity be opened equally to all." The bishops called for programs that included education, job training, housing, and family support. "Where welfare relief is necessary, it should be given in a context that favors family stability and respects the human dignity of those who cannot earn their living." The statement called for nongovernment religion-administered programs as well as government programs. "It is our hope that all our Catholic people will join with their Christian and Jewish brothers, and indeed with all men of good will, in common projects which affirm and realize the dignity of all men." Over the next decade the bishops issued additional statements focusing on poverty, race relations, antipoverty legislation, farm labor, welfare reform, the food crisis, feeding the hungry, and economic policies.[13]

Religious organizations that had long been involved in healthcare, orphanages, and poor relief became active partners in daycare provision under modifications included in the 1962 Social Security Act, the staffing of community mental health centers under mental health legislation passed in 1963, and preschool programs created by the Head Start program of 1964. An effect of the expansion of government programs was to channel religious efforts into distinctive niches, for example working more comfortably with family and mental health assistance than with job training and housing, and partnering more readily through interdenominational and interfaith organizations than as local congregations. Another connection consisted of clergy working as employees of public service agencies or serving on advisory boards. Having been directly involved in low-income neighborhood ministries, working with youth gangs, or administering foster care and health clinics, clergy were invited to serve on municipal and county public welfare commissions both for their expertise and for the real and symbolic linkages they provided with various segments of the community.

Besides partnering with publicly funded antipoverty programs, another role that religious organizations played was to vouch for programs' credibility. A case in point occurred in 1968 when The Woodlawn Organization (TWO), which administered block clubs and neighborhood associations in southeast Chicago, received nearly a million dollars from the Office of Economic Opportunity for a job training program and in turn hired several members of the Blackstone Rangers, a street gang, to work in the program. News reports about the gang's alleged criminal activities and Woodlawn's support provided grist in the US Senate to legislators critical of the OEO. The critics' attempt to shut down the Woodlawn program faltered, though, partly through its connection with half a dozen churches in the immediate neighborhood and with Chicago's First Presbyterian Church, a well-established mixed-race congregation whose pastor was well known in the city and who, from conversations with the Blackstone Rangers, was able to publicize the positive side of what they were doing. When he was criticized by members of the clergy, his arguments received backing from other religious leaders who communicated to the Senate on his behalf.

This was an instance in which an underrepresented community's interests and activities were made known both to the public and to public officials through a channel provided by religious organizations. In addition to defending the Woodlawn effort, the clergy group also criticized the critics' tactics. Noting the racial tensions present that summer in the aftermath of Dr. Martin Luther King Jr.'s assassination, one of the clergy called the Senate subcommittee to task for the incendiary language in which its investigation was conducted. "It does not seem to be an investigation at all; rather a trial in which charges are made, witnesses summoned to prove the charges, but cross-examination by lawyers not allowed, opposing witnesses not admitted." Not only that, but the senator in charge of the investigation, the pastor wrote, was rude to the witnesses and made remarks about their religion that were out of order. Whether anyone other than those immediately involved took note of the exchange, it was but one of many in which clergy and religious organizations were involved. That summer alone, religious leaders also weighed in on gun control legislation, civil rights, crime, schools, international human rights, suppression of freedom in Eastern Europe, the Peace Corps, and the role of religious organizations in international economic development.[14]

Where the churches took differing positions, then, was in whether they should assist the poor principally through voluntary charitable efforts under the churches' own auspices or whether they should support and indeed cooperate with government programs. In the 1960s the one side was sympathetic to the Republicans' criticisms of the welfare state, while the other side was supportive of the Democrats' antipoverty legislation. Both were motivated by a biblical concern for the poor. Both were interested in individual freedom and responsibility, although the one stressed moral uplift to a greater extent and the other emphasized human rights. The two also reflected the differing positions of religious organizations in the social landscape, on the one hand oriented toward the routine acts of caring that could be conducted in relatively stable middle-class congregations, and on the other hand influenced by participation in large-scale social assistance programs. As National Catholic Conference for Interracial Justice director Raymond Hilliard observed in a 1965 lecture, "It must be realized that because of the growing complexity of modern society, the disadvantaged, in particular, more and more lose the very ability to make choices, to be responsible, to know what must be done and to take action."[15]

A third perspective was in some ways more interesting because it straddled the division represented by the other two. This third perspective was best illustrated by a case that bore a resemblance to the story Reagan told about the impoverished mother of six. At 8:30 p.m. on Wednesday, April 14, 1965, Mary Etheredge, a twenty-seven-year-old mother of five, died in the psychiatric ward at the District of Columbia General Hospital. She was reported to have been going from one public or private welfare agency to another for several days in hope of securing food for her children. An autopsy determined that the cause of death was a massive pulmonary embolism accompanied by marked bilateral congestion of the lungs.[16] According to the chief psychiatrist who had examined her when she was admitted, she was "detached," "uncommunicative," and "unable to give a clear story." In her last letter to her mother in North Carolina, she wrote, "I know you're worried about me. I just want you to know I'm doing fine. The Lord has wonderfully blessed me."

Mary Etheredge's death prompted an investigation of what had gone wrong. She was said to have been a popular girl at the high school she attended in North Carolina and was elected secretary of her class. Married shortly after graduation, she and her husband moved in 1960 with their two children to Washington, DC, where he found work as a baker and cook. But the work was unsteady, the income too meager to live on, and the couple lost their home. Mary and the children moved in temporarily with a woman who became her godmother and went on public assistance, which was never enough. In her final days before a social worker at Family and Child Services arranged with the police to have her taken to the hospital, she and the children had sought help from the Women's Bureau and found shelter at a nearby convent. The Bible Way Baptist Church she and the children had attended—a predominantly Black congregation—had tried to help by taking up a small offering. "They were good people, both of them," the pastor said, "but they just couldn't work things out."[17]

The *Washington Post* covered the story for a few days, but Mary Etheredge would have been forgotten had it not been for an organization called the DC Coalition of Conscience. The coalition, under the direction of Reverend Walter E. Fauntroy of New Bethel Baptist Church, was an association of some forty churches, civil rights groups, and civic organizations concerned about the administration of the metropolitan area's welfare programs. Black pastors, like Fauntroy, headed most of the churches. As the coalition followed the Etheredge case, it learned that Mary's mother in North Carolina, who was now caring for the children, had received fifty dollars from an anonymous donor, was expecting to receive only a dollar a day from public assistance for each of the children, was still waiting after two months to receive anything, and was on the verge of being evicted from her home for being unable to pay the rent.[18]

The DC Coalition of Conscience under Fauntroy's leadership was one of a growing number of inner-city organizations that worked directly with the poor through African American churches and neighborhood centers but that also advocated for human rights and reforms of public assistance programs. After graduating from Yale Divinity School, Fauntroy returned to the inner-city neighborhood where he was raised, and as pastor at New Bethel he became an active critic of redevelopment projects that he saw benefiting absentee owners while displacing resident families. In addition to the Coalition of Conscience, Fauntroy played an active role in several other community organizations that dealt with housing and welfare policies and forged ties among churches and with the NAACP, Congress of Racial Equality, Archbishop's Committee on Community Relations of the Catholic Archdiocese, and other advocacy organizations. In 1966 the coalition joined in creating and supporting Free DC, a network of civil rights organizations advocating for home rule in the district, and after further work on housing, Fauntroy was elected as the district's nonvoting delegate to Congress. In 1965 the coalition's chief concern was bringing Mary Etheredge's death to a wider audience in the interest of welfare reform.[19]

That audience was the US Congress. At a demonstration of some three hundred to four hundred people organized by the coalition, marchers carried a gray casket representing Etheredge. An Episcopal bishop derided the welfare system as a violation of the principles of democracy, religion, humanity, and justice. Other speakers called for a list of reforms that included assistance for the children of unemployed parents, an extension of the daycare program for children of working mothers, an increase in support for foster children, and an increase in emergency services. A report of the event noted that one of the speakers had denounced Senator Robert C. Byrd, the West Virginia Democrat who chaired the Senate Subcommittee on Health, Education, and Welfare, as "a little man, hardhearted, biased, and segregation oriented." Byrd was in fact segregation oriented; he had been in the Ku Klux Klan in the 1940s and filibustered the Civil Rights Act of 1964, and he would soon vote against the Voting Rights Act of 1965.[20] But he was adamant that his conscience was clear and to that end launched a hearing to probe the circumstances of Etheredge's death.

The hearing exonerated the various welfare agencies from any failings in the case and placed the blame for Etheredge's struggles on her husband, but stopped short of criticizing Etheredge herself. "I am impressed with the Christian character of this woman," Byrd said. "I feel she tried to live an honest, upright, and Christian life"—a statement resonant with the view that Black citizens merited fair treatment *if* they led exemplary moral lives.[21] The value of the hearing was the opportunity it provided to air the concerns the Coalition of Conscience had raised about the welfare system. These concerns included levels of funding and criteria of eligibility that were eventually decided in Congress but went beyond them in prompting a discussion about rights, compassion, decency, and civic responsibility. Late in the hearing, the discussion turned to the perennial question of work and whether those who were not working should be supported on public assistance or denied assistance. Several of the witnesses posed examples of people they had assisted personally who were unable to work or were working intermittently, seeking work, or busy tending their children. These were people, one of the pastors observed, "who have been eroded, who have been so violated by this system they are lost to the productive process and simply don't qualify psychologically, spiritually or whatever for what we call work." The conversation moved on to the important "man-in-the-house" rule that determined a mother and her children to be ineligible for public assistance if she was in a relationship with a man willing and able to provide support. In all, thirty-four factors were proposed that could contribute to ineligibility.[22]

A year earlier, Yale law professor Charles Reich had published an article that was to become a classic in the debate about welfare, rights, and dignity. In his best-selling *Greening of America* a few years later, Reich would celebrate the new freedoms of lifestyle and expression he saw happening among the young and better-educated segments of the White middle class. In the law review article, though, he focused on

the constraints that were impinging on the freedom of those who benefited from "government largess." Welfare, he argued, was one of numerous forms of "new property" deriving from government: jobs, services, benefits, farm subsidies, franchises, licenses, contracts.
Everything from highways and airport terminals to defense contracts
and the postal service could be counted as coming from the government's giant "syphon," which extracted money from citizens through
taxes and fees and returned it in these forms. The new property was
subject to laws that aimed to be in the interest of the general public.
This meant that it gave the government new opportunities to impose
conditions. It could require universities receiving government grants
to report the racial composition of their faculty. It could deny a junk
cart license because the applicant had been charged at some point with
a crime even though the crime was dismissed. Welfare recipients were
especially at risk. Reich cited a case in New York in which an elderly
man was denied public assistance on grounds that he slept in a barn
and thus was living in unsanitary conditions. "He has no right to defy
the standards and conventions of civilized society while being supported at public expense," the judge declared.[23]

Welfare recipients' right to privacy was another concern. The thirty-
four factors of ineligibility discussed at the Senate subcommittee hearing in 1965 left welfare investigators the task of determining whether a
man was present in the household. To ferret out fraud, investigators
made surprise visits to recipients' homes to see whether fathers, stepfa-
thers, or surrogate fathers who were alleged to be absent were in fact
present. Typically the visits occurred after midnight and in many cases
occurred more than once. One family consisting of a mother, teenage
son, and younger daughter were awakened at three o'clock in the morning by two men who without identifying themselves said they were
looking for the father. Several weeks later, they came again at one o'clock
in the morning. In another instance, the investigator arrived while the
mother was taking a bath, was let in by her nine-year-old daughter,
searched the closets, found a suit belonging to the mother's boyfriend
who visited occasionally, and discontinued the family's assistance. The

man-in-the-house rule was to be modified and states were given greater discretion in its enforcement. And yet reporting, monitoring, and collecting information were established features of welfare provision.[24]

Welfare and Democracy

When President Reagan spoke to New York's leaders at the Waldorf Astoria in 1982, the community groups and volunteers he had in mind were religious organizations as well as businesses and nonprofit associations. If every church and synagogue adopted ten poor families, Reverend Billy Graham had told him, all government welfare—federal, state, and local—could be eliminated. It would cost infinitely less, and it would actually help more because it would come from the heart. Welfare, the president said, was demoralizing. Private programs run by volunteers and administered by churches and community groups were better. As evidence, he pointed to the church-supported Jubilee Housing effort in Washington, DC, that "changes lives." He listed other groups in Massachusetts, Illinois, and California that harnessed generosity with lessons in personal responsibility. This, he said, was the meaning of the Bible's emphasis on faith, hope, and charity. The Good Samaritan practiced generosity that accrued to the goodness of both the victim and himself. "He didn't hurry on by and then when he got to town tell a caseworker that there was someone out there . . . that needed help." Caring of the kind the Samaritan delivered was inspirational. It resonated with Reagan's inherent optimistic belief that the nation's best days were ahead. "If we believe in ourselves and in the God who loves and protects us, together we can build a society more humane, more compassionate, more rewarding than any ever known in the history of man."[25]

The religious climate in 1982 was markedly different from what it had been in 1964. Then, the mainstream Protestant denominations that supported the National Council of Churches—Episcopalians, Lutherans, Methodists, Presbyterians, and what would soon become the United Church of Christ—were growing and sufficiently well funded to engage in a variety of domestic and international ministries on behalf of the needy; now, they were declining in membership and revenue. African American churches, mostly Protestant, were still concentrated in low-income neighborhoods in cities, but more of their members were now middle class and lived in suburbs. Jewish groups remained strong across the theological spectrum, but leaders voiced greater concern about the loss of active members through interreligious marriage and secularity. Roman Catholics who had been solid supporters of the Democratic Party in 1964 were now increasingly Republican. Evangelical Protestants who had been known earlier for steering clear of politics were now a larger and more vocal presence in national politics.

Division within Protestant denominations had ramifications for public welfare provision. The Palmer Home for Children was an interesting example. Founded as an orphanage in 1895 by the First Presbyterian Church of Columbus, Mississippi, the facility had a 120-acre campus, multiple buildings, and an annual budget in excess of $500,000, a focus of intrachurch conflict by 1980. The difficulty began in 1970 when a doctrinal dispute led to a split in the congregation. Like many Presbyterian congregations at the time, one of the factions remained loyal to the denomination while the other joined the more conservative Presbyterian Church in America. A struggle for control of the Palmer Home ensued through proposed amendments to the facility's charter and contested elections of trustees. Central to the dispute was whether it should be run more as a nonsectarian welfare agency or more like a church, which was the view that prevailed. Over the following decade, the organization became an example frequently cited in the debate about government funding. As one of the former residents explained, "If we ever get to the point that we take government assistance, that's the end of the value of Palmer because the government that gets involved in these social things . . . is a sure sign of failure."[26]

The larger division between theologically conservative and moderate or liberal Protestants also mapped onto political alignments, with conservatives favoring Republican candidates and policies, and liberals opting for Democrats. African American churches were similarly divided, although conservative theology more easily aligned with progressive political views than it did among White Protestants. Jewish groups were more often supportive of Democratic than Republican candidates, but there were many exceptions. Roman Catholics were divided on important social teachings about birth control and gender roles in the church, and they differed from other traditions in how parishes were governed, but there was one issue on which they and conservative Protestants agreed.

The major issue on which Roman Catholics and conservative Protestants grew closer together was abortion. When the US Supreme Court in 1973 decided for the plaintiffs in *Roe v. Wade,* the decision was of special interest to religious organizations that had mobilized on both sides of the issue. In Texas, where the case originated, Catholic Charities had been on record against proposals easing restrictions on abortion for more than a decade, while the United Presbyterian Church in the USA and the Union of American Hebrew Congregations had expressed modest approval. The Southern Baptist Convention initially instructed its Christian Life Commission to publish materials on both sides of the issue but shifted increasingly toward the conservative side. Grassroots "right-to-life" groups attracted conservative Protestants as well as Catholics.

By 1980 abortion had also become a pivotal topic in discussions of human dignity. The connection was, on one side, that human dignity was violated when a mother died whose life could have been saved by an abortion. Arguments were voiced too about the right of choice as a means of family planning among low-income families. On the other side, the connection was that human dignity necessitated protecting the life of the unborn. The Vatican and US bishops had been the most vocal advocates for dignity, broadly conceived, since the 1950s and in statements about its importance drew on teachings much older. In 1965 at the conclusion of the Second Vatican Council, Pope Paul VI issued *Dignitatis Humanae* in strong defense of religious freedom and the dignity of the human person. During the 1970s the church's focus was increasingly on abortion. In his 1979 Christmas message, for example, Pope John Paul II asserted that the child is "a test of our respect for the mystery of life, upon which, from the very first moment of conception, the Creator places the imprint of his image and likeness."[27]

Like abortion, homosexuality posed fundamental questions about human dignity—toward which religious groups also took differing positions. Conservative Protestants and traditional Catholics generally held that homosexuality was morally wrong, while mainline Protestant denominations and Jewish organizations were divided or held "progressive" views on questions of biblical teaching and about nondiscriminatory public policy. Activist groups emerged to mobilize on one side or the other around particular issues such as the right of homosexuals to be ordained or welcomed as members of congregations. On the conservative side, groups such as Presbyterians United for Biblical Concerns and an evangelical Methodist caucus called Leaders of Good News launched campaigns to oppose gay ordination, publicize what they regarded as biblical teachings against homosexuality, and in some cases advocate for gay repentance and conversion. Opponents of homosexuality gained national attention in 1977 through singer Anita Bryant's "Save Our Children" campaign, which was endorsed by the Southern Baptist Convention and church groups across the South and Midwest.[28]

Other groups organized to advocate for gay and lesbian rights and legal protection. Although public opinion remained more disapproving than approving of homosexuality, by the late 1960s examples of grassroots groups advocating for greater understanding and acceptance of gay and lesbian identity included a clergy-led organization in California, a coalition of Episcopal priests in New York City, a clergy council in Connecticut, a gay Reform Jewish congregation in Los Angeles, and the ministries of Glide Memorial Methodist Church in San Francisco. In the 1970s, social action departments within the United Church of Christ, Presbyterian, and several other mainline denominations that had advocated for civil rights and against the Vietnam War turned their attention to advocacy on behalf of sexual identity. Another response was the Fellowship of Metropolitan Community Churches, initiated in Southern California in 1968—and within a decade in forty-six other locations—to facilitate open communion, worship, and support among lesbian, gay, bisexual, and transgender families. Yet another response was the formation of gay and lesbian caucuses—Catholics,

Episcopalians, Lutherans, Methodists, Mormons, Presbyterians, and Unitarians, among others—that served as supportive networks, published newsletters, and submitted reports within their denominations challenging traditional heteronormative practices.[29]

Attitudes toward welfare divided along lines similar to those separating attitudes toward abortion and homosexuality. A national survey conducted in 1984 by the Gallup Organization showed the public divided almost evenly along a continuum from self-identified religious "liberals" to self-identified religious "conservatives," with the two differing significantly on attitudes toward "government spending on social programs" as well as on views about abortion. One of the most outspoken critics of public assistance was Reverend Jerry Falwell, the pastor of Thomas Road Baptist Church in Lynchburg, Virginia. He had briefly served on the board of a federally funded War on Poverty program in the 1960s but resigned to devote himself full time to the church, and in 1979 he founded the Moral Majority to advance conservative social and cultural values. A strong supporter of Reagan, Falwell declared in numerous forums that the nation was becoming a welfare state, remarking on one occasion that America was creating a "generation of bums that don't know how to take care of themselves." The National Council of Churches, in contrast, charged that Reagan's cutbacks of welfare expenditures constituted a compromise of the government's obligation to "promote the general welfare."[30]

African American churches were positioned to address firsthand the necessity of combining arguments about compassion and rights with arguments about justice. A few weeks before President Reagan addressed the city's business elite at the Waldorf Astoria, for example, New York's African American churches and community activist groups organized a rally to protest the administration's welfare policies. Black Solidarity Day, as it was called, attracted some two thousand participants to meetings at the Ebenezer Baptist Church in Flushing and the House of the Lord Church in Brooklyn. The chief organizer was Brooklyn Pentecostal minister Reverend Herbert Daughtry, whose Black United Front was spearheading efforts in New York, Pennsylvania, Oregon, Illinois, and Mississippi to protest welfare cutbacks, police violence, and unemployment and to cultivate Black leadership.[31]

In other communities, networks of African American churches provided direct assistance to poor families, made trips to Washington to advocate for antipoverty programs, spoke with legislators about holes in the social safety net, held rallies, and staged protest marches. In a 1982 report for the Urban League, National Conference of Black Churchmen president Dr. Kelly Smith of First Baptist Church–Capitol Hill in Nashville, for example, described the Black church as "the moral authority of the black community" and its buildings as where the community gathered. Divorcing the political from the spiritual or moral, he wrote, was "diametrically opposed to the black church's self-understanding." The line between strictly religious activities, such as preaching and worship, and "secular" activities, such as providing charitable assistance and advocating against injustice and oppression, the report concluded, was nearly invisible.[32]

It was invisible especially in the case of some of the African American churches and pastor-led social movements that developed large urban ministries in the 1970s and 1980s with federal as well as private funds. One of the largest of these was the Allen African Methodist Episcopal Church in Jamaica, Queens, under the pastorate of Reverend Floyd H. Flake. Its 3,200 members and well-educated pastor gave it an outsized role in the community. When a hospital merger was proposed that would reduce healthcare for low-income families, Reverend Flake and pastors of nearby churches led a protest march, and when a group called Black Youth for Survival protested the police shooting of a fifteen-year-old boy in the neighborhood, Reverend Flake served as the group's adviser. The church's primary role in combating poverty was through housing development and rehabilitation. In the early 1980s with a federal Housing and Urban Development grant it completed an $11 million 300-unit senior citizen housing complex. It also purchased and rehabilitated dilapidated stores and provided subsidies for homeowners. Its other large-scale project was a $3.8 million elementary school, which it built without federal funds to ensure that students could pray and study the Bible in school. In 1980 Reverend Flake was appointed to New

York's Public Utilities Review Board, in 1983 he became an active supporter of Reverend Jesse Jackson's Operation PUSH, and in 1987 he was elected to the US House of Representatives.

Black churches' direct engagement with families in poverty gave them a distinct forum for contributing to the discussion of human dignity. Operation PUSH was one of the more visible examples of enlisting churches, other nonprofit organizations, and businesses to attack inner-city poverty by creating jobs and job training opportunities, advocating against racial discrimination, and encouraging youth to stay in school. The idea was that dignity could be enhanced at least for some by making greater use of opportunities for self-improvement through education, jobs, and investment. Some of the proposals found encouragement in projects like Reverend Flake's, which harnessed the spiritual and moral power of traditional church teachings with opportunities to bring jobs to the community by investing in schools, housing, and business. Other programs emphasized a wider movement of self-improvement that would rely heavily on the churches. The Black Leadership Family Plan formulated by staff of the Congressional Black Caucus in 1982, for example, called on African Americans everywhere to attend and participate in the community service activities of Black churches, and for the churches in turn to mobilize voter registration and support of African American–owned business and more generally to be the "primary means by which black people find the spiritual strength and understanding to be effective moral agents in their quest for freedom and justice."[33] While enlisting churches, organizations like Operation PUSH, the Urban League, and the Congressional Black Caucus were also the vehicles through which legal and policy expertise could be mobilized.

The early 1980s case that aroused public sentiment similar to that surrounding Mary Etheredge's death in the 1960s was the death of Dwayne Harrington. On the evening of December 1, 1981, a city ambulance brought seven-year-old Dwayne Harrington to the Cardinal Glennon Children's Hospital in St. Louis, Missouri. He was underweight, unconscious, and breathing with difficulty. He never regained consciousness and died two days later. The autopsy determined that he had a streptococcal infection of the throat that had ruptured into the lungs. The official cause of death was pneumonia. The autopsy also discovered lacerations on his torso and buttocks and particles of foreign matter caked on his feet. These particles were determined to be rat feces.

Dwayne's thirty-year-old mother, Sandra, and his seven stepsiblings lived in a rented ground-floor flat without heat or hot water and a bathroom that was no longer functional. After Dwayne's death an inspection estimated that twenty to thirty rats roamed the rooms. The inspection also found dangerously hazardous levels of lead paint. Sandra, who was one of twelve children and had only a ninth-grade education, had worked on an automobile assembly line and then as a housekeeper but was no longer employed. The family's only income was a monthly check from the federal Aid to Families with Dependent Children program and food stamps. They were under the supervision of a protective services agency for suspected child abuse. Ten days before Dwayne's death the agency informed Sandra that her case was being closed because of "excellent progress."[34]

The death prompted an investigation that led to a wide-ranging discussion of child abuse, its relationship to poverty, and the role of family services and child protection agencies. After details of Dwayne's death and graphic photos of the squalid conditions in which the Harringtons lived were published in the *St. Louis Post-Dispatch*, the director of Missouri's Division of Family Services sent an aide to collect additional information. Medical staff at the hospital where Dwayne was taken reported seeing three cases a day on average of children who were beaten, whipped, or abandoned without food. During the previous twelve months, the St. Louis County Division of Family Services had received more than four thousand reports of child abuse or neglect. Statewide, more than thirty thousand reports were filed. As a result of budget cuts, the agency had approximately 12 percent fewer caseworkers than during the previous year and was struggling to keep up with its increasing caseload. An examination of the Harringtons' records showed repeated meetings with caseworkers and home visits but left doubts as to whether their case had been closed prematurely because the agency was understaffed. The inquiry discovered that Dwayne's teacher had phoned the same day the case was closed to report that Dwayne appeared to have been abused when he arrived at school. The director of family services threatened to fire everyone involved with the case but was dissuaded from doing so because it was impossible to determine who had bungled it the most. Sandra Harrington was arrested for negligent homicide, but prosecutors decided not to pursue the case. The children were placed in foster homes. Six months later they were returned to their mother.[35]

The reality that children like Dwayne Harrington were dying from malnourishment and illness and in other instances from child abuse or gun violence contributed to the wider debate about how a democracy that purported to embrace human dignity could better serve that aim. The only role that religion played in the immediate case was the Salvation Army temporarily providing foster care for one of the Harrington children. The popular idea that religious organizations could fill the gap from cutbacks in public assistance, though, put a distinct spin on the discussion. Whereas previous arguments held that both were necessary or that one was more effective than the other, now the prospect of religion assuming a greatly magnified role in welfare provision posed constitutional issues as well as practical questions. The principal question was whether religious freedom could be upheld under such an idea, even if it were practical for religious organizations to expand their role. One aspect of the question related to the possibility that religious organizations would receive government funding and, if so, what regulations might be added. Another was whether recipients would be given preference for being members of religious communities. Yet another was whether the public that was not involved in religious organizations was benefiting unfairly by not having to shoulder its share of welfare expenditures.

Charitable Choice

In 1995 Senator John Ashcroft of Missouri proposed an amendment to the welfare reform bill currently under consideration that would alter the debate about religion's role in antipoverty work for the next decade. Charitable Choice, as it was called, included provisions allowing religious and other private charitable organizations to engage in social service programs under government contracts, called for religious organizations to submit proposals, and eased the constraints under which funds would be administered. As it happened, the discussions that the deaths of Mary Etheredge in 1965 and Dwayne Harrington in 1981 had prompted figured in small unanticipated ways in the deliberations. Senator Byrd, who had overseen the hearing in which Etheredge's death was discussed, was the originator in 1985 of the "Byrd rule," which prevented budget reconciliation bills from including extraneous provisions, among which were any changes to Social Security. Charitable Choice was deemed extraneous by the Senate parliamentarian and excluded from the bill unless at least sixty senators voted to reinstate it. Ashcroft's defense of it, arguing that "America's faith-based charities and non-governmental organizations, from the Salvation Army to the Boys and Girls Clubs of the United States [which contract with governments], have been very successful in moving people from welfare dependency to the independence of work and the dignity of self-reliance," won the Senate's approval by a vote of sixty-seven to thirty.[36]

The connection with Dwayne Harrington's death was the debate to which it contributed about childcare. In 1980 Republican Kit Bond won the election for governor in Missouri by defeating Democrat incumbent Joseph P. Teasdale. Bond had been elected governor in 1972, was defeated by Teasdale in 1976, and was challenged in the 1980 primary by Republican lieutenant governor Bill Phelps. Bond's victory was credited in large measure to his pledge to dramatically reduce the state's welfare expenditures. The cuts, though, posed two questions that the Harrington case helped publicize: How could child neglect and abuse be monitored if fewer caseworkers were employed, and how could welfare mothers like Sandra Harrington be forced to work when they had children needing their care? Inevitably the discussion turned to private daycare. It was not argued that private daycare could entirely fill the gap—but it could help. The same discussions that criticized inadequate caseworker attention to children like Dwayne Harrington noted the success of private facilities, such as the St. Louis Christian Home, Raphael House, Residence for Children, and Emergency Lodge, which were run by churches or supported by donations and volunteers from churches. These church-run and church-supported programs were inexpensive and seemed to provide the personalized care lacking in budget-stretched public assistance. They also posed questions about separation of church and state.[37]

The church and state questions that church-run daycare programs posed proved to be sufficiently controversial that critics suggested it would be better if religion were not involved at all. Indeed, church-run daycare centers were a reminder to lawmakers that religion wasn't a matter only of private convictions that people quietly expressed in their congregations. Religion was also woven into the social fabric organizationally: as parochial schools, church colleges, foundations, charities, church-run orphanages and hospitals, international relief funds, and increasingly as church-run daycare programs, church-run homes for indigent or abused boys and girls, and church-run housing projects. Whether they received government funding or not, they were subject to the kinds of regulations and licensing standards that Charles Reich had identified in 1964. That was especially true when it came to children and of special concern when child abuse was as prevalent as it seemed to be.

On November 2, 1982, a private plane en route from Corpus Christi, Texas, to Kansas City crashed, killing the crew and five passengers. One of the passengers was radio evangelist Lester Roloff. Roloff was the founder of three "wayward children" homes, which by 1973 housed 180 girls and 100 boys. Complaints about practices at the facilities had led Texas authorities to open an investigation, which discovered widespread abuse of the children, including beatings, denial of food, and solitary confinement. Such abuse, another court in Texas had declared, was not only a derogation of law but also a degradation of human dignity. Authorities threatened to close the facilities unless state licenses were obtained and state health and safety standards were observed. Roloff sued on grounds that church-run facilities should be exempt because of separation of church and state. As the case made its way through the courts it was widely publicized through Roloff's radio broadcasts on hundreds of stations and at conservative churches as evidence of big government's agenda to persecute religion. When he died, some of Roloff's childcare facilities were still operating without a license, now under the aegis of his People's Church, but that option was about to expire as well. In 1985 Roloff's staff relocated the last of his facilities for wayward children to Kansas City, Missouri.[38]

The benefit of Missouri was that it had the most lenient policy of any state toward the licensing of church-run facilities. Despite health and welfare professionals insisting on licensing that would protect children from neglect and abuse, antigovernment church groups had successfully persuaded lawmakers to resist. The reason to exempt church-run facilities, they argued, was twofold: it was a violation of separation of church and state and it would raise the facilities' cost of operation. Church leaders worried especially that licensing would prevent the religious instruction they thought was essential to the moral development of children under their care. Fiscal conservatives in the legislature argued that licensing would impinge on grandparents' and friends' freedom to care for children in their own homes. With welfare, in their view, already costing too much, the legislation they passed exempted church-run and other private facilities from licensing and sought to save money by making it illegal to report child abuse anonymously. When Roloff's staff brought the remaining children and teens to Kansas City, a spokesperson for the new governor said the governor welcomed them and thought their arrival would be good for the economy. He was also committed to keeping church-run facilities license-free. The new governor was John Ashcroft.[39]

Ashcroft was an active member of the Assemblies of God Church and as governor was the denomination's first member to achieve elected office at that level. He firmly believed in the value of church-based charity and social service. The experience with church-run programs in Missouri contributed to his understanding—now as a senator—of the complexities of church-state relations. The Charitable Choice provision Ashcroft included in the Personal Responsibility and Work Opportunity Reconciliation Act of 1996 was designed to circumvent as many of these complications as possible. It stipulated that agencies could not discriminate against clients on the basis of religion, religious belief, or refusal to participate in a religious practice and required that a secular alternative be provided for any client that objected to the religious character of the program. It further stipulated that government funds had to be used only for the fulfillment of public social service goals and could not be diverted to activities such as worship, religious instruction, and proselytization. As a protection of the religious practices and beliefs of the agencies, it did permit them to discriminate on religious grounds in their employment practices and did not require them to change their form of internal governance or remove art or other religious symbols from the facilities in which government-funded services were provided. It did, however, require agencies to adhere to state laws and be subject to audit for the government funds received.[40]

Charitable Choice and the Faith-Based Initiative that followed under the presidency of George W. Bush significantly enlarged the debate that had been going on for the past half century about how best to uphold principles of human dignity with respect to the general welfare of persons living in poverty. The Bush White House made it a priority to roll out a plan to promote faith-based programs across federal agencies, which it did in Bush's first months in office; by the end of his first term faith-based offices in varying form had been founded in at least thirty states. Their mission was to facilitate religious organizations' involvement in welfare provision by hosting conferences, clarifying or eliminating barriers, and networking with the leaders of faith-based agencies.[41]

The Faith-Based Initiative was popular among White evangelical Protestants. But Black leaders were skeptical. Only 10 percent of African American voters had voted for Bush. Black communities faced continuing systemic racism, which they had seen Bush's predecessors—his father and Reagan—do little to combat. When Black clergy got involved in politics, discrimination and injustice were the issues they most cared about. However, it was essential for Bush to demonstrate that the Faith-Based Initiative was appealing to a wide diversity of religious groups—including Black churches—not just his White evangelical base. Anticipating that Black clergy who were engaged in foster care, housing, job training, and homeless ministries in their communities might be interested in receiving financial support from the initiative, Bush reached out to them.

Reverend DeForest "Buster" Soaries was one of the Black leaders the initiative enlisted. As a young pastor in the 1970s, Soaries had served in New Jersey as a community liaison on civil rights issues and headed a county-level chapter of Operation PUSH, but then separated from Jackson's organization in the 1980s. By 1996 when Charitable Choice went into effect, Soaries's church had grown to 3,700 members, and his First Baptist Community Development Corporation was working to build low-income housing, attract small businesses, and provide job training. Soaries's ministries also provided daycare, loans, and pregnancy counseling. In 1999, Republican governor Christie Whitman appointed Soaries as secretary of state of New Jersey. In 2001 the White House considered him one of the top candidates to lead the new Office of Faith-based Initiatives.[42]

As before, Republicans were more favorable toward faith-based initiatives than Democrats, but both parties included supporters and opponents. Soaries, for example, opted to stay in New Jersey and, while working with government funding to expand community development and launch a foster parenting program, resisted the sectarian direction other faith-based initiatives were taking.[43] In many instances religion contributed to partisan polarization and was a means to advance partisan agendas. Religion's diversity, however, meant that even the most politically salient arguments were met with counterarguments. Organizations as varied as the American Jewish Congress, Baptist Joint Committee on Public Affairs, Church of the Brethren, Interfaith Alliance, and United Methodists, for example, opposed the legislation. Similarly, those who supported it held varying views that reflected their distinctive traditions and interests, whether as Catholics or Protestants or as Jews or Muslims.

The argument for Charitable Choice was that welfare reform shifted more of the task of caring for the poor to religious organizations, and therefore it made sense for religious organizations to receive government funding for that purpose as long as certain rules were in place, particularly preventing religious organizations from proselytizing those who came for assistance and prohibiting the funds from being used for regular religious activities. It was generally agreed that religious organizations had a role to play. They were already involved and, in many cases, had a well-established infrastructure of staff and volunteers with experience in social service work. They had two other assets: religious organizations often interacted with the needy on a personal basis, which increased the likelihood that interactions would respect individuals' desire to be treated with dignity; and a transcendent faith in the value of every person was capable of inspiring compassion and perhaps an interest in working for social justice.

The theological argument that for some provided a rationale for Charitable Choice reflected an interpretation of human nature that included a Judeo-Christian understanding of human dignity. In this understanding the human person was created in the image of God but was separated from God through sin, both the original sin of Adam and Eve that afflicted all humans and the specific sins that individuals committed when they violated the Ten Commandments and other biblical teachings. Human dignity therefore was lost and could be retrieved only by confessing one's sins and seeking redemption through divine grace. An additional interpretation put the theological argument in a historical narrative. In that interpretation the modernist teachings that had crept into mainstream churches early in the twentieth century had subverted this biblical understanding of sin and redemption. Modernism taught instead that humans were naturally good and were prevented from doing good only by the impediments of their environment. The differences in views about how best to care for the poor were thus theological as well as political.[44]

In a best-selling book that leaders engaged in welfare reform (including Ashcroft, George W. Bush, and House Speaker Newt Gingrich) credited with shaping their thinking, historian Marvin Olasky linked the shift from traditional theology toward modernist theology to the trajectory of welfare reform. The New Deal, he said, had been furthered by the changing conceptions of human nature but had been necessitated only by the severity of the crisis and was regarded as temporary. The War on Poverty in the 1960s, in contrast, came at a time when "God is dead" had become a popular slogan and was not necessitated by an economic downturn. It was a "disaster," he wrote, "not so much because of its new programs but because of their emphasis on entitlement rather than need." Compassion based on "discernment" and "bonding" was replaced by "legal circuses and depersonalization."[45] Olasky, Gingrich wrote, "unlocked for me the key of how to replace the welfare state."[46]

These arguments were not new. However, a defensive posture was present in the debate about Charitable Choice legislation that had not been as pronounced before. The aim was to protect the rights of religious organizations. It was, as Ashcroft put it, to keep them from "having to compromise their religious integrity or of being hobbled by excessive government regulation and intrusion." It was to protect "the rights of faith-based providers as well as the religious liberty of the individuals they may serve." This was the concern that White evangelical Protestant groups especially were asserting. They believed their churches were embattled and their service ministries were up against a federal welfare establishment that was imposing unnecessary licensing and certification requirements. As the head of one agency complained, "faith-based programs are continually under assault by the professional poverty industry."[47]

Some of those who opposed Charitable Choice also did so on grounds that religion needed to be protected. Their argument was that religion's integrity was more likely to be compromised by taking government funds than by not taking them. "One cannot assume that tax dollars will not change the nature, even the freedom and effectiveness, of faith-based programs," a Baptist leader argued. No religious organization, he thought, should want "the rules and regulations or even the reporting that goes with government-handled money."[48] Others anticipated that religious organizations would be differentially harmed, with larger and more politically connected groups benefiting from government grants, and smaller and less politically influential groups at a disadvantage.

Interpretations registered less agreement about what Charitable Choice implied for the government's role in providing assistance. The disagreement hinged partly on how much of the overall task could be performed by religious organizations. One view held that religious and other nongovernment associations, formal and informal, could do nearly all the service work required. A view at the other extreme held that religious organizations were a stopgap measure at best and perhaps a diversion from achieving a more effective solution through public assistance. The question of human dignity was also present, although more often in the background. The argument about religious organizations upholding dignity was an implicit acknowledgment of the accusations that public welfare frequently fell short on this dimension. The argument that public welfare should be a national priority also implied that the dignity of all Americans was at stake even if there were contending views about what that meant.

From its inception in 1996 through the end of the Bush administration's Faith-Based Initiative in 2008, the practical ways in which faith-based organizations participated in social welfare provision were marked by the fact that religion was diverse in organization and belief, constitutionally separate from government, and yet engaged in activities that inevitably had political and policy implications. Few doubted that human dignity should be upheld, but much disagreement was expressed about whose dignity was most at stake. Model faith-based programs demonstrated exceptional success in dealing with addiction recovery and rehabilitation, but some of these programs violated the rights of clients and potential clients.[49]

The practical solution to protecting the integrity of religious organizations was to establish separate nonprofit service organizations that were independent of congregations in terms of regulations and reporting requirements. Separate organizations such as religiously affiliated schools, orphanages, hospitals, and daycare centers already existed in large numbers and provided models for the new ones that emerged in response to Charitable Choice. Their administrative separation from congregations eased the restrictions on receiving government funds. Yet they were in many cases indisputably religious in purpose, providing religious instruction, holding worship services, employing staff on the basis of religious affiliation, operating in buildings also used for religious services, and being administered by ordained clergy.

It was not surprising, therefore, that countless questions arose despite the general provisions included in Charitable Choice about what religiously affiliated childcare and service organizations could legally do and whether they were exempt from any of these regulations because they were religious. Licensing was the regulation that states considered in varying ways, with Missouri at one extreme and other states usually adopting policies that provided for some accommodations. In neighboring Kansas, for example, religiously affiliated childcare centers were required to be licensed, but when an Independent Fundamental Baptist church-run center declared licensing would prevent it from practicing corporal punishment, which it said the King James Bible demanded, the state responded that administrative remedies were available on a case-by-case basis at parents' discretion.[50]

Licensing was but one of the many issues that arose. In several instances a childcare facility sought exemption from providing Social Security numbers because doing so would diminish God's authority. In another instance a California church found itself in legal jeopardy when an automobile crashed through a fence, killing several children on the playground of the daycare center leased from the church. Other questions emerged about finances: Were employees terminated from religiously affiliated childcare centers eligible for unemployment compensation, or excluded because they worked for a religious organization? Was a program for children at a church that operated from 6:30 a.m. to 6:00 p.m. like an ordinary Sunday school class, or was it in fact a childcare program? Was it necessary for a facility to bill the welfare department for fewer hours if some of the children were sick or on vacation?

In the Courts

The frequency with which these questions came before the courts provides an opportunity to view an interesting and often overlooked way in which religion's connections with public welfare assistance contributed to interpretations of human dignity. What dignity means in practice reflects the values we hold dear. When a seven-year-old living in

squalid housing dies from pneumonia it offends human sensibilities as
an instance of indignity. The offended sensibilities may disappear before
anything is done to prevent other children from dying. Or the causes
may be determined to have been beyond prevention. And yet one of the
considerations in welfare provision, public and private, is to reduce the
chances of indignities occurring. To advocate for human dignity is thus
to argue concretely for provisions protecting the health and safety of
children. The meaning of dignity is not only an abstract assumption
about the common dignity of all humanity but also a specific interpretation about the value of health and safety.

Religion's relevance, then, is operative concretely as well as abstractly.
Religious values are themselves likely to be a reason for protecting the
health and safety of children. On that account, religion contributes
when it advocates explicitly for certain values. It does so by affirming
values deemed important to human dignity. But another, less obvious
way of thinking about religion's contribution is useful. The Constitution
protects religious liberty in competition with other values. And deliberations about that competition illuminate what those other values are.
Religious liberty may take precedence in the competition, for instance,
but not if it involves protecting the nation from attack, because that is
an even higher value. Some of the competing values with which religious liberty is paired are valued because we define them among the
ways in which human dignity is manifest. One such value is the health
and safety of children. Others relate to justice, fair treatment, and
nondiscrimination.

In 1966 a Michigan farm couple who spent much of their time volunteering for an evangelical youth ministry founded an organization they
called Teen Ranch. The organization served as a residential center for
abused, neglected, and delinquent children who were committed to or
placed in its care by state courts. By the end of the century, Teen Ranch
was one of ninety-six private childcare centers that Michigan's Family
Independence Agency contracted with to provide stays of four to twelve
months. Thirty-five of the centers were faith based. Teen Ranch advertised itself as a place for young people and their families to acquire hope
though life-changing relationships and experiences from a Christian

perspective. Participation in its religious programming, including worship services, prayers before meals, and discussions of Christian faith, was voluntary.

The legal question that came before the US Court of Appeals for the Sixth Circuit in 2006 was whether Teen Ranch's clients were being subjected to religious instruction against their will and at government expense. Teen Ranch insisted that its freedom to provide religious instruction would be unfairly compromised if it were denied funding or if funding were contingent on abandoning its religious orientation. It argued that clients were free to opt out of worship services and prayers if they wished or be provided with alternative study materials and be exposed to religious teachings with no expectation of becoming believers themselves. Ways in which they could transfer to a nonreligious center were also suggested. The difficulty, though, was that Michigan dealt with approximately seventy-five thousand such cases annually and was under pressure to lower its costs. In fact, an influential conservative policy institute at the time suggested that many of the state's programs to assist delinquent and at-risk youth be eliminated.[51]

The precedent the court relied on in determining that Teen Ranch was not eligible for government funding was a case in Ohio that ultimately went to the US Supreme Court. In 1995, in response to evidence that public schools in Cleveland were failing to provide satisfactory education, the state of Ohio established the Pilot Project Scholarship Program to give children an opportunity to attend private religiously affiliated schools, nonsectarian schools, and charter schools. Whether it was appropriate for religiously affiliated schools to benefit from government funding as participants in the program was determined on the basis of whether "true private choice" was present. True private choice meant that parents were free to choose for themselves whether to send their children to a religiously affiliated private school, a private school that was not religiously affiliated, a subsidized charter school, or a public school. In Cleveland, true private choice was present because the state did not decide where children should attend. At Teen Ranch, true private choice was not present because teens were assigned to their respective facilities by a computer algorithm.[52]

True private choice became the standard by which other cases of religious freedom were decided, including cases about faith-based programs in prisons and government-funded scholarships for students at sectarian schools. It specified that religious organizations could receive government funding as long as individuals were free to choose whether they wanted to be exposed to religious instruction. This was different from saying that religious organizations should never receive government funding because of separation of church and state. It differed too from arguments about the intrinsic value of religious instruction, its effectiveness, or its efficiency. It was an example of how the courts, in having to render decisions about religious liberty, reinforced the value of individual choice without ascribing value to either religion or nonreligion. It was of course considered a win by some and a loss by others even though it affirmed the importance of free choice as an expression of human dignity.[53]

The cases also registered a shift in how religious organizations defined their interests. In some cases, religious diversity was the overriding issue to the extent that freedom of religion meant being able to practice according to the distinctive beliefs of one's denomination or tradition. But in these cases the possibility that clients might want to choose a Baptist rather than a Lutheran or Catholic program seemed not to matter. The possibility that funding decisions might stir up religious divisions also did not matter. As one statement by a coalition of religious organizations in the Ohio case argued, all denominations pretty much agreed that religious instruction was integral to religion, which was what truly mattered. Another statement acknowledged that earlier arguments reflected Protestant anti-Catholicism and argued that these wrongheaded sentiments should no longer be considered. True private choice was satisfied as long as being able to choose religion or nonreligion was possible.[54]

These arguments were shaped by being made not by clergy, but on behalf of clergy and the congregations they represented. Unlike when public advocacy came primarily from spokespersons such as Reinhold Niebuhr or Stephen Wise or from the US bishops or an elected head of the Southern Baptist Convention, arguments in these cases were advanced by spokespersons with a different kind of specialized training. This shift was masked because some clergy (Jerry Falwell, Pat Robertson, and a few others) were still in the public eye. But their role was declining relative to that of organizations such as the Christian Legal Society, Center for Law and Religious Freedom, Family Research Council, and Focus on the Family, which generally argued on one side of major issues, and on the other side, the Council of Religious Freedom, Interfaith Religious Liberty Foundation, ACLU, and Americans United. These organizations' expertise was devoted not to articulating theological distinctions but to providing an understanding of the law and speaking for a cross section of faith communities. It was a conduit through which the diverse arguments and counterarguments that originated in considerations about religion made their way into legal decisions.[55]

In contrast to the instances in which true private choice was the determining principle, health and safety issues generally took priority over freedom of religion. Licensing requirements were imposed to protect health and safety, and when church-run programs were exempt from licensing they were often still required to meet health and safety standards and undergo inspections. Most states also had laws protecting facilities at which children were present, including childcare centers, schools, and sometimes public playgrounds, by prohibiting registered sex offenders from "entering school property." But there were exceptions, such as for a parent or guardian who could seek special permission from authorities to attend a school function. Religion necessitated additional considerations. For example, under Indiana's Religious Freedom Restoration Act, a case came before the courts in which three registered sex offenders claimed the state's sex offender law prevented them from attending church and thus placed a burden on their free exercise of religion. Their claim, which pertained to the particular churches in which they were active members, raised the interesting question of whether and under what circumstances churches are schools: whenever church services are held at which children are present, when a church-run childcare center is present, when children are present at the childcare center, or never? The court determined that the offenders' free exercise of religion was in fact violated by the state's law but took account of particular circumstances such as the fact that the offenders were known to the churches' leaders as well as whether the state's law was overbroad and imprecise. Other cases were also decided on narrow grounds. For example, in one case a regulation was upheld even though it kept drug use and liquor establishments farther from churches than from schools; in another case, the court decided in a church's favor when the parents of a child molested by the child's babysitter argued that the molestation occurred because the babysitter had been recommended through a contact and information obtained at the church. In the California case in which two children were killed when an automobile crashed through the fence on property leased from a church, the court decided that the layout of the fence and playground were adequate protection against any foreseeable intrusion but that the driver had committed a criminal act that could not have been foreseen.[56] Insofar as a child's dignity meant being protected against unhealthful and unsafe childcare conditions, then, these deliberations contributed to clarifying the meaning of those protections.

The issue that proved particularly controversial for faith-based programs was emotional health. By late twentieth-century standards, positive self-esteem was often regarded as a mark of human dignity. Many states included something about emotional development as a requirement for licensed daycare centers. Faith-based organizations that challenged state licensing requirements, though, routinely included these among their objections. A case initiated by a Baptist daycare organization in Michigan, for example, challenged the state's emotional development requirement by arguing that self-concepts should not be subjected to testing and standardized curricula. The ensuing discussion affirmed the twin principles of protecting children from emotional harm on the one hand, and on the other hand of acknowledging that families have varying views about emotional development.[57] Religion's contribution in these cases was not in advocating for a specific definition of emotional harm but in forcing further consideration of how emotional harm should or should not be defined.

Economic issues largely fell into a different category. It was harder to argue that clients' dignity was compromised on economic grounds than as a matter of health and safety, and by the same token it was difficult for claims about religious freedom to be based strictly on financial considerations. The questions that faith-based service organizations posed nevertheless dealt frequently with issues that brought together the contested relationship of religion and money. The topic that often implied something basic about human dignity was fair treatment. Employees were protected against unfair treatment such as discrimination on the basis of race or sexual orientation when funding was from government sources but could be discriminated against for religious reasons when religious funds were used. The complexities involved in making that determination were evident, for example, when Alicia Pedreira, an employee of the Kentucky Baptist Homes for Children (KBHC), was fired for being homosexual, which KBHC said violated its religious teachings. KBHC was the recipient of approximately $12.5 million annually from Kentucky and was explicit about its "Christ-centered" values, which it said permeated its ministry "like the very blood throughout our bodies." Through prayer and religious instruction, the agency sought to make converts of its clients: "The angels rejoiced last year as 244 of our children made decisions about their relationship with Jesus Christ." Pedreira brought suit and was joined by three additional plaintiffs. After thirteen years in the courts, a settlement was reached that satisfied none of the parties involved. The case nevertheless brought national attention to the need for civil rights legislation to protect gays and lesbians from employment discrimination, which at the time had been enacted in only a minority of states. It also brought to light the need for clearer rules and stricter monitoring to protect children at faith-based facilities from coerced indoctrination.[58]

Fair treatment of faith-based organizations' beneficiaries could be especially problematic when beneficiaries doubled as employees or volunteers, as they often did in church-run rehabilitation programs. A US Army rehabilitation center run by the Salvation Army in San Francisco, for example, kept the distinction clear on paper yet found itself in court when a beneficiary sued for having worked as an employee, as he saw it, for less than minimum wage. The case was one of many in which the claim required consideration of the specific circumstances under which fair treatment applied, including whether the beneficiary was engaged primarily in rehabilitation (in this case, yes) and whether the organization was essentially a commercial enterprise (in this case, no). Similar questions occurred in cases asking whether an employee was truly an employee or a volunteer.[59] Economic considerations also came to bear on faith-based organizations in cases of criminal damages and penalties. In several cases involving arson, for example, the courts were asked to determine whether the punishment might be more severe because the structure met the definition of interstate commerce, perhaps because its clients or employees lived in more than one state or because it was the property of a national denomination.[60] Thus, in these instances the fact that faith-based service organizations were businesses became the occasion for clarification about fair treatment.

The other values that litigation illuminated were generosity, privacy, and familial relationships. Generosity was rarely a decisive consideration in litigation but figured broadly in determining whether an organization's primary purpose was altruistic or commercial. This determination was complicated when an organization's funding was partly from charitable donations and partly from government contracts or fees. For example, in a suit brought by a woman injured in an accident while attending a meeting of a group that paid a rental fee to a church, the New Jersey Supreme Court decided that the church's general altruistic orientation toward "good works" in the community was determinative and not the specific sources and amounts of its funding.[61] Privacy concerns arose in connection with the solicitation and reporting or nonreporting of information about clients, including cases in which Native Americans or conservative Christian groups objected to personal information being collected. Obligatory reporting in instances of sexual abuse in other cases prompted reflection on the limits of norms of pastoral care within religious communities. For example, a suit in California found the pastor liable for knowingly withholding information from the authorities about a credible allegation of sexual abuse. The case also posed questions about churches sharing information informally at church meetings, as was commonly done, without permission of the parties involved. Parents of an infant who died under the care of a babysitter recommended by a church in Indiana, for example, sued for invasion of privacy when the church put out a press release without their permission. Familial relationships were also among the values given priority in cases involving visitation and the rights of parents and foster parents.[62]

In most of the cases considered in this chapter, religious organizations did not themselves advocate for democracy, other than when defending religious freedom, but provided the occasions on which advocacy for democracy occurred. In defending their own rights, religious leaders evoked discussion of other rights and principles that required adjudication, such as privacy, safety, and health. The advocacy and litigation demonstrated the porous boundaries separating church and state and indeed the imprecision of what counts as religion. Religion was variously defined as private choice, religious instruction, and religious purpose, or simply as what was declared in statements of religious mission, and as sectarianism, as well as being defined as what it was not by its secular alternatives. Indeed, as religious studies scholar Winnifred Fallers Sullivan observes, the definitions of religion were so varied that "religion" no longer seemed serviceable as an acceptable referent in legal contexts.[63] Moreover, the advocacy for varying priorities that specified the meanings of human dignity and religion was made by an ever-widening assemblage of public welfare officials, caseworkers, childcare administrators, special interest organizers, lawyers, and judges, and on occasion by religious professionals themselves.

How public assistance should be provided was thus a matter not only of determining who should pay for what and whether it was effective but also of deciding on policies that were consistent with principles of human dignity. What that meant in practice was that people had certain minimal rights to be treated with respect and in keeping with the law. Dignity meant generally that society had an obligation to concern itself with the needy and disadvantaged. It was a mark of democracy that deliberation about how that obligation was fulfilled should be conducted fairly and with openness toward alternative perspectives. Religious organizations played an active role in those deliberations. Their role at times was to assert that human dignity was founded on religious teachings about all persons being formed in the image of God. Their role more often was to prompt consideration of specific indignities that warranted redress, redefinition, or renewed attention.

The indignities that Mary Etheredge and Dwayne Harrington experienced were tragic. They were the kind of indignities that illustrate the all too frequent failures of public welfare provision. The Etheredge and Harrington cases also illustrate the complex intersection of religious, civic, and government organizations. The changing relations of government programs and faith-based services was not a story that could be understood in terms of values and theology alone or through the speeches of presidents and other public officials. Above all, it was the frontline caseworkers, caregivers, volunteers, beneficiaries, and recipients who forged the connections between theory and practice.

5

Inclusion

IMMIGRANT RELIGION AND
IMMIGRANT RIGHTS

THE SEPTEMBER 11, 2001, attack on the World Trade Center and the Pentagon had a profound and lasting impact on the nation both in its continuing military engagements in the Middle East and Afghanistan and through the questioning it evoked about our responsibilities to one another as citizens. Immigration was an immediate focus of these questions. Muslims were attacked, Sikhs mistaken for Muslims were attacked, and calls were made to shut down entry points and tighten requirements for citizenship. Beyond the outrage toward Muslims, the attack prompted a wider sense that perhaps America had become too diverse, too open toward the rest of world, and too accommodating to newcomers. Religious advocacy would play an important role in the ensuing debates, contributing in the process to the meanings of citizenship and its implications for democracy.

During the decade preceding 9/11, the number of legal immigrants entering the United States totaled approximately ten million. That was three times the number that immigrated during the 1960s and higher even than the previous peak between 1905 and 1914. In the year following the attack the number of refugee approvals fell 72 percent because of heightened safety concerns, delays in processing, and new security requirements. During the same period the number of criminal terrorist cases increased 304 percent. Border patrol operations shifted from apprehending undocumented immigrants after they entered the United States to preventing and deterring their entry in the first place. Even on the US-Mexico border where the likelihood of terrorists seeking entry was minimal, arguments about national security surfaced repeatedly.[1]

After a brief post-9/11 downturn, though, the number of persons obtaining legal permanent resident status returned to approximately one million per year, of whom about half were new arrivals. In 2010 the US Census Bureau reported that forty million people representing 12.9 percent of the total population were foreign born.[2] The clearest evidence of immigration's impact on religion was the growing numbers of residents who identified as Muslims, Hindus, Buddhists, or members of other non-Christian religions. Polls were at best crude approximations because of low response rates and because what it meant to affiliate varied among religions. However, polling conducted in 2012 suggested that approximately a quarter of recent immigrants who were legal permanent US residents identified with religions other than Christianity. Ten percent of the legal immigrant residents polled identified as Muslims, double the number who had done so in 1992. Seven percent identified as Hindus, up from 3 percent in 1992. Eight percent identified as Buddhists, slightly higher than in previous polls. And 3 percent identified with other non-Christian religions. In raw numbers, approximately 2.75 million Muslims, 1.8 million Hindus, and 3.6 million Buddhists were residents in the United States.[3] In addition, an estimated 11 million undocumented immigrants were living in the United States, 42 percent of whom had arrived during the past decade.[4] Nearly all were from Mexico and countries in Central America that were predominantly Catholic or evangelical Protestant. It would be the undocumented immigrants, both the ones already living in the United States for much of their lives and the new ones seeking entry, who would become the focus of divisive policy debates, with the debates being complicated by concerns about national security, religious diversity, and ethnic nationalism.

The public's attitudes toward immigrants, polls suggested, were mixed but generally more favorable than unfavorable. The polls also suggested that the 9/11 attack had relatively little impact on attitudes toward immigrants. In a September 2000 poll, for example, 50 percent said "immigrants today strengthen our country because of their hard work and talents," while 38 percent thought "immigrants today are a burden on our country because they take our jobs, housing, and health." In June 2003, the same question resulted in a 46 percent to 44 percent split. And over the next decade, the unfavorable attitude never exceeded 50 percent.[5]

Polls suggested that attitudes about Muslims were mixed, too, but may have been affected by officials' responses to the 9/11 attack. In March 2002, when public spokespersons were still attempting to frame Islam in a positive way, only 25 percent in one poll thought Islam was more likely to encourage violence than other religions, but by July 2003 the same response increased to 44 percent. The polls also suggested that a majority of those responding felt Islam was quite different from their own religion and that Muslims were mostly anti-American.[6] Further analysis demonstrated that the media's framing of Islam subsequently became increasingly partisan, with the effect that by 2006 a majority of those who said they knew little about Islam had adopted an unfavorable attitude toward it.[7]

Attitudes toward immigrants also revealed a widening partisan divide. Polls conducted between 1994 and 2003 showed Democrats and Republicans holding similar attitudes toward immigrants. However, by 2006 only 34 percent of Republicans compared with 49 percent of Democrats felt that immigrants "strengthen the country," and over the next decade the response among Democrats grew to 78 percent while it remained only 35 percent among Republicans.[8] What the polls partially reflected was the growing influence within the Republican Party of conservative leaders in the House of Representatives whose views were dominated by concerns about illegal immigration. Thus, the Comprehensive Immigration Reform Act of 2006, which provided a pathway for illegal immigrants to gain legal status, passed the Senate but failed in the House.[9]

Religion had been profoundly affected by immigration in the past. The first immigrants were predominantly Protestant but varied in denominational affiliation and were preceded by Catholic explorers and trappers from Spain and France and by Native Americans who practiced their own religions. Enslaved people initiated religious practices that included both African and Christian beliefs. During the nineteenth and early twentieth centuries, Protestant denominations diversified into branches of German Baptists and Methodists and Swedish and Norwegian Lutherans, among others; Roman Catholic parishes variously reflected the arrival of immigrants from Ireland, Italy, and Poland; Jewish immigrants from Eastern Europe founded synagogues that reflected both religious and cultural customs; and Chinese and Japanese immigrants organized Buddhist temples and in some cases Christian churches. For many, the path to citizenship and democratic participation ran through the diverse religious organizations that assisted in the transition. They perhaps "could find nothing in their life in the Old World or the New," Oscar Handlin wrote, "that would confirm the democratic hypothesis that they themselves could participate meaningfully in the exercise of power." But in their congregations, just as in the ethnic associations they initiated, they were able to make a start in that direction. "They elected officers, and conducted debates, and made rules," Handlin observed. "If these affairs had little effect upon the world outside, they nevertheless gave the members a taste of what politics involved."[10]

The generation of scholarship to which Handlin contributed saw religion as a dynamic component of the assimilation process. Its role in the lives of first-generation immigrants was to ease the transition, keeping some of the traditions from their countries of origin intact while they adapted to a new language and way of life. Its role among their children and grandchildren diminished as these generations identified increasingly as "Americans" and as religious traditions became a kind of "symbolic ethnicity" expressed through home rituals, holiday festivals, and participation in their places of worship. In the process, religion itself underwent a transformation, becoming less distinctly ethnic, adopting English as the preferred language for worship, and engaging in denominational mergers. Finnish, Danish, and Swedish Lutherans, for example, gave up their separate denominations to become the Lutheran Church in America. Similarly, the Roman Catholic Church became increasingly

"Americanized." In these ways, both the immigrants who participated in America's various religions and the religions themselves were involved in a process of democratization.[11]

The new immigration that increased in large numbers after the 1965 Immigration and Nationality Act was similar to earlier waves of immigration but also different. It was similar in that it added diversity to American religion, as in the founding of hundreds of Korean, Vietnamese, and Hispanic congregations. It was similar, too, in that studies identified processes of assimilation and Americanization taking place within these congregations, which in large measure held services at the same times and conducted business in the same manner as established congregations. It was different in that nearly all of the immigrants in the past, with the exception of Jews, had come from Christian traditions, whereas the new immigrants included significant numbers of adherents of other religions. It was also different in the pattern that assimilation took. What scholars had identified earlier as "straight-line assimilation" was now being replaced by "segmented assimilation," which meant that substantial numbers of immigrants, especially those from poorer countries, were being channeled permanently into low-wage jobs. The new immigration was also shaped by the globalization of international economic relations and by greater ease of travel, meaning that immigrants more often retained ties with their countries of origin.[12]

These characteristics of the new immigration shaped the discussion about immigration policy. In addition to the perennial questions about immigration's effects on the economy and the culture, questions about its implications for American democracy were also debated. The pro-immigration argument held that democracy is strengthened by diversity—strengthened because diversity encourages people to expand their horizons, think new thoughts, and learn how to deal respectfully with people who have different values and lifestyles. The anti-immigration argument held that democracy is weakened by diversity—weakened because democracy depends on holding core beliefs and values in common and thus is threatened by newcomers who are presumed not to share those beliefs and values. There were arguments in the middle too. One was that immigration was neither good nor bad for democracy but if immigration had to happen, democracy was the best way to cope with it. Another was that it all depended on who the immigrants were, which implied that immigrants who understood democracy were fine but immigrants who didn't were a problem.[13]

Religion was relevant to the debate about immigration in three ways. First, religion was integral to the lives of many of the immigrants, woven into their habits of worship, their ethnic traditions, and their family relationships. Second, religious beliefs and practices among the native-born population affected their views about immigrants. And third, religion mobilized advocacy groups that supported immigrant rights and countermovements that opposed immigration. In each of these ways religion was part of the process of deliberation and policy making through which the United States figured out yet again, as it had done before, who should be welcomed as citizens, who should not, and what the reasons should be for welcoming some and rejecting others.

Immigrant Religion

The literature on new immigrants reveals that levels of participation in religion among immigrants vary depending on countries of origin, religious tradition, socioeconomic status, how recent or traumatic the move may have been, and the religious composition of the new community. There is little to suggest that across-the-board conclusions can be drawn as to whether immigration increases or decreases immigrants' participation in religion; much depends on how involved in religion they were before they came, where they settle once they arrive, and why they decided to make the transition.[14] However, thousands of examples show immigrants starting their own congregations—sometimes with the assistance of established religious organizations—and these new congregations function as the places in which traditions are preserved even as participants adapt to their new communities. Religious participation in these ways serves as a refuge within the wider culture and as a resource composed of social networks that assist in securing jobs and negotiating the procedures involved in becoming naturalized citizens. Identifying with a religious congregation is for many immigrants, as it has been in the past, a way of becoming "American," which means fitting in, perhaps by adopting a form of Christianity similar to the beliefs of many native-born Americans or by adapting some other religious practice (such as Islam or Buddhism) to be more like a voluntary organization in which people meet to socialize and engage in charitable activities.[15]

The Muslim Community Association (MCA) of Santa Clara, California, typifies the process of immigrant adaptation. Founded in 1981, MCA grew to about three thousand participants at Friday prayers by 1995—the year it launched a plan to make a difference in the civic life of its community. As the plan went into action, MCA members heard lectures encouraging their involvement in civic activities, held voter registration drives, ran for public office, hosted forums at which local and congressional candidates spoke, organized open houses attended by hundreds of non-Muslim neighbors, hosted bake sales to benefit local nonprofit organizations, initiated a legal clinic for free consultations, and developed ties with regional food banks and American-Islamic relations groups.[16]

Although many immigrant groups have been less intentional about civic involvement than the leaders at MCA, participating in congregations is often a way for immigrants to gain leadership skills by serving on or chairing committees, to secure assistance in becoming citizens, and to make connections with social service agencies and school administrators. The affiliation of many immigrant congregations with national, regional, diocesan, or denominational organizations also facilitates connections with municipal, state, and federal agencies. A study of Haitian immigrants in Miami, for example, showed that Catholic parishes served Haitian families directly but also used diocesan networks to secure resources from local, state, and federal agencies.[17]

But, if religion can be a way of bridging into the wider culture, it can also be a barrier. Spending a great deal of time in a congregation can limit one's contacts in the wider community. It can also reduce opportunities to learn a new language. The bridge-or-barrier question has been the focus of numerous studies, which on balance suggest that it all depends on the congregation, the people involved, and the contexts in which it occurs. Congregations composed of Muslims, Sikhs, Hindus, or Buddhists often find it harder than congregations composed of Protestants, Catholics, or Jews to bridge into the wider culture because of the religious differences involved. Racial, ethnic, and language barriers also present difficulties. Children of immigrants, unsurprisingly, are more likely to transcend these barriers than their parents. Language is interesting, too, in that extensive participation in a non-English-speaking congregation can be a barrier for some but a resource for maintaining one's first language for others.[18]

Immigrant religion's implications for democracy vary along similar lines. Insofar as democracy is stronger when people vote, learn civic skills, and feel that they belong, congregations that facilitate these kinds of inclusion benefit democracy. Congregations that pose barriers can have the opposite effects. In ethnographic studies, immigrants also vary in how they think about democracy, some equating it with flag-waving superpatriotism, others with adhering to democratic processes of governance while taking a critical stance toward particular issues. Ethnographies also demonstrate the significant extent to which congregations shape how immigrants view their civic obligations, focusing in some instances on nurturing fellow congregants and coethnics, while in others emphasizing nonethnically bounded relationships. However, the larger result is the additional diversity immigrant religion provides. Many immigrant congregations are ethnic enclaves in which participants find ways to be citizens without giving up distinctive traditions. Many others are connected with White-majority Protestant denominations and Catholic parishes. Still others are multiethnic aggregations that serve as centers of community activity as much as for worship.[19]

Attitudes toward New Immigrants

Religion's second way of influencing deliberations about immigration policy is by shaping attitudes toward immigrants among the native-born population. Attitudes toward immigrants vary considerably among the majority Christian population depending on which of several theological frameworks their adherents espouse. In a large national study that included both a survey and hundreds of in-depth interviews, "exclusivist" Christians who believed that salvation was to be found only through Christ and who often identified themselves as evangelicals were the least welcoming toward immigrants, especially immigrants who were Muslims, Hindus, or Buddhists—but also toward immigrants in general, many of whom were Catholics or Protestants. "Inclusivist" Christians who believed that truth could be found in religions other than Christianity and who more often adhered to mainline Protestant and Catholic churches were more welcoming than exclusivists. And "spiritual shoppers" who personally drew on multiple religions and spiritual practices were the most welcoming. Of course there were exceptions, but in general, these theological differences had more of an impact on attitudes toward immigrants than other commonly discussed factors did, such as age, gender, and level of education. The public divided about equally among these three orientations (a quarter or so of the public did not identify with any religion). The study found other differences among adherents of the three orientations as well: exclusivists were the most likely to say that the United States was founded on Christian principles and that democracy is based on Christianity, spiritual shoppers were the least likely, and inclusivists were in the middle. The differences were theological but also sociological: exclusivists were least likely to have traveled or lived outside the United States or had personal contact with non-Christians, spiritual shoppers were the most likely, and inclusivists were in between.[20]

Theological divisions such as the ones found in this study were closely associated with partisan preferences and voting. Polling showed a consistent pattern of White evangelical Protestants favoring Republican candidates who wanted tighter restrictions on immigration, while White mainline Protestants, Black Protestants, Catholics, and Jews preferred Democratic candidates who favored immigration reform. These differences notwithstanding, a live-and-let-live attitude toward immigrants—and toward religious differences in particular—generally prevailed, no matter which of the three categories best described a person's theological orientation. Exclusivist Christians related to non-Christian coworkers and neighbors mostly by ignoring their religious differences, although the most devout exclusivists occasionally engaged in proselytizing. Inclusivist Christians also mostly avoided talking about religion with people who belonged to different religions. Spiritual shoppers' engagement with other religions was usually selective, focusing mostly on enriching themselves spiritually. It was the members and leaders of Muslim, Hindu, and Buddhist groups, in contrast, who reached out most often to their Christian neighbors in efforts to seek greater understanding and to engage in dialogue across religious communities.[21]

How the growing numbers of immigrants since the 1960s may have affected the *practices* of established religious groups—not just their attitudes—was harder to gauge. One possibility that some scholars of religion entertained was that the larger presence of immigrants— especially immigrants with religious practices differing from majority US traditions—may have motivated some established religious groups to work harder to retain or expand their numbers, although little evidence suggested that this was happening on a measurable scale. However, some groups—especially White evangelical Protestants— increasingly imagined themselves as a beleaguered minority, which was possibly a factor in why they became more interested in policies they considered essential to the protection of their religious freedom.[22] Among inclusivists and spiritual shoppers, the value they attached to diversity and tolerance as civic ideals seemed to be reinforced by interacting with people who adhered to different religions. For some Americans, though, immigration represented a threat, not in any immediate way to their family, jobs, or community, but to what they thought America should be. They wanted a strong border that could serve symbolically as well as physically to protect against this threat, and the threat level was higher if they believed America was a Christian nation that was in danger of losing that identity.[23]

The missing piece in much that has been written about religion's role in shaping attitudes toward immigrants is the extent to which these attitudes are refracted through the lens of local conversations and social networks, the media, and national events. The language in which attitudes are expressed is always intertwined with personal experience and

the stories of friends, neighbors, and public figures. That was evident in
the immediate aftermath of the 9/11 attacks when public opinion toward
immigrants and especially toward Muslims reflected all of these influences. It was evident again in 2016 when the presidential election dramatically increased public rhetoric about immigration. An ethnographic
study of a low-income neighborhood in Detroit offered a revealing example. A seemingly straightforward meeting at a local church to discuss
the resettlement of Syrian refugees generated an unexpected negative
reaction from the neighborhood. A "Trump lens" emerged, the study
found, that precluded any possibility of calmly considering the refugees'
plight. People with newly discovered ethnocentric language declared
they were outraged that the US government was trying to help outsiders
while ignoring their own needs and concerns.[24]

Activist Support and Resistance

In addition to its role among immigrants and in attitudes toward immigration, religion has been an important part of early twenty-first-
century advocacy for—and sometimes against—immigrant rights. Religious advocacy groups have weighed in on debates about policies
toward immigrants, taking different sides on border security, sanctuary
for undocumented immigrants, asylum, and resettlement. In addition,
advocacy groups have frequently participated directly in providing legal
counsel, arbitrating disputes about visas and citizenship, obtaining support for refugees, providing English language and citizenship classes,
and registering new citizens to vote. Advocacy itself has become more
diverse as new ethnic congregations and organizations have joined coalitions of native-born Protestants, Catholics, and Jews. In their attempts to influence immigration policy, advocacy groups have typically
advanced claims about the values they thought democracy should uphold. For example, the plight of refugees fleeing wars in Syria and Iraq
has led some advocacy groups to argue that Christian refugees should
be given preference because Christianity is the majority religion in the
United States, but other advocacy groups cite separation of church and
state as a reason for not granting Christian refugees special treatment.[25]

In short, immigrant rights debates provide another topic with which to consider religious diversity's role in deliberations about democracy. Citizenship is the key question: Who is "in" and what are the nation's responsibilities toward those at the edge?

Policies toward undocumented immigrants are among the issues in which religious advocacy groups have been most involved. Activists' involvement has been particularly notable in protest demonstrations. Between March and early May 2006, for example, large demonstrations in support of immigration reform were staged in towns and cities across the country. Under the rubric "A Day without Immigrants," May Day marches sought to demonstrate immigrants' value to the national economy through their temporary absence in the workplace and their presence in the streets. Other demonstrations that spring called for comprehensive immigration reform and support for the rights of undocumented immigrants: the Mega March on April 9 in Dallas attracted 350,000 participants, a May Day rally in Chicago turned out 400,000, in Los Angeles between 500,000 and 650,000 participated, and Washington, DC, New York City, Phoenix, and San Jose each reported demonstrations of 100,000 participants or more. In all, some three million to five million persons participated in rallies at more than 150 scattered locations.[26]

The demonstrations' organizers drew on expertise learned in previous grassroots protests, strikes, and boycotts on behalf of immigrant workers. These events included major demonstrations, marches, and boycotts organized by the League of United Latin American Citizens (LULAC) in Texas and the United Farm Workers in California. Churches, synagogues, mosques, and interfaith organizations also contributed to the protests, drawing on decades of activism and advocacy. Since the 1940s priests in border parishes had been providing English language instruction and mediating with employers against harsh working conditions. In the 1980s many churches participated in the sanctuary movement that sought to shield Central American immigrant families from deportation. Through short- and long-term missionary work churches had also been involved in planting and supporting congregations, building faith-based schools, operating fair-trade businesses, and advocating against corporate exploitation of workers.

The 2006 Mega March in Dallas—one example of immigrant rights advocacy—was spearheaded by a multiethnic ecumenical organization called Dallas Area Interfaith. In another example, advocacy along the Texas-Mexico border was led by Bishop Raymunda J. Peña—one of the state's most outspoken critics of immigration policies. Peña summarized his views: "If the undocumented knock on our door or meet us on the street and ask for help, we will generously address their need, lovingly. Their legal status cannot deter us, since in God's eyes, no one is illegal."[27] In yet another example, under the leadership of Cardinal Mahoney in Los Angeles, where 70 percent of the immigrant population was Catholic, the church contributed to the May Day events by providing "parish kits" with information about church teachings on social justice and "how-to guides" for contacting public officials, and by following the May Day demonstration with a petition drive, a month-long series of masses and processions, and meetings to protest deportations and detentions of undocumented immigrants.[28]

A national survey of the US Latino population shortly after the 2006 demonstrations found that 36 percent of Latino noncitizens and 18 percent of Latino citizens had participated at some point in one of the marches and demonstrations. Taking account of other differences, the study showed that noncitizens who identified religiously as "charismatics" were more likely to have participated than other noncitizens, while among citizens participation was highest among Catholics and mainline Protestants. Among citizens and noncitizens alike, those who did volunteer work through their congregation were more likely to have participated in protests than nonvolunteers. The study also showed that almost a third of noncitizens and approximately a fifth of citizens belonged to congregations that had participated in organizing immigrant rights marches.[29]

Opposition to immigration—documented and undocumented— also mobilized religious constituencies. One of the most effective of these organizations, NumbersUSA, kept mostly under the radar but played an important role in killing immigration reform efforts in 2007 through a campaign involving a million faxes to legislators. Numbers-USA was a nonreligious organization that worked closely with

conservative Republicans but understood the value of recruiting supporters based on religious appeals. Lawmakers, the group claimed,
would respond better if they thought people with religious beliefs similar to their own were involved; for example, the movement's leadership
said it helped when criticizing the Catholic bishops' proimmigration
stance to reveal that 26 percent of the movement's 1.5 million members
were Catholic; similarly, it should help to cultivate legislators of other
faiths by showing that 17 percent of the group's activists were Baptist,
9 percent were Methodist, and smatterings were Mormon, Jewish, and
Episcopalian.[30] Another advocacy group that took a strong stand against
immigration reform was Christian Coalition, the conservative group
created in 1989 by evangelical broadcaster Pat Robertson. "The American people are backed up by the Bible in their demands that America's
national boundaries are to be respected," its president, Roberta Combs,
argued. "The left wing in this nation is thoroughly wrong when they
argue that because Christ showed compassion to all of God's children,
Christians should ignore violations of the law by aliens."[31]

    Although much of the advocacy either supported or resisted policies
liberalizing immigrant rights, the advocacy and counteradvocacy was
also *interactive*, which meant that each side influenced the other. As one
side mobilized, the other side countermobilized. Activism in Hazelton,
a working-class community of thirty-one thousand in eastern Pennsylvania, was a typical example. With nearly a third of its population composed of recent Hispanic immigrants, Hazelton's Anglo citizens organized to restrict housing and employment opportunities, winning
praise from conservative television commentators. The publicity
prompted one of the local Pentecostal churches that had never been
involved in politics to organize in support of the immigrants. Its pastor
and members began attending public meetings, speaking out, offering
English language classes, cooperating with kindred spirits at the local
Catholic church, and monitoring harassment of Hispanic citizens. This
was an example of conflict elevating attention to an important national
issue. Freedom of religion and the diversity it facilitated provided the
forum for the issue to be debated.[32]

Another way in which advocacy and counteradvocacy were interactive was in mobilizing adherents of the same religious tradition to take opposing positions. White evangelicals, for example, were known during the Bush administration for supporting Republican policies, but Hispanic evangelicals were more supportive of Democratic policies, which they considered to be more in keeping with minority representation and inclusion. The National Hispanic Leadership Conference, patterned after the Southern Christian Leadership Conference, became the vehicle through which more than twenty-five thousand evangelical churches organized. As the 2010 census approached, the organization worked closely with two secular groups, the New Democratic Network and America's Voice, to pressure the Census Bureau to obtain an accurate count of the Hispanic population and encouraged church members to participate in the count.[33]

Amid the back-and-forth about immigration, the reality was that because of immigration America was more diverse religiously and ethnically than it had been a few decades earlier. Conversations about the meaning of democracy took into account this reality whether they embraced or opposed it. But the reality was present in ways other than population and polling statistics. Diversity made it possible for organizations to form that embodied this diversity in their membership and action. Advocacy for immigrant rights was a way for new immigrants to join longtime residents in activities that furthered grassroots democracy.

One of the most diverse sections of the country was just outside the nation's capital. Northern Virginia was a hub for cloud computing, advanced technology, government contracts, and national intelligence agencies. It was a magnet for skilled immigrants with training in information technology and programming and for low-skilled immigrants in the dynamic construction industry that was being driven by rapid population growth. Many of the public schools were minority majority with large percentages of South Asians, East Asians, and Hispanics. Politically, it was "purple," with a varying balance between moderate Republicans who sided with the state's rural conservative voters and moderate

Democrats who favored inclusive social policies and economic growth.[34]

Among Northern Virginia's strongest advocacy groups was VOICE. The acronym stood for Virginians Organized for Interfaith Community Engagement. Modeled on the Industrial Areas Foundation's community organizing efforts of the 1960s, VOICE was a coalition of more than forty congregations with a total of 125,000 members. The congregations were Catholic, Protestant, Unitarian, Jewish, and Muslim, united around a common agenda of justice and community participation. Among its principal activities, VOICE convened conferences, wrote reports, lobbied, and worked directly with the region's new immigrants to incorporate them into the democratic process as fully participating citizens. One of its projects was assisting immigrants whose applications for citizenship were being unduly delayed. Muslim immigrants were frequently the targets of these unexplained delays. Another was meeting with school principals to learn about the challenges they were facing. Yet another was working with the state legislature and governor's office to facilitate the reinstatement of driving privileges for residents with unpaid court fines, a problem that severely affected the region's low-income Hispanic immigrants.[35]

Reston Interfaith

How a large regional coalition like VOICE functions in practice can be seen more clearly through the activities of its constituent organizations. An organization that illustrated these activities at the local community level was called Reston Interfaith. Reston, Virginia, was founded as a planned community in the early 1960s by wealthy New York real estate developer Robert E. Simon, who named it using his initials. It was an unlikely place for an interfaith center devoted to religious, racial, ethnic, and socioeconomic diversity. By the early twenty-first century, household incomes, education levels, and housing prices in Reston were among the highest in the region. Most of its growth, mushrooming from 5,700 in 1970 to 36,000 in 1980, was driven by the rapid expansion of high technology and government contracting firms—and happened before the large influx of immigrants from Asia and Central America.[36] But Simon was a visionary and when he purchased the seven thousand acres for the community with proceeds from the sale of Carnegie Hall, he wanted it to be different from the homogeneous suburbs he was familiar with on Long Island. He specifically wanted it to be a community of diversity, a goal reflected in its mission statement of building "a community where barriers created by race, income, geography, education, and age are removed" and including language about "housing for different needs and incomes."[37]

That was a tall order in the early 1960s when the state of Virginia was doing everything it could to deter and delay school integration and when de facto residential segregation was the prevailing pattern. Sociologist Herbert Gans, who was writing a book about the huge Levittown planned community in New Jersey, visited the development as it was under construction and predicted that residents would socialize among their friends and family and at their houses of worship but were unlikely to forge a wider sense of being an inclusive community.[38] In 1967 the hope for diversity suffered a serious blow when Simon, facing financial difficulties, sold the development to the Gulf Oil Corporation. Gulf's interest was to maximize its profits by selling houses to upscale buyers at the highest possible prices.

Having been attracted to the community by its promise of diversity, residents formed the Reston Citizens Association (RCA), which its founding officers described as a "union" or "voice" organized to combat the big money that was threatening to undermine the kind of community they wanted.[39] In 1972, RCA's president, John Dockery, drafted a document to guide the association's tactics. A nuclear physicist who worked at the Pentagon and who would go on to write influential papers about artificial intelligence and chaos theory, Dockery was fluent in four languages and read widely. The document he wrote for the RCA was titled "Tactical Considerations for 'New Town' Citizens Groups: An Urban Guerrilla Warfare Manual." It was based on Brazilian leader Carlos Marighella's recently translated *Mini-Manual of the Urban Guerrilla*. Although it rejected Marighella's engagement in violence, it adopted the manual's advice in other respects. Terming the community's new developer "a gray, amorphous, corporate conglomerate," it argued that the community needed to counteract the "natural drift toward human complacency" by organizing at the grassroots, engaging in a long campaign on familiar ground against a very wealthy organization, carefully husbanding its resources, strategically selecting its targets, limiting its objectives, and creating a well-developed information network.[40]

RCA served as the hub for Reston Interfaith's activities. Organized in 1970, Reston Interfaith became the institutional vehicle through which Simon's vision of diversity was carried forward. The group's existence was made possible by the inclusion of space for the establishment of churches and synagogues in Reston's master plan. In addition, the planners worked with the Council of Churches of Greater Washington to solicit input about the kinds of religious organizations that should be represented and how to attract them. By 1970, the congregations that formed Reston Interfaith included the Roman Catholic Church of Saint Thomas à Becket, the Northern Virginia Hebrew Congregation, the Washington Plaza Baptist Church, and the United Christian Parish, which was a coalition of members from five denominations.[41] All were committed to social justice and social service engagement. Reston Interfaith became the coordinating agency for the congregations' job counseling, food pantries, thrift shops, and homeless shelters. It also spearheaded the Reston Interfaith Housing Corporation, which in the early 1980s worked with regional and federal agencies and engaged in litigation to bring affordable housing to the community. Still, it was an uphill battle to shape the community against the trend toward upscale development and homogeneity. When sociologist Sylvia Fava studied it in 1985, Reston seemed destined to become the privileged, predominantly White enclave that it did in fact become over the next two decades.[42]

In 2006 Reston became the center of national attention in the debate about immigration. In cooperation with local officials and religious groups Reston Interfaith had organized a formal day-labor center in neighboring Herndon—where a third of the population was Hispanic, many of whom were recent immigrants—at which day laborers gathered to await work. Almost immediately questions were raised about the immigrants' legal status. The 2005 Virginia gubernatorial campaign used immigration as a campaign issue on both sides and drew Reston Interfaith's day-labor center into the debate. Two national anti-immigrant groups (Minuteman Project and Judicial Watch) filed a lawsuit charging the center with using public money to assist illegal immigrants. In 2006, when proimmigration marches gained national attention, local officials pressured Reston Interfaith to require proof of legal residency for immigrants registering though the center. The center refused and Herndon officials shut it down.[43]

Nationwide in 2006 approximately five hundred day-labor centers were in operation. In many of the communities, residents were divided. Day laborers in their communities inspired fear on one hand and compassion on the other.[44] The failure of comprehensive immigration reform legislation left the issue open for debate. Reston Interfaith had little choice but to shift its attention toward other programs. In 2012 it changed its name to Cornerstones, a name it considered to be meaningful in all religious traditions without referring explicitly to religion. It continued the programs it had begun in the 1970s: affordable housing, childcare, and emergency food assistance. It also initiated a citizenship class through which immigrants from more than thirty countries became citizens.

Reston Interfaith's short-lived role in assisting immigrant day laborers was a failure as far as effecting change on a larger scale. Its participation in that effort nevertheless underscores several aspects of religion's connections with democracy. First, organizations such as Reston Interfaith depend on the support of religious congregations but are also complexly intertwined with nonsectarian community associations, developers, local officials, state and national policy makers, advocacy organizations, and the media, all of which are involved when projects focus on controversial issues such as housing, day laborers, and immigrants. These are the kinds of cross-sectoral social networks that strengthen civil society. Second, democratic procedures are learned, instituted, and reinforced, not only through legislation and the courts, but also within religious and nonprofit associations such as Reston Interfaith. This was true especially in the formation of the United

Christian Parish, which involved numerous meetings to work out by-laws and procedures that honored the various modes of church governance among the denominations represented. Democratic procedures were also evident in the Reston Citizens Association's reformulation of "urban guerrilla tactics" to focus on information, pressure, and activism. Another benefit of an organization like Reston Interfaith is its staying power and adaptability. The congregations that supported it were in the community for the long haul. They provided stability and resources. They also adapted to changing circumstances. They worked at times as a coalition, at times as separate organizations, and at times as participants in new coalitions. Thus, when anti-immigrant groups won the battle to shut down the day-labor center, Reston's congregations assisted immigrants in other ways. United Christian Parish, for example, was one of a dozen Christian, Jewish, and Muslim congregations in Northern Virginia that formed a new Congregation Action Network, rooted in religious teachings about sanctuary, refuge, and welcoming the stranger, to provide support for families being detained, deported, and profiled by immigration authorities.

The New Sanctuary Movement

The New Sanctuary Movement, as it was called, began in early 2007 when five churches in New York City offered shelter to a family from Haiti and a second family from China to protect them from deportation orders filed against them by the federal government. The movement spawned a network that included churches in Chicago, Los Angeles, San Diego, and Seattle. Its impetus was a sixfold increase in deportations following conservative Republicans' blockage of comprehensive immigration reform in Congress. It was a risky move. In the 1980s, when a similar movement had been in operation, church workers were convicted of criminal conspiracy for providing sanctuary to refugees from Central America.[45]

The movement gained national attention in August 2007 when federal immigration agents arrested Elvira Arellano outside a church in Los Angeles. Arellano was thirty-two, a single mother living in Chicago with her American-born son. She had come from the Mexican state of Michoacán in 1997, been arrested and deported, come back to the United States, and lived in Washington State for three years before moving to Chicago, where she cleaned planes at O'Hare International Airport. During a post-9/11 security sweep she was arrested and convicted; she then pursued various legal reprieves until the last one failed in 2006. In the interim she became a volunteer for a Methodist advocacy group working to keep unauthorized immigrant families together. To avoid being deported and thus separated from her son, she took refuge at a Methodist church in Chicago where she and her son lived for a year before she was in fact deported. Having been a leader in the spring 2006 immigration reform demonstrations in Chicago, and then forming her own activist group to oppose the forcible separation of undocumented parents from their children, she was featured in *Time* as one of the year's "people who mattered" for giving immigration reform a human face. In September 2007, three weeks after she was deported, activists from Chicago, New York, Rhode Island, and Texas rallied in Washington on behalf of the estimated four million to five million US-citizen children facing the possible deportation of one or both of their parents. Arellano's eight-year-old son, Saul, and other children carried homemade banners through the House of Representatives' Rayburn Building urging lawmakers to stop raids and deportations separating families.[46]

Adalberto Methodist Church, where Elvira Arellano took refuge, was a storefront congregation on Division Street near Humboldt Park in northwest Chicago. Settled in the late nineteenth century by Norwegian and Danish immigrants, the neighborhood attracted Jews and Eastern European Catholics in the 1930s and then in the 1970s Puerto Ricans, who started Spanish-speaking businesses and community organizations that attracted growing numbers of Mexican immigrants through the end of the century. When immigration agents started post-9/11 security sweeps at O'Hare International Airport, agents also raided immigrants' homes in Humboldt Park, usually at night, sometimes detaining US citizens. Adalberto's pastors, Walter Coleman and Emma Lozano, organized protests at the airport with the cooperation of the Chicago Interfaith Committee on Worker Issues, the Illinois Coalition to Protect

Political Freedom, and Pueblo sin Fronteras, of which Lozano was president. In addition to assisting immigrants facing deportation, the church leveraged the publicity it received to advocate for change in US trade relations with Mexico. The North American Free Trade Agreement (NAFTA), which went into effect in 1994, prohibited protective tariffs and resulted in US corn and other staples flowing into Mexico, lowering the prices of Mexican-grown crops, raising consumer food prices, and devastating the livelihoods of Mexican farmers. Jobless Mexicans migrated to the United States in the hundreds of thousands after NAFTA.[47]

Grace Yukich, a social scientist who spent two years studying churches that participated in the New Sanctuary Movement, concluded that it had enlarged the debate about immigration, trade, and citizenship. Although it generated as much opposition as it did support, it brought human dignity, conscience, and compassion into the picture alongside arguments about legality and border security. If it did not persuade lawmakers, it sharpened the sensitivities of the people involved. "When religious people use religious reasons in the public sphere," Yukich wrote, "they are not only trying to win people over to their particular political position—at times, they are also attempting to define and argue over what it means to be religious in the first place." In the short run it meant helping individuals like Elvira Arellano; in the long run, it meant reaching across new lines of ethnic difference and cultivating an enlarged political perspective.[48]

A decade later, when families were being torn apart in large numbers through a more aggressive border security policy, municipalities as well as churches began defining themselves as sanctuaries, at least to the point of refusing to cooperate with draconian enforcement practices. In the meantime, Adalberto Methodist Church provided live-in sanctuary for a succession of immigrant families. In Tijuana, Elvira Arellano founded the Casa Refugio Elvira, where she sheltered recently deported women and advocated for immigrant rights. In 2014, she returned to the United States under a short-term visa to advocate for passage of the immigration reform proposal known as the DREAM Act. The advocacy group she started in Chicago, Familia Latina Unida, served as a connecting point among Mexican immigrants of Protestant and Catholic background and their families in Mexico, carrying on traditions such as honoring the Virgin of Guadalupe as well as providing legal advice. Emma Lozano, who copastored a second Spanish-speaking church in the neighborhood, continued her advocacy work. In March 2016, the second church was twice vandalized. In white paint, vandals scrawled swastikas and the message "Rape Mexico."[49]

Vandalism and violence were the public edge of fear, anger, and resentment toward immigrants. A few weeks after the 2006 proimmigrant May Day marches, four Long Island teenagers attacked, robbed, and beat two Mexican immigrants, demanding to see their green cards. In 2008, seven teenagers attacked and killed a Salvadoran immigrant. In 2011 the FBI reported 6,216 hate crimes, 20 percent of which were motivated by bias against the victims' religion and 12 percent by ethnicity bias. Mosques and temples were vandalized. Immigrants also experienced microaggressions ranging from ethnic slurs to discrimination based on language and personal grooming.[50]

White evangelical Christians, when polled, were the least welcoming toward immigrants; nearly two-thirds thought newcomers threatened traditional values and jobs. They did not form church-based advocacy organizations to resist immigration and they were noticeably absent among the leaders of secular anti-immigrant groups. Their quiet inhospitality was puzzling enough that writers speculated about the possible reasons. It was plausible that evangelicals in White churches in White communities had so little contact with immigrants that all they knew was what they heard and saw on conservative television. It was equally plausible that evangelicals in multiethnic communities experiencing an influx of immigrants were guided by concerns about their jobs and perceived threats to the familiar norms of their communities.[51]

The Muslim Ban

On January 27, 2017, at the end of his first week in office, Donald Trump announced his first Muslim ban. It banned entry into the United States for 90 days of people from seven Muslim-majority countries: Iran, Iraq, Libya, Somalia, Syria, Sudan, and Yemen. It also banned entry of all refugees from eleven countries, nine of which were mostly Muslim, including spouses and children of refugees already living in the United States. Thousands of people were stranded in airports, students were kept from returning to the colleges where they were enrolled, people were deprived of life-saving healthcare, and families were separated. The ban was sudden but not unexpected. Trump had been denouncing Muslims and Islam to enthusiastic crowds throughout his campaign. The ban was challenged in the courts, but after a year and a half the US Supreme Court upheld a version of the ban that applied to five of the original seven Muslim countries.[52]

It was unclear whether the Muslim ban was something religious groups could do anything about, and if they could, whether there was interest enough to try. The Supreme Court determined that it was certainly within the right of the president to protect the country's national security. How that was done was up to the executive branch of the federal government. The countries at issue were reasonably considered as sources of possible terrorist attacks. As far as discrimination against Muslims was concerned, the administration argued that the countries affected just happened to be majority Muslim and promised that individuals from those countries could go through a process to request a waiver. As for the public, the ban was of obvious concern to American Muslims and possibly to a few others, but Trump seemed to have solid support from evangelical Christians.[53] The ban, though, posed another occasion on which religious advocacy groups asserted claims about the principles for which democracy was supposed to stand.

News of the initial ban spread immediately among US Muslims gathered for Friday prayers. In New York City a rally hastily convened by Muslim and interfaith groups was joined by Jewish speakers commemorating International Holocaust Remembrance Day. The gathering also included Franciscan friars, an Episcopal priest, and a representative of a Hindu organization. Khalid Latif, executive director of the Islamic Center at New York University, told the crowd, "We have to be the reason people have hope in the world." The next day crowds gathered at JFK International Airport to protest the ban as ACLU lawyers filed for an injunction. As protests spread, leaders of organized religious groups condemned the ban. Joining other Baptist leaders, Cooperative Baptist Fellowship's executive director Suzii Paynter stated, "The love of Christ compels us to stand in solidarity with our global neighbors—the oppressed, the unheard and those on the margins." The US Conference of Catholic Bishops' Committee on Migration chair, Bishop Joe Vasquez, said, "We believe that now, more than ever, welcoming newcomers and refugees is an act of love and hope." USCCB president Cardinal Daniel N. DiNardo added, "The church will not waiver [*sic*] in her defense of our sisters and brothers of all faiths who suffer at the hands of merciless persecutors."[54]

Litigation challenging the ban evolved into a coordinated effort under the direction of attorneys working with Jewish Family Service of Seattle. JFS was a private nonprofit organization in the Puget Sound region, founded in 1892 by local Jewish women with the mission of helping people live with dignity, achieve health, and enjoy safe sustainable housing. Over the years it had been extensively involved in assisting immigrants and refugees, focusing on Jewish refugees during and after World War II, and by the early twenty-first century resettling approximately three hundred refugees annually from many countries including the ones subject to the Muslim ban. The suit, which was joined by the ACLU, was brought on behalf of specific individuals from Somalia, Egypt, and Iraq, including two whose lives were threatened for having served as interpreters for the US Army.[55]

Like the New Sanctuary Movement, the travel ban lawsuit prompted lawmakers and the public to acknowledge that ideals were at stake other than the administration's claims about national security. Of the three arguments JFS attorneys presented, one was procedural, challenging the manner in which the Trump administration had arranged the travel ban and forcing revisions that brought it closer to conformity with procedural rules. The second challenged the ban on First Amendment grounds, arguing that it unfairly infringed on the rights of Muslims by singling them out under the guise of identifying Muslim-majority countries as the reason for the ban. The third argued that the ban was inhumane, particularly in violating families' fundamental right to be together, which had long been a principle of refugee and immigration policy. Citing judicial precedent, the plaintiffs asserted that "the right to live with and not be separated from one's immediate family is 'a right that ranks high among the interests of the individual.'"[56]

In upholding the ban, Supreme Court chief justice John Roberts argued that the president had satisfactorily signaled that entry of people from the named countries would be detrimental to the interest of the United States, and that whatever prejudicial statement the president may have made against Muslims was irrelevant. In an impassioned dissent, Associate Justice Sonia Sotomayor argued that the decision failed to safeguard the fundamental principle of religious neutrality in the First Amendment and turned a blind eye to the pain and suffering of countless families and individuals.[57]

Citizenship

Throughout its history, US democracy has been a contest about citizenship and thus an evolving question about who is in and who is out, who has rights and who does not, and how much to accept or reject those at the edge. Religion has participated at each step of the way, offering opinions about gender, race, national origin, property ownership, and character. Religion's participation in recent debates about immigration has continued this precedent. The contribution to democracy has consisted of arguments about both inclusion and exclusion, the one being evident in congregations of native-born members welcoming immigrants and refugees and in activist groups advocating for immigrants' rights, and the other consisting of hunkering down to protect traditions and beliefs.

The biblical backstory against which the differing perspectives have played out is the narrative of the "stranger" whom the people of God variously welcomed or shunned, engaged in sexual relations with, intermarried, made peace with, or slaughtered. The stranger was always the person or group who symbolized the community's identity by being at the gates. For faith communities that drew from the biblical tradition, the narrative was a reminder that the definition of community was always fraught. It was impossible to decide once and for all that a particular group of immigrants or refugees should be allowed in or kept out. The decision had to be negotiated. It was negotiated mostly in terms of what was good or bad for the economy and sometimes for foreign relations and the nation's image in the world. Religious advocacy, along with the advocacy of human rights and humanitarian groups, expanded the discussion to include consideration of what was most representative of the values democracy was intended to uphold.

Religion's role in these deliberations is further evidence of its tendency to be influenced by partisan politics. When Democrats welcomed immigrants and worked for comprehensive immigration policy reform, progressive religionists were on board, and when conservative Republicans championed border security, evangelical Protestants registered their support.[58] But religion's voice on immigration, as on other issues, also cut across partisan divisions. Interfaith advocacy, legal assistance, intervention for low-income housing, and sanctuary were examples of religious organizations engaging in democratic governance through nonpartisan coalitions with secular organizations and working with local, state, and regional policy makers.

White evangelicals' nonparticipation in many of these activities did not in all cases indicate a lack of concern for immigrants' struggles. Churches that would never have provided sanctuary for undocumented immigrants staffed food pantries, opened their facilities for immigrant congregations' worship services, sent relief to refugee camps, and operated international adoption agencies. Insofar as these activities contributed to the inclusion of immigrants, they also facilitated their integration into the community as citizens. The gap was at the national policy level where anti-immigrant arguments were more often coming from political interests rather than being guided by humanitarian concerns.

When the Trump administration decided to phase out the DREAM Act provisions that gave work permits to undocumented immigrants who were brought to the United States as children, evangelical leaders joined mainline Protestant, Catholic, and Jewish leaders in opposing the idea. The National Association of Evangelicals, for example, acknowledged varying views on the topic but reiterated its call for legislation that treated immigrants with respect and mercy. Baptist, Quaker,

Lutheran, Methodist, Presbyterian, United Church of Christ, Jewish, Unitarian, Muslim, and Catholic leaders all denounced the decision. The US Conference of Catholic Bishops called it "reprehensible." The president of Church World Service termed it "deeply disappointing and hurtful."[59]

Immigration and religion gained national attention again in 2018. On the US-Mexico border, thousands of children were being held in detention camps, separated from their parents who were being detained and deported, some never to see their children again. The government's policy was sufficiently heinous that religious leaders across the board denounced it. Pope Francis, representatives of the Greek Orthodox Church, Jewish organizations, the Church of Jesus Christ of Latter-day Saints, and Methodist and Episcopal leaders all went on record opposing it. Evangelical leaders also weighed in, sending a letter to the White House signed by representatives of the Southern Baptist Ethics and Religious Liberty Commission, National Association of Evangelicals, Council for Christian Colleges and Universities, and National Hispanic Christian Leadership Conference. "As evangelical Christians guided by the Bible, one of our core convictions is that God has established the family as the fundamental building block of society," the letter said. "The state should separate families only in the rarest of instances."[60]

The use of the Bible on both sides of the issue was reason to believe, as skeptics did, that religion was servant to whatever interests it might be put. Yet if that were true, it was still important to consider how it was used. Its rhetorical use to condemn or defend immigration policies was one way. Its behind-the-scenes use was equally important, if not more so. Immigration policy was always about more than who was legal and who was not. That distinction was complicated by considerations of deservingness—that is, by the question of who deserved to be welcomed as an aspiring legal citizen and who did not. Were immigrants more deserving if they were refugees, children, or the children of refugees? If their children were citizens and had always lived in America? If they had spouses or parents or aunts and uncles living in the United States? If they could contribute to the economy? If they spoke English? If they were students? Refusal of entry and immediate deportation on the one hand, and on the other hand temporary admission, pathways to citizenship, exceptions to the rule, and methods of accommodation reflected the answers to these questions. And behind these policies were political and economic interests and differences in political philosophy.[61] But deservingness is fundamentally a question about morality, and morality is a topic on which religion has had much to say. In recent decades, religious groups have advocated among the various definitions of deservingness. Immigrants have also used religious resources to demonstrate deservingness: joining local congregations, becoming Christians or Buddhists or Muslims, utilizing clergy as references, becoming "American" because being religious was part of what it meant to be American.[62]

Although the rhetorical uses of religion were important, advocacy for immigrant rights also illustrated what the social science literature calls "performative citizenship."[63] In this view, citizenship is defined, illuminated, and revised through acts that dramatize something about the rights of citizens and the differences between citizens and noncitizens. Performative acts transgress the boundaries separating "us" and "them," bringing the distinction into sharper relief and challenging its legitimacy. Charles Tilly termed them "contentious performances." They function by violating the taken for granted, gaining publicity through numbers, media coverage, celebrity involvement, and declarations. The huge marches that took place in 2006 were an example. Marches to the US-Mexico border in 2018 in protest of family separation policies were another. Religious groups were not the only ones staging performative acts of citizenship. But religious participants are often among the activists most familiar with the power of such ritual acts and the symbolism that goes with them. Marchers frequently convene in houses of worship, invoke divine blessings, carry crosses, and wear liturgical garb.

The Trump administration's family separation policies seemed justifiable to some Americans. In their view, immigrant families and refugees—from what the administration said about them—were trying to enter the United States illegally and thus deserved to be punished. Even if separating children from their parents seemed harsh, in their view that was how justice worked. Some of the same Americans interpreted family separation less through the lens of religion. They wanted the predominantly White Christianity with which they were familiar to be preserved. They feared that immigrants were one more threat to worry about. The tragedy of the Trump administration's family separation policy, as many other religious groups saw it, was that an "America First" ideology was driving policies that paid no attention to the values of compassion and humanitarianism that religious teachings embraced. Under those conditions, it seemed imperative to these religious groups that religious communities were speaking against government policies in the name of alternative values.

Deplorable as critics said it was that a democracy based on principles of freedom, dignity, and respect could imprison children with no plan of what to do with them, this was only one of the threats the nation faced in the early years of the Trump administration. Voter suppression, gun violence, racism, tense foreign relations, election interference, and untruthfulness at the highest levels of government were among the others. Informed analyses identified another threat, the unraveling of goodness and decency amid the grip of severe economic inequality, materialism, and its manifestations in corporate greed and public indifference. As if that were not enough, sufficient political discord was present to prompt questions about the future of democracy itself.

6

The Wealth Gap

RELIGION, WEALTH, AND
ECONOMIC INEQUALITY

WEALTH, WHEN CONCENTRATED in the hands of the few, has been deemed a threat to American democracy from the nation's earliest days. Thomas Jefferson, writing to James Madison in 1785 from Fontainebleau, a village forty miles from Paris, said a conversation on his walk that morning with a woman living in poverty prompted him to reflect on the misery effected by the "unequal division of property" in France where property was concentrated in "a very few hands." The result of this concentration was a large amount of uncultivated land and a large number of unemployed poor. "It is clear," Jefferson wrote, "that the laws of property have been so far extended as to violate natural right." Although he considered a truly equal division of property to be impracticable, he pondered distributive inheritance laws, subdivisions of the land, and a progressive tax as possibilities for equalization.[1] Against the concentration of property in Jefferson's own hands and the hands of Robert "King" Carter and other wealthy slave owners in colonial Virginia, the ideal of democratic governance came to be associated with yeoman farmers, freeholders, self-employed artisans, traders, and small business owners. "The basis of a democratic and a republican form of government," Noah Webster wrote in 1790, "is a fundamental law favoring an equal or rather a general distribution of property."[2]

In the early republic it was possible to imagine that democracy's adherence to natural rights—to life, liberty, and the pursuit of happiness—was firmly upheld as long as the majority of citizens (slaves and indentured servants being the notable exceptions) were free to own property in some small amount or to imagine being able to do so in the future. Concentrated wealth in itself was not regarded as problematic for democracy as long as there was sufficient opportunity to claim new land and to benefit from economic expansion. Owning some of the nation's wealth, moreover, was thought to strengthen democracy by ensuring that citizens felt they had a stake in the common good. However, recognition was growing that concentrations of wealth also implied an aggregation of power that could be used for the self-interested benefit of the rich rather than for the good of all. Self-interest, Alexis de Tocqueville cautioned when he wrote about American democracy in the 1830s, needed to be "rightly understood" in terms of serving the common good.[3]

Movements in protest of concentrated wealth emerged throughout the nineteenth century. In the 1830s Jacksonian democracy championed greater rights for the "common man" in opposition to the aristocracy that Jacksonians perceived to be arising among the coastal elite. The antislavery movement was in part a protest against the unfair advantages that politically entrenched slave owners were perceived to enjoy in raising cotton, tobacco, and other crops in competition with small freeholders on the expanding frontier. At the end of the century, populism spread across the Midwest and South in protest of wealth concentrated in East Coast banks. In Pittsburgh, Chicago, and other manufacturing centers, and in mining towns and lumber camps labor disputes resulted in protests, strikes, and violence. By the end of the century, the Gilded Age had become known for its vast corruption. Critics of the wealth gap understood it as a problem not because inequality itself was undemocratic, but because a concentration of wealth at the top gave the wealthy an excess of power that they could use to their advantage and against the rights, freedoms, and pursuit of happiness of the citizenry at large.

Religion contributed to these popular movements against economic inequality: through the grassroots revivals of the 1830s that produced

converts by the thousands who sided with Democrats in their repudia-
tion of Whigs under the banner of Jacksonian democracy; through the
leadership of Henry Ward Beecher, Frederick Douglass, and kindred
abolitionists who drew inspiration from the scriptures; and through the
labor agitators and populists who sang hymns and gathered at churches
to condemn the mine owners and banking trusts whose exploitative
practices they sought to overturn. Less visible but equally significant
was the democratic strand that ran through the everyday teachings of
ordinary houses of worship. Communities of faith appealed to the common person, asserting that God could speak in diverse ways to spiritually inform the consciences of all. If these ideas were not a basis for active dissent, they were an antielitist orientation that prompted
skepticism toward the high and mighty.[4]

The difficulty that kept antielitism from spreading more widely in
the churches was that religious leaders depended on the rich to advance their work. The colleges and seminaries in which the first clergy
in the colonies were trained benefited from the benefactions of the
wealthy. Prior to disestablishment, clergy salaries depended on taxes
and the income from crops raised on parish glebes. The new denominations that distanced themselves from ecclesial hierarchies were not
immune to ideas that favored the rich. Such was the temptation to seek
approval from the rich that leading clergy tried to prevent it from happening. Methodist leader Francis Asbury, for example, warned preachers against locating in towns where the wealthy "settle themselves to
purchase ministers." It was against this temptation that Methodists also
rotated clergy from congregation to congregation on a three-year
cycle.[5] Later, the industrial wealth that grew from trade, commerce,
and the infrastructure that opened the West through canals, shipping,
and railroads influenced religion, shaping it even when its popular appeal was to shopkeepers, farmers, and factory workers. Dwight L.
Moody's evangelistic meetings were supported by J. Pierpont Morgan
and Cornelius Vanderbilt in New York and by John Wanamaker and
Anthony Drexel in Philadelphia. The Student Volunteer Movement
attracted funding from John D. Rockefeller and Mrs. Cyrus McCor-
mick.[6] The pattern continued in the twentieth century through the

philanthropy of John D. Rockefeller Jr., J. Howard Pew, and H. L. Hunt. When James W. Fifield Jr. expanded his Congregational ministry in Los Angeles into a national movement for "spiritual mobilization," he did so with the support of Pew, Harvey Firestone, Armstrong Cork president H. W. Prentis Jr., and ranking executives at General Motors, DuPont, and Gulf Oil. Similarly, when Billy Graham launched his televised crusades in the 1950s, early supporters included grocery retailer Howard E. Butt Jr., industrialist R. G. LeTourneau, oil barons Nelson Bunker Hunt and Sid Richardson, and networks of business leaders in California and Texas.[7]

Although these examples suggest the difficulties religious leaders sometimes had in distancing themselves from the wealthy, it mattered that American religion was as diverse as it was. Where local clergy were too deeply in the pocket of the wealthy to venture criticisms of concentrated wealth, others were sufficiently independent to speak on behalf of the common person. At the end of the nineteenth century, the Social Gospel movement brought progressive Protestants, liberal Catholics, and Reform Jews together with labor leaders, muckrakers, and populists to advocate for social reform. Drawing on biblical teaching and political theory, the Social Gospel movement set forth a vision of an alternative social order that would distribute wealth more equitably than industrial capitalism did. The movement's preeminent leader, Walter Rauschenbusch, who taught at Rochester Theological Seminary after having served a congregation in the Hell's Kitchen section of New York City, regarded wealth inequality as the source not only of economic problems but also of a cultural malaise that elevated worldly pursuits above spiritual values. His vision of social reform regarded democratic socialism along with spiritual renewal as the means of perfecting American democracy. "The great sin of modern humanity," he wrote, was that "men learned to make wealth much faster than they learned to distribute it justly."[8]

The Social Gospel movement also launched activities within denominations that ministered directly to the poor and worked cooperatively with labor leaders and union heads. These activities included the work of leaders such as Methodist pastor Harry Ward, who preached about wealth disparities on street corners near the Chicago stockyards and then organized the Open or Industrial Church League to promote antipoverty efforts in churches across the country. Another leader was Charles Stelzle, a machinist during his youth who went on to head the Presbyterian Church (USA)'s Workingmen's Department, which morphed into the denomination's Department of Church and Labor. Stelzle also worked with labor leaders during the violent struggle between mine owners and miners at Cripple Creek in Colorado and the bloody McKees Rocks strike in Pittsburgh, as well as supporting Ward's Open or Industrial Church League and forming a Department of Immigration to work with Hungarians, Italians, and Jews. The idea motivating his activities, Stelzle said, was that labor and the church working together could put democracy into practice in ways that strengthened it in the nation at large.[9]

The papal encyclical *Rerum Novarum*, which set forth the moral duties of capital and labor in 1891, honored the rights of property owners but cautioned the wealthy about their responsibilities toward the poor and before God. "The rich should tremble at the threatenings of Jesus Christ," Pope Leo XIII warned. Moreover, because the wealthy were capable of taking care of themselves, the pope argued, government had a special obligation to protect the poor. Monsignor John A. Ryan, whose influence on Catholic thought matched Rauschenbusch's among Protestants, formulated one of the most thorough treatises of the period about the wealth gap in his 1916 book *Distributive Justice: The Right and Wrong of Our Present Distribution of Wealth*. Ryan conceded that the "indefinitely large profits" earned by some of the business leaders of the day were justified because of the work and risks involved and because of their adoption of new methods in progressive industries. "Nevertheless," he wrote, "it would seem that those businessmen who obtain exceptionally large profits could be reasonably required to transfer part of their gains to their employees in the form of higher wages, or to the consumers in the form of lower prices." How to achieve that transfer, however, was a difficult question. Ryan doubted that a cap on profits would discourage investments very much as long as the cap was high, but he worried that it would be impractical to administer such a law because of the intolerable level of minute supervision it would require. It was perhaps untenable to expect much in the way of economic reform, he concluded, short of a religious revival effecting changes in the human heart. But that difficulty did not suggest doing nothing. A fair living wage could be advocated and greater efforts could be made to advance social policies beneficial for the poor. Ryan's ideas also represented an important development in arguments about what those beneficial social policies might be. Whereas in the 1880s Catholic social practice had focused on charitable activity, by the end of the century it was directed toward reform in labor and industry as well as charity. Church leaders worked increasingly with trade unions, assisting immigrant families and serving as arbitrators on strike commissions.[10]

Historians of the Social Gospel argue that the movement had a powerful impact on twentieth-century church practices, orienting the ministries of upscale congregations and parishes toward the struggles of the expanding urban working class and guiding these ministries with ideas about prayer and faith that churchgoers could embrace when they would not have accepted the views of secular socialist leaders. Scholars also note the movement's limitations, among which were its emphasis on reforming the social order by perfecting the piety of individual believers and its location at seminaries and churches that depended on the very concentrations of wealth it criticized.[11] Illustrating these limitations, Rauschenbusch called for repentance and a new spirit of evangelism while acknowledging that the church "has furnished no adequate principles either for the distribution or the consumption of wealth." Throughout his time at Rochester Theological Seminary, Rauschenbusch maintained a close relationship with the seminary's chief donor, John D. Rockefeller, and refrained from directing his most pointed criticisms of capitalism at Rockefeller.[12] Stelzle, for his part, approached Rockefeller's son, John D. Rockefeller Jr., who he hoped might be pushed toward social reform, but without much success. "Let us everlastingly pound him," Stelzle wrote in criticizing Rockefeller, "when, for any reason, he goes contrary to the great principles of social justice and democracy for which most of us stand."[13] Ryan carefully distanced himself from socialism but was known to have been mistrusted by one of

Catholic University of America's potential donors, who declared, "I won't give a cent so long as the University keeps that dashed Socialist, John Ryan."[14] The reformers' other limitation was another faction of the wealthy elite who patronized a different branch of Christianity that had greater appeal to the working class of farmers and small business owners who enjoyed incomes above the poverty line. Fundamentalism spread rapidly between the 1890s and the 1920s, with popular fervor at the grassroots and generous philanthropy at the top.[15]

By 1929 the Social Gospel still enjoyed support among northern Methodists, Episcopalians, Presbyterians, Unitarians, and Reform Jews but was already declining as an organized movement and would decline further after World War II. Its impact on the New Deal was chiefly through the involvement of Roosevelt adviser and Works Progress Administration architect Harry Hopkins, whose Methodist upbringing combined Social Gospel ideals with progressive politics. Threads of the Social Gospel continued into the 1950s and 1960s in ideas that ranged from Christian socialism to advocacy for birth control as a means of lowering the economic burden of large numbers of children on lower-income families, and from teachings about civic responsibility to civil rights. But these ideas focused less on wealth concentration and redistribution than on poverty and racial reconciliation.[16]

Rising Inequality

Around 1979, the share of the nation's wealth owned by the top 1 percent began to increase after having remained relatively constant since the end of World War II, and by the early twenty-first century it had grown to the point of being widely regarded as a serious threat to democracy. One comparison noted that in Ancient Rome the top 1 percent controlled 16 percent of society's wealth, compared to as much as 40 percent in the contemporary United States. Comparisons with Ancient Rome implicated inequality in its downfall and posited a similar fate for America. Other comparisons likened the United States to "banana republics" where the few rich at the top dictated the terms on which government exploited everyone else.[17]

Data compiled by the Congressional Budget Office demonstrated
that between 1979 and 2007, average real after-tax household income for
the 1 percent of the population with the highest income grew by
275 percent, while comparable growth among the 60 percent of the
population in the middle of the income scale was just under 40 percent,
and growth among the 20 percent of the population with the lowest
income was only 18 percent. Investigations identified multiple reasons
for the rise in inequality: technological innovation increased the demand for high-skilled labor; automation reduced the demand for low-
skilled labor; women's increasing participation in the labor force contributed to higher household incomes for married women but lower
household incomes for single women; executive compensation and
capital gains contributed to the rise of income for the top 1 percent;
stagnant government transfer payments for the poor and elderly reduced income growth among low-income households; and federal tax
policies shifted more of the burden from top-income households onto
middle-income households. Another source about which there was
speculation was that the rising number of immigrants, especially in low-
wage jobs, was putting downward pressure on wage rates for workers at
the bottom of the income distribution.[18]

The 2008 recession furthered concern about the widening gap between high- and low- or median-income households. During the recession household income among the highest-income households declined by only 4 percent, whereas median household income declined
by 9 percent, and bottom household income decreased by 20 percent,
largely because of an increase in unemployment.[19] Furthermore, over
the next decade nearly all of the recovery accrued to the highest-income
households. By 2017, research showed that the richest 10 percent of US
households held 70 percent of the nation's wealth, while a record
30 percent of households owned no nonhome wealth at all (up from
only 19 percent in 2007).[20]

But was this a problem? Was a high level of income inequality detrimental to democracy? The literature that tried to address the question
came up with different answers. Studies comparing the histories of
countries in Europe and the Americas concluded that it was impossible

to demonstrate that greater wealth inequality delayed or deterred the adoption of democratic forms of government. Nor was there compelling evidence that democratic government, once in place, reduced wealth inequality. Studies of late twentieth-century legislative decisions in the United States did show—unsurprisingly—that they favored the interests of the wealthy. The studies did not demonstrate, however, that these decisions threatened democracy, just that they went against public opinion on certain issues such as estate taxes and support for a minimum wage. Other studies identified conditions that might mitigate or exacerbate the possible effects of wealth inequality on democracy, such as ethnic, racial, and regional divisions. The contemporary increase in the wealth gap, moreover, was the result of multiple features of the economy itself that could not be directly attributed to or remedied by the legislative process. Still, one conclusion stood out: wealth inequality that was perceived to be *unfair* was the kind of inequality most likely to also be regarded as a threat to democracy. When enough of the public believed the wealthy were not contributing their fair share and when the wealthy were perceived to be damaging the well-being of others by manipulating things to protect their wealth, that was a threat. Moreover, the basic trust in government and in other institutions on which democracy depends was said to be undermined when the fortunate few dictate what they want against the interest of the many.[21]

After the 2008 recession, criticisms of the wealth gap's unfairness emphasized that the rich were getting away with not shouldering their share of the tax burden. Large majorities of the public told pollsters that the wealthy should be paying higher taxes, but tax rates on the ultrarich and on corporate profits remained low. The democratic system seemed incapable of remedying the situation. Ordinary taxpayers were carrying the burden of providing relief to the poor; in addition, infrastructure was falling into disrepair. Hedge-fund managers and subprime lenders were being bailed out at the public's expense while homeowner foreclosures and bankruptcies were skyrocketing. Productivity was increasing but average working families' incomes were failing to keep pace. If democracy was supposed to provide for the interests of the majority, it was being replaced by an oligarchy that favored the few—an oligarchy of wealthy families united in defending their wealth. Moreover, wealth was becoming all the more important as a source of entrenched political power because of the declining power of labor unions, the high cost of elections, and the waning of antitrust enforcement.[22]

Religion's relevance to the wealth gap was unclear. Discussions of rising inequality focused on tax policies, regulations or the lack thereof, and shifts in the composition of the economy itself, but these discussions agreed that public attitudes about fairness, trust in government, and economic policies should be considered. Studies showed that attitudes toward economic policies were related to questions about religion, but in varying ways. For example, like studies of attitudes toward poverty in the 1980s and 1990s, studies conducted more recently found that religious conservatives favored private charity rather than redistributive policies.[23] Taking a different approach, several quantitative cross-national studies suggested that higher levels of religiosity and more acute religious polarization were associated with lower government spending on social services and thus with greater income inequality. A comparison of US data at the state level found a relationship between religious heterogeneity and greater income inequality that was probably attributable to attitudes toward welfare spending. However, the cross-national data identified significant variations among different religious traditions. Other research suggested a more complicated relationship among religion, wealth, and inequality, including variations in asset formation and wealth concentration in different religious traditions.[24] In short, religious views seemed relevant to how people thought about wealth, but it was impossible to draw generalizations about these relationships— perhaps because of a key feature of religion: its diversity.

When researchers shifted attention to what was happening on the ground, they found that congregations across the theological spectrum were engaged in poverty relief efforts of all kinds—soup kitchens, clothing drives, mission trips to poor communities, and special offerings for the support of bishops' funds and denominational ministries.[25] In addition, some ministries encouraged wealthier members to be mindful of materialistic tendencies and to be more active in philanthropic efforts. Addressing income inequality at the congregational level, though, was constrained by the funding patterns on which congregations relied. Contributions of time and money that supported service ministries depended on these programs showing tangible results, which was easier to demonstrate in stories about individuals being directly helped in small ways than in arguments about larger issues that often seemed intractable. As in the past, congregations depended on the goodwill of wealthier members to support the general expenses of salaries, buildings, and maintenance, which worked against pastors' incentive to criticize wealth or to redirect it toward outside philanthropic giving. Furthermore, pastors and lay leaders were often selective in what they considered appropriate to address about public policy, which meant refraining from speaking about antipoverty legislation on grounds that doing so was "political," while openly discussing abortion and homosexuality because those issues were "moral." When ministries to the poor did include advocacy, it typically depended on congregations having formed coalitions and then focused on such issues as low-income housing, food, shelter, and job training. This emphasis was relevant to the wealth gap insofar as it addressed the needs of the poor but differed from advocacy focusing on wealth.[26]

As the wealth gap began to increase, advocacy in which religious groups played a role also began to increase, rarely directed specifically at the wealth gap itself but addressing the production, uses, and implications of wealth. These efforts were guided by the assumption that religion's voice should be heard on matters relating to the common good but also with awareness that religion's capacity to challenge corporate policies and lawmakers' ideas about taxes and budgets was limited. Religious groups' advocacy fell largely into four categories: corporate social responsibility, "trickle-down" economics and small government, the attainment and responsible use of wealth through "wealth ministries," and ameliorative legislation through community-based organizing and interfaith networks. These approaches shared an interest in shaping the uses of wealth, the values underpinning these uses, and the implications of wealth for the health of democracy. They differed dramatically in the support they received from various segments of the religious community.

Corporate Social Responsibility

Advocacy for corporate social responsibility took as its starting point the fact that large corporations are major producers and holders of wealth and as such play a powerful role in shaping society, including how well society functions to provide for the freedom, justice, and happiness that democracy aims to preserve. The idea of corporate social responsibility does not presuppose that the wealth gap should be reduced. The idea is rather that corporate wealth should be used in ways that do not contribute negatively to the common good and that may specifically include being concerned about disparities between the incomes of top management and ordinary workers, protecting the environment, avoiding militaristic incentives leading to war, and upholding human rights domestically and abroad. Religious groups that advocate for corporate social responsibility do so on grounds of teachings about peace, justice, environmental stewardship, human dignity, and compassion. Religious groups' tactics for achieving these goals include shareholder resolutions, boycotts, informational publications and meetings, and social networking. The resources religious groups have been able to deploy for these activities include sympathetic supporters in congregations, the teachings in their traditions about money, and leaders with training in business, law, and public relations. These resources are limited, though, so advocacy for corporate social responsibility often falls short of stated goals. Yet, the efforts give voice to the values being advocated.

In 1971 an organization in New York City called the Interfaith Center on Corporate Responsibility (ICCR) was founded that represented a coming together of several strands of activism toward wealth inequality. These strands included activism concerned with consumer rights, peace, the environment, and racial justice. The common idea was that wealth was concentrated in the corporations in which wealth was invested and that what corporations did could be influenced by boycotts, public shaming, and above all shareholder resolutions. The strategy was not to challenge corporations' role in producing wealth or to address the wealth gap directly but to shape how the wealth produced was used,

which could range from reducing pay disparities between top officers
and ordinary workers to providing employees with better healthcare,
refraining from activities that exploited low-wage workers in other
countries or that perpetuated racial discrimination, and reducing the
corporate footprint on the environment.[27]

One of the strands that fed into the formation of ICCR was the civil
rights movement. Boycotts of bus companies, drugstores, restaurants,
and other local businesses were an effective means of protesting segregation. A related strategy was to purchase goods only from companies that adopted equal opportunity hiring practices. In addition to
encouraging members to make purchases accordingly, religious groups
used their own purchasing power—estimated at approximately $2 bil-
lion annually for everything from building materials and maintenance
to utilities and supplies—to accomplish a similar end. In 1967 the
Catholic archdiocese in St. Louis published a "buyer's guide" for its
parishes rating 930 area firms on racially inclusive hiring. Also in 1967
a national network called Project Equality was able to coordinate the
work of six thousand Catholic dioceses and Protestant, Jewish, and
Orthodox groups around a similar idea. Another connection was civil
rights leaders' advocacy toward the investment strategies of denominations, for instance as evidenced in Methodist and Presbyterian leaders
speaking as shareholders at Kodak about the company's employment
practices.[28]

A second strand in forming ICCR was advocacy against the Vietnam
War, specifically activism directed at companies involved in manufacturing weapons. Critics of the war regarded its supporters as being motivated in part by the profits—and the prospect of future profits—the
war generated for oil companies and military contractors. A means of
expressing opposition to the war was thus to divest from these companies. The Community Church of New York, where Reverend John
Haynes Holmes had advocated for pacifism during World War I, for
example, divested its stock in the chemical companies supplying napalm
in Vietnam. On a larger scale, Clergy and Laity Concerned (CALC), a
national organization founded in 1965 to protest US military escalation
in Vietnam, engaged Protestant, Catholic, and Jewish activists in "Stop

the Draft" demonstrations, provided assistance to conscientious objectors, circulated information critical of the war and civil defense measures, coordinated with other antiwar and pacifist groups, and organized protests against corporations engaged in war-related activities. CALC's most publicized effort to persuade religious organizations to use their investments against the war was a campaign in 1970 against Honeywell for its manufacture of antipersonnel weapons—a campaign that failed but became a model for other stockholder actions. By the end of the 1970s, CALC had thirty thousand members in forty-two locations and was among the first to protest US military involvement in Central America and assist refugees from the region.[29]

A third strand in ICCR's development was the corporate social responsibility movement, which initially was separate from the efforts of religious organizations but developed tactics similar to the ones ICCR put to use. Although the idea that corporations should be socially responsible was not new, groups engaged in pressuring corporate investment strategies gained interest in the 1960s just as civil rights and antiwar advocacy did. In 1970 a nonprofit organization calling itself the Council on Economic Priorities was founded in Washington, DC, to promote corporate social responsibility. The organization publicized information and threatened shareholder action against corporations that practiced discrimination, contributed to pollution, and produced munitions. Its initial publications focused (like CALC) on antipersonnel weapons being produced by Honeywell and by General Tire and Rubber for use in Vietnam. About the same time, universities with large endowments such as Harvard, Yale, Princeton, Stanford, and MIT mobilized internal projects to examine the potential social implications of their investments. Reports called for greater transparency of information about safety, pollution, and hiring.[30]

The initial interest in social responsibility was met with skepticism from corporate heads who considered it impossible to factor in public costs that would lower profit margins, reduce their competitive edge, and at the same time satisfy shareholders. It seemed to many of the corporate spokespersons that social responsibility initiatives could work only if government intervened in the marketplace. The executives who expressed interest in social responsibility opted for initiatives that did not threaten profits. For example, General Foods pledged to include more African Americans in its commercials and Quaker Oats offered to reduce its impact on urban congestion by locating new plants away from cities. Economist Milton Friedman succinctly summed up the prevailing view among corporate executives in a *New York Times* essay: "The Social Responsibility of Business Is to Increase Its Profits." Although the 1970s saw an increase in discussions of social responsibility at business schools and in business publications, what that meant was compatible with Friedman's summary. To be socially responsible, one survey of corporate executives suggested, was to be mindful of minority hiring, the environment, and contributions to education and the arts.[31]

The founding of ICCR was prompted by the fact that groups such as CALC and several Protestant denominations were already engaged in shareholder actions, and yet they shared little information about who was doing what or how best to coordinate it. In 1971 the National Council of Churches at its offices in New York established the Corporate Information Center to create a rating system that churches could use to identify companies from which they might want to divest. During the previous three years, separate initiatives had developed, including the United Presbyterian Church forming an independent development corporation to guide its investments toward greater social responsibility; the United Methodist Church Board of Missions divesting holdings in two banking firms involved in South African business; an Episcopal bishop calling for divestment from General Motors; and a Lutheran body calling for shareholder activism. Besides divestment in protest of apartheid, the various agencies were also issuing statements about the military-industrial complex, Vietnam, racism, and the environment.[32]

Although ICCR's founders represented the national offices of large Protestant denominations, local groups formed its infrastructure. The first local group to affiliate with ICCR was the Milwaukee-based Seventh Generation Interfaith Coalition for Responsible Investment, also known as SGI. SGI began in 1972 when members of the Capuchin Franciscan Province of St. Joseph committed themselves to a province-wide "thrust toward justice and peace," a commitment inspired by the gospel as a response to the Vietnam War and the racism that remained un-abated in the city five years after the riots against housing discrimination and police brutality in 1967. A year later, SGI's new Justice and Peace Center joined the School Sisters of St. Francis in Milwaukee and five other midwestern religious communities to form the responsible invest-ing coalition called Seventh Generation Interfaith, drawing its name from the Iroquois teaching that decisions should be made taking ac-count of their effects for seven generations. SGI's plan of action was "Catholic Church Investments on Corporate Responsibility," a treatise written by its director, Capuchin friar Michael Crosby, who had realized that corporations were central to the quest for peace and justice during a trip to Washington to participate in antiwar protest demonstrations. The treatise was a call for action based on solidarity and compassion and oriented toward challenging companies to "bring good news for the poor and the planet."[33]

Many of the local and regional groups that participated in corporate responsibility advocacy had similar origins. The Midwest Coalition for Responsible Investment, which merged with SGI in 2017, for example, was founded in St. Louis in 1977 by Catholic leaders and joined ICCR shortly thereafter. Among its first activities was a resolution asking Mc-Donnell Douglas to reduce its involvement in military contracts. An-other early participant was the Sisters of St. Francis in Philadelphia, which kept its retirement fund in savings accounts and certificates of deposit but after selling thirty acres of suburban land in the late 1960s decided to invest in stocks and bonds. That decision prompted it to set up a procedure to screen its investments against corporate activities that it deemed contrary to human dignity.[34]

From the 1970s through the end of the century, these advocacy groups expanded their efforts. Much of their attention focused on South Africa. Between 1973 and 1988 ICCR cooperated with hundreds of cam-pus, secular nonprofit, labor, municipal, and regional groups to sponsor dozens of shareholder resolutions and proxy statements against US companies doing business in South Africa. The companies included Bank of America, Control Data, Exxon, General Electric, Gulf Oil, IBM, Mobil, NCR, and Sperry Rand, among others. In conjunction with the

Corporate Information Center, ICCR also produced documents and held conferences for stockholders, journalists, and clergy highlighting the extent of US, European, and Japanese investments in South Africa and summarizing church groups' arguments against investment. The center also distributed information about companies working in Chile, Namibia, Rhodesia, and Zimbabwe. Besides ICCR, antiapartheid fund-raising walkathons, demonstrations, and shareholder resolutions engaged the support of the Church World Service, Clergy and Laity Concerned, Episcopal Church, Mennonite Central Committee, Northern California Ecumenical Council, Presbyterian Church (USA), Seventh Generation Interfaith, and United Church of Christ.[35]

ICCR's second focus in the 1970s and 1980s was the corporate marketing of infant formula in developing countries, which health organizations were criticizing on nutritional and economic grounds. In 1974 ICCR and member groups, along with the Ford Foundation and Rockefeller Foundation, initiated proxy battles and educational campaigns against the leading US producer of infant formula, Bristol Myers. One of the coordinators was Milwaukee Justice and Peace Center director Reverend Crosby, who served as a negotiator with Bristol Myers and a year later arranged a lawsuit brought by the Dayton, Ohio, religious order Sisters of the Precious Blood. Over the next five years other ICCR affiliates including the Illinois Committee for Responsible Investment, Adrian Dominican Sisters, and Sisters of Mercy brought shareholder resolutions against Bristol Myers, Borden, and Abbott Laboratories, culminating in the widely publicized international boycott of Nestlé and the adoption in 1984 by the World Health Organization of the International Code of Marketing of Breast-Milk Substitutes.[36]

The infant formula battle led to health-oriented campaigns in the 1990s against tobacco, hormone additives in milk, and pharmaceutical pricing, and by the end of the decade shareholder resolutions and publications were also directed toward advancing sustainable environmental policies, albeit with limited success. In 2009 when Reverend Crosby, whose efforts had turned toward battling the international marketing of tobacco products, was asked to summarize ICCR's effectiveness in promoting corporate social responsibility, he observed that the tobacco companies had made "no real changes," but that Eastman Kodak had left the filter business, Kimberly-Clark had divested from making tobacco paper, Sara Lee was no longer involved in tobacco production, and resolutions against McDonald's and Wendy's had contributed to their going smoke-free.[37] An ICCR report concluded that the campaign for sustainable environmental policies had also achieved limited results: 150 shareholder requests asking fossil fuel companies to evaluate risks from climate change had been ignored or met with a dismissive reply.[38]

Most of these ICCR initiatives focused only indirectly on the wealth gap, doing so by targeting employee rights and remuneration and topics of concern to the general public such as tobacco and the environment. However, by the end of the century a growing number of shareholder resolutions also focused directly on executive compensation, with some success in challenging its contribution to the wealth gap. A study of several hundred shareholder filings concerned with CEO pay between 1997 and 2007, for example, found that filings were more likely to be directed at CEOs with higher pay and were more likely to be successful at firms with "excess" CEO pay relative to a predicted level based on economic performance. Filings brought by religious investors were distinguished by seeking to link compensation with socially beneficial criteria and with lowering CEO-to-worker pay ratios.[39]

Studies evaluating the impact of the larger socially responsible investment movement suggest that its impact on corporate policy was modest but not negligible. A study of information collected by ICCR on 2,310 shareholder resolutions filed between 1997 and 2004 concluded that about 10 percent could be deemed to have affected management decisions. The decisions concerned a range of issues including board diversity, equal employment, energy and environment, international labor, and human rights. Resolutions filed by religious investors constituted 38.2 percent of all the proposals filed and 30.8 percent of successful filings. Another study, covering thirty-five years, found that religious investors were the most prolific type of shareholder resolution filer and the most innovative in terms of being the first to file on new topics.[40]

Although most of the shareholder filings failed, a number of considerations encouraged the strategy to persist. The simplest of these considerations was that a few successes were better than none. The data also showed that successful filings against large companies had spillover effects on smaller companies. Unsuccessful filings, moreover, frequently generated further dialogue about the issues raised. Studies also pointed to the incentives of advocacy groups to persist in filing shareholder resolutions: resolutions were inexpensive in terms of the amounts of investment required, they could shift easily to new topics once an advocacy organization such as ICCR was in place, they often furthered the careers of activists, and they complemented other activities such as demonstrations and private negotiations.[41]

Shareholder advocacy was also characterized by activities that the social science literature associates with strengthening democracy. These activities amplify relationships between shareholders and management, which under other conditions are usually distant and impersonal. Shareholder activism fosters relationships beyond the wealthy elite by representing a more diverse set of investors. It also forges relationships among advocacy organizations, as shown by the many Protestant, Catholic, Jewish, and secular organizations that interact through ICCR meetings and in other contexts. As new issues and strategies emerge, these networks also serve as hubs that provide the kind of social capital political scientists argue is beneficial to the functioning of democracy.[42]

In addition, shareholder advocacy consists of what is sometimes called "symbolic politics," which means activities that are of worth in their own right because they publicly express procedures and values that advocacy groups consider important. As expressions of procedural democracy, shareholder resolutions show the processes through which shareholders can participate. Whether the filings succeed or fail, they generate publicity about responsible investment, health, the environment, racial and ethnic diversity, workers' rights, and various other topics. They have also provided occasions for speaking about broader values. A notable instance occurred at a 1980 congressional hearing about corporate criminal liability when Reverend Crosby argued that legislation requiring corporations to disclose information about dangerous working conditions was basically a matter of truthfulness, which was essential to a just society. Quoting a statement by Pope John Paul II that was remarkably prescient about the shape of political discourse in decades to come, Crosby said, "Selective indignation, sly insinuations, the manipulation of information, the systematic discrediting of opponents—their persons, intentions, and actions—blackmail and intimidation: these are forms of non-truth working to develop a climate of uncertainty aimed at forcing individuals, groups, governments, and even international organizations to keep silence in helplessness and complicity."[43]

The 2008 financial crisis challenged the shareholder advocacy movement to shift some of its attention toward corporations' role in causing the crisis. ICCR sent letters to Congress on behalf of its members supporting the Dodd-Frank Wall Street Reform and Consumer Protection Act and the creation of the Consumer Financial Protection Bureau. ICCR's membership by that point had grown to a coalition of nearly three hundred organizations, including faith-based institutions, socially responsible asset management companies, and unions and other pension funds representing over $100 billion in investments. In its letters ICCR took the occasion to address the protection of small businesses and to register concern about payday lending and student loans as well as the financial crisis. ICCR also produced a white paper for distribution to its members about predatory subprime lending and derivatives and, in conjunction with Sustainalytics, an international investment analysis firm, created a scorecard ranking the seven largest banks on risk management, lending practices, and executive compensation. Notably, these documents emphasized ICCR's history and the scope of its membership and appealed for transparency and responsibility in the interest of the common good but did not assert claims on the basis of religion itself. Although ICCR originated from religious groups and was based on the deeply held religious convictions of its founders, as well as on the faith commitments of many of its current members, its operational power was mainly its ability to threaten corporations with "reputational risk"—that is, to generate facts and figures and deploy this information to embarrass corporations in ways that damaged their relationships with shareholders and customers or clients. ICCR's successes in implementing this strategy were often the result of quiet work behind the scenes and were accomplished by persuading corporations that reforms were in their own interest as well as the public's.[44]

The Tea Party

The shareholder advocacy movement appealed to the progressive religious groups whose antiracist, antiwar, social justice, and environmental concerns had led to the coalition that formed its core. The advocacy that appealed to conservative religious activists interpreted corporate wealth quite differently. But they too had ideas about the wealth gap and what it meant for the common good. The conservative view was that corporate wealth functioned best when left alone to be guided by the free market, and when it was, it would produce economic benefits for all. The impediment to be advocated against was government regulation. Smaller government kept power in the hands of those who were best at producing wealth. Small government was also the idea that conservative religious groups considered to be in their interest. These were ideas that had been clearly expressed by the small-government opponents of the New Deal and by critics of the Great Society. In response to the 2008 recession conservative religious groups again found common ground with critics of big government.

The Tea Party movement that mobilized in 2008 and played a significant role in the 2010 midterm elections was galvanized by citizens concerned about the size and scope of government, by which they meant primarily the federal government. Lower taxes and less government interference in the daily lives of families and businesses were ideas that had wide appeal. Ideas about wealth were more complex. On the one hand, Tea Party leaders regarded the Troubled Asset Relief Program (TARP) and the American Recovery and Reinvestment Act (ARRA) as economic stimulus programs that benefited the already wealthy and powerful Wall Street and banking interests. On the other hand, the Tea Party received backing from lobbyists and donors representing wealthy interests that considered it beneficial for government to be less involved in their affairs. Among grassroots supporters of the Tea Party the prevailing view was that smaller government was best and that corporate wealth was not a problem. Polling in 2010, for example, showed that 88 percent of Tea Party supporters considered the federal government wasteful and inefficient, 83 percent thought it had gone too far in regulating business, and 82 percent thought it was too big and powerful; in comparison, only 30 percent thought corporations made too much profit.[45]

Why a movement organized around fiscal policy should have been of interest to conservative religious leaders was from one perspective puzzling. It should have been in the interest of religious leaders whose congregations were intent on helping people whose homes were being foreclosed and whose jobs were lost because of the recession to support the government's economic stimulus programs. Polling nevertheless showed that the more often people attended religious congregations the more likely they were to support the Tea Party. In a 2010 poll, for example, 49 percent of weekly attenders said they agreed with the Tea Party compared with 30 percent of monthly or yearly attenders and only 18 percent of those who seldom or never attended. The poll also showed that White evangelical Protestants were more likely than other faith communities to support the Tea Party. Another national study found that the odds of expressing positive views toward the Tea Party were two and a half times greater among born-again Christians than among other respondents even when controlling for race, gender, marital status, income, and age.[46]

Investigations of the link between the Tea Party and conservative churchgoing identified several connections. For one thing, Tea Party voters supported social issues that also happened to be supported by members of conservative churches. These issues included opposition to abortion, homosexuality, and immigration. A study that surveyed the same people over time showed that being involved in antiabortion activities and holding strong opinions about it in 2006 were in fact good predictors of support for the Tea Party four years later. These connections were reinforced by the antiabortion movement and the Tea Party having similar demographic locations in small towns and rural areas and among older or lower-income White working-class families in suburbs. Additionally, Tea Party leaders worked to enlarge the movement's appeal beyond sexual politics by focusing on broader themes of interest to conservative churches, such as the idea that America had been founded on Judeo-Christian principles and was now endangered by liberal interpretations of the US Constitution. These broader themes, moreover, were cultivated by clergy who spoke at Tea Party meetings and by conservative political leaders who spoke at churches.[47] In interviews, clergy spoke of things being out of control in Washington and of politicians no longer working for the common good. A pastor in Texas, for example, thought deficit spending was against the "principles of scripture." Others expressed concern about tyranny and moral decline. At "God and Country" rallies they mixed calls for freedom of religion with appeals for fiscal conservatism.[48]

The relevance of these views to religious advocacy about the wealth gap was that conservative religious groups mobilized against or at least refrained from supporting the groups that were interested in reducing wealth inequality or directing corporate wealth toward socially responsible policies. While ICCR supported the Dodd-Frank Wall Street Reform and Consumer Protection Act, for example, the Tea Party strongly opposed it. The reason to reject it on religious grounds, critics of the legislation argued, was that it posed a threat to religious freedom. It would endanger religious freedom, they feared, by giving government agencies power to tell religious organizations whom they could hire and to enforce antidiscrimination laws that religious organizations opposed. Similar concerns were expressed about the Affordable Care Act. As for wealth inequality, polling in 2014 showed that a large majority (66 percent) of the public agreed that "the government should do more to reduce the gap between rich and poor," but among White evangelicals nearly half (47 percent) disagreed.[49]

Like the groups that promoted corporate social responsibility, the ones that opposed measures to reduce wealth inequality consisted of diverse coalitions. The diversity was less in terms of race and religious traditions beyond Christianity and more in terms of White evangelical Protestants, conservative Catholics, libertarian groups, and political action committees. As ICCR pressed companies toward sustainable environmental programs, for example, one of the most outspoken opponents of renewable energy was Minnesota congressional representative Michele Bachmann. Bachmann's victory in the 2010 midterm election and subsequent presidential campaign were part of the Tea Party movement but also illustrated the diverse coalitions that supported her. These included the Christian Coalition, which television evangelist Pat Robertson had founded in the 1980s; the Freedom Coalition, run by former Christian Coalition leader Ralph Reed; the Minnesota coalition of religious leaders that had mobilized against same-sex marriage in 2004; and the Maple River Education Coalition, which had launched Bachmann's political involvement against abortion in the 1990s.

The idea that wealth could best serve the common interest when it was freed of government intrusion was implicit in Bachmann's and other Tea Party activists' opposition to environmental regulations. Nowhere was the idea more explicit, though, than under the administration of Governor Sam Brownback in Kansas. Winning the Kansas governorship by a landslide in 2010 and having a sizable majority of Republicans in the state's House and Senate, Brownback had a rare opportunity to demonstrate that lowering taxes, cutting regulations, and luring businesses to the state with loans and tax incentives would benefit everyone by helping the rich—"a shot of adrenaline into the heart of the Kansas economy," he said. The "Kansas Experiment" was watched nationally as an example of "trickle-down economics" and when the results were in proved disappointing to its advocates. When Brownback took office the richest 5 percent of households in Kansas had incomes nearly 12 times as large as the bottom 20 percent. Over the next four years average incomes of the bottom 20 percent grew by 11 percent while incomes of the top 5 percent increased by 22 percent. Moreover, in each of those years the annual change in real GDP for Kansas lagged behind that of the United States. The tax cuts' most serious consequences were cuts of funding for schools, healthcare, and social programs benefiting low- and middle-income families.[50]

In 2004 Thomas Frank's best-selling *What's the Matter with Kansas?* argued that conservatism in Kansas was a prime example of "a movement whose response to the power structure is to make the rich even richer." Political conservatism worked, he said, by appealing to the religious convictions of middle- and working-class voters who attended conservative Catholic and evangelical Protestant churches, heard sermons about the evils of abortion and homosexuality, and voted overwhelmingly for Republicans even though it was not in their best economic interests to do so.[51] Frank's argument seemed to predict the state's support for Brownback. Brownback was a conservative Catholic with an evangelical Protestant background and during his fourteen years in the US Senate had been a champion of the antiabortion movement, a sponsor of anti–gay marriage legislation, and an outspoken defender of religious freedom. He was a member of a conservative Christian leadership group in Washington called the Fellowship that sponsored the National Prayer Breakfast, and in Kansas he enjoyed the support of Kansans for Life, which was one of the state's most active lobbying groups among conservative Catholics and Protestants. His principal sources of financial support were the libertarians David and Charles Koch. Indirectly the "Kansas Experiment" was a referendum on an idea about wealth that certain Christian conservative groups had long held. However, it was a better example, as Frank had argued, of advocacy on particular issues—abortion, freedom of religion, small government—mobilizing people to participate in the democratic process with the result of their advocacy having unanticipated spillover consequences for other issues.[52]

The Tea Party ideas that Brownback and fellow religious conservatives supported were widely criticized, not only by economists but also by other religious leaders. "Some people continue to defend trickle-down theories which assume that economic growth, encouraged by a free market, will inevitably succeed in bringing about greater justice and inclusiveness," Pope Francis observed in an apostolic exhortation released in 2013. "This opinion, which has never been confirmed by the facts, expresses a crude and naïve trust in the goodness of those wielding economic power and in the sacralized workings of the prevailing economic system. Meanwhile, the excluded are still waiting." The pope's statement, which also spoke at length about the "idolatry of money," was widely discussed in the American press. Unremarkably, it drew a mixed response. "I love this pope," Missouri senator Claire McCaskill, a Catholic, said. "Jesus focused so much on helping the poor and the downtrodden [and this refocusing on that] has been a breath of fresh air." US House of Representatives Budget Committee chair Paul Ryan, also Catholic, welcomed the dialogue but dismissed the pope's understanding of the US situation. "The guy is from Argentina," he said. "They haven't had real capitalism in Argentina. They don't have a true free enterprise system."[53]

But if the Tea Party was wrong about trickle-down economics, it represented a contribution to democratic participation. Sociologist Arlie Hochschild, who spent several years interacting with Tea Party supporters in Louisiana, wrote that the movement demonstrated a healthy democracy's capacity to hash things out. Political scientists Theda Skocpol and Vanessa Williamson went further in their appraisal. The movement was composed of ordinary men and women, they wrote, who turned out to organize rallies, set up chairs, print leaflets, and prepare refreshments. Beforehand, these men and women studied the issues and at meetings asked knowledgeable questions about taxes and healthcare; afterward they followed up with speakers, discussed what they had heard, and planned what to do next. Although Skocpol and Williamson disagreed with these Tea Party activists, they saw the movement as a model of grassroots citizenship. "The Tea Party meetings have the same 'let's pitch in and get it done' air about them," they wrote, "as clubs and lodges and church societies throughout America's past as 'a nation of joiners.'"[54]

Wealth Ministries

"Wealth ministries" were another response to the wealth gap. These ministries consisted of programs of education and action directed at wealthy individuals themselves and at persons aspiring to be wealthy. Unlike shareholder initiatives and unlike the Tea Party, wealth ministries were organized mostly within congregations, but they also involved networks that connected individuals and religious organizations. They were ministries that aimed to instruct and support the wealthy in relating their wealth to theological frameworks and in directing it toward practices consistent with those frameworks. Like shareholder initiatives, they focused on the rich rather than on the poor and they dealt with the use of money in the private sphere rather than seeking to guide it through government involvement. Their relationship with democracy was similarly indirect, aiming to facilitate thinking about common values and the common good. They varied widely in how they saw the relationship of religion and wealth, but the rubrics under which many of them fell were prosperity gospel ministries, philanthrocapitalism, and faith-friendly leadership.

Prosperity gospel ministries encouraged adherents to understand wealth as a divine blessing and taught those who aspired to wealth that it would be attainable if they followed God's will. In these terms, the prosperity gospel was concerned not with reducing wealth inequality but with providing a justification for it. The wealthy, according to prosperity gospel teachings, were people whom God had chosen to bless either because they were doing the right things or because of an inscrutable divine plan for their lives. Those who did not have wealth could hope to improve their situation by drawing closer to God. Prosperity gospel ministries therefore focused more on what was possible for individual believers than on social structures and policies in the nation or world. Testimonials in congregations related stories of people praying and being lifted out of debt or finding jobs. Pastors of large prosperity gospel congregations were often the most visible personifications of wealth, demonstrating through the size of their congregations, the ambience of their worship spaces, and sometimes their lavish lifestyles that God blessed those who wanted to be blessed. The key to the success of these ministries was their leaders' willingness to ask for generous contributions and to forge connections between these donations and possibilities of material blessings in return. The ministries varied in theology and location as well as in the socioeconomic and racial composition of their members but offered a way for people to make sense of their own position within the realities of wealth inequality.[55]

Studies of prosperity gospel ministries observed their fundamental compatibility with neoliberal economic arguments about financial success being the result of individuals pursuing wealth on their own by working hard and having faith in the outcome. The role of prosperity gospel theology was to reinforce convictions that things would work out for the best because God promised that they would. Prosperity gospel ministries were also compatible with Americans' penchant for material goods. An analysis of prosperity gospel preacher Joel Osteen's widely read books, for example, found a prevailing message of optimism about seemingly extravagant discretionary consumption going hand in hand with godliness. As well as its effects on individuals' beliefs and habits, the prosperity gospel also struck some observers with its possible impact on voters' views about public policy.[56]

A second kind of wealth ministry is philanthrocapitalism. Philanthrocapitalism is the term given to the idea that the wealthy can be good citizens through their generous involvement in philanthropy and by their application of business methods to their giving in the interest of rendering the results more efficient and effective. Philanthrocapitalism resembles the prosperity gospel in suggesting that wealth is deserved; however, it differs in that it provides legitimacy not only for wealthy individuals' privileged lifestyles but also for the economic system through which wealth is generated. Support for the idea that a wealth-producing economy is good for everyone comes from the frequent contribution of philanthrocapitalism to the common good through projects devoted to health, education, and the alleviation of poverty. Criticisms of philanthrocapitalism argue that it is fundamentally nondemocratic, granting wealthy individuals the power to decide with very little accountability what projects to fund, which recipients to assist, and how public policy should respond.[57]

Philanthrocapitalism's intellectual origins can be traced to religious teachings in early modern Europe and America about the morality of capitalism. The recent connection with religion lies less in religious organizations and teachings per se than in an expression of exceptional gift giving that, as some scholars have noted, resembles divine

beneficence and earns the benefactor the kind of respect that in previous eras would have been reserved for the gods.[58] One of the early
twenty-first century's leading examples of philanthrocapitalism is the
Bill and Melinda Gates Foundation. During the foundation's first fifteen years, the Gateses donated more than $3 billion annually to fund
projects on educational opportunities in the United States and healthcare and poverty globally. In 2005 *Time* magazine honored the Gateses
as persons of the year. Other early twenty-first-century philanthrocapitalists include Amazon founder Jeff Bezos and Facebook founder Mark
Zuckerberg. In addition to the causes these and other donors have supported, studies have shown that philanthrocapitalism was influencing
the overall shape of charitable giving. Specifically, larger shares of total
giving were coming from the few who gave in the largest amounts, thus
skewing the nonprofit sector increasingly toward the interests of
wealthy donors.[59]

Philanthrocapitalists' prominence has been notable not only in charitable giving but also in defending the wealth gap. For example, in 2014
the best-selling English translation of French economist Thomas Piketty's book *Capital in the Twenty-First Century* presented evidence suggesting that economic inequality was having far-reaching negative consequences. In a response to Piketty, Gates agreed that high levels of
economic inequality are potentially a problem for democracies, turning
them toward powerful interests and against the idea that all people are
created equal. Gates further agreed that wealth concentration does not
automatically correct itself and that government can play a corrective
role. But Gates disagreed that things were as bad as Piketty said. The
reason, Gates argued, was that concentrated wealth generated goods
and services that benefited consumers. An additional reason for believing that economic inequality was less of a problem than Piketty believed, Gates suggested, was the presumably growing number of wealthy
people engaged in philanthropy. "Philanthropy done well," Gates said,
"not only produces direct benefits for society, it also reduces dynastic
wealth." This was in fact true in Gates's case, but whether it was true in
terms of concentrated wealth overall was unclear. Data on charitable

giving among the wealthiest families, moreover, showed that giving as a percentage of income declined when income inequality increased.[60] But philanthrocapitalism did contribute in several positive ways to the debate about wealth inequality. It provided a comparison point from which to criticize self-interested billionaires whose wealth benefited only themselves. It served as inspiration for small entrepreneurial charities, many of which originated from religiously motivated donors. Its idealism also set a standard against which to criticize its results, such as the mixed consequences of its wilderness conservation projects and its inner-city schooling programs.[61]

Few of the best-known philanthrocapitalists have been noted for their personal involvement in religion. Wealthy philanthropy motivated by religion is commonly identified as "traditional," meaning that money is given to recipients who are vetted in terms of religion or some other mark of worthiness and are then in charge of how the funds are spent rather than becoming involved in business activity that is closely guided by the donor. None of the wealthy evangelicals Michael Lindsay interviewed, for example, were engaged in philanthrocapitalism.[62] The line separating traditional philanthropy and philanthrocapitalism, however, is indistinct. A study of World Vision, an international relief organization to which many evangelical Christians donate, for example, showed a decisive shift in orientation toward philanthrocapitalism through grants to projects involving small businesses producing consumer goods. A more explicit example of philanthrocapitalism was initiated by Partners Worldwide, a faith-based organization with a $5 million annual budget that links US business leaders with entrepreneurs in countries with high rates of poverty. Faith-based philanthropy has also been involved in microfinance projects encouraging local entrepreneurs to engage in profitable business ventures.[63]

Philanthrocapitalism shapes the environment in which religion functions in ways that influence how religion relates to society as well. These influences vary but include concerns about a "crowding out" effect that further limits religion's role. A single philanthropist such as Gates or Bezos, for example, can fund larger projects each year than most Protestant denominations can support. Moreover, these philanthrocapitalist projects may promote effectiveness metrics that contrast sharply with values favored by religious communities such as compassion for the neediest, humility, sacrifice, congeniality, and evangelization.[64] Some evidence suggests that small philanthropic organizations founded by religiously motivated individuals have increasingly adopted philanthro-capitalist business models as well.[65] Beyond these indirect influences, religion itself is also shaped by the funding that comes from a few highly capitalized foundations with interests in promoting agendas such as integrating religion and science, promoting prosocial activities, and producing polls about religion.

These influences on religion have a potential impact on how religious organizations are able to engage in advocacy regarding the wealth gap and concerns about democracy. Philanthrocapitalism can either weaken or amplify religious organizations' advocacy about wealth inequality depending on those organizations' political stance. Religious organizations aligned with conservative politics may view philanthrocapitalism as a benefit that supplements their own private charitable efforts. For other organizations, it may be harder to criticize wealth inequality if it appears that the wealthy are donating generously to social causes. In either case, religious advocacy is likely to be taken less seriously if activism addressing social problems is taking place without also addressing questions about wealth.

The third kind of wealth ministry is "faith-friendly" leadership. Originating in the 1980s, the faith-friendly leadership movement sought to enlist CEOs and other wealthy persons with deep religious convictions in an effort to improve society by enabling their employees to integrate their various faith commitments into the workplace. From the start, faith-friendly leadership was less an organized movement than a scattered array of activities at companies like Tyson Foods, Coca-Cola Bottling, Chick-fil-A, and Walmart where the owners or top managers were evangelical Protestants or devout Catholics. These "faith at work" initiatives, as they were called, were not directly concerned with addressing the wealth gap, but indirectly they sometimes did so as leaders attempted to practice their faith by reducing management-worker pay disparities or providing better working conditions. In addition, some wealthy CEOs and business owners conducted seminars in financial management, addressed issues of corruption and unethical practices, sponsored scholarships for low-income students, and donated to religious charities.[66]

Studies suggested that faith-friendly leadership initiatives did make workplaces more accepting of diverse religious practices, including those of Muslims and Hindus, and often supplied employees with on-site chaplains and opportunities for Bible study, prayer, mindfulness training, yoga, and meditation. The initiatives created networks among like-minded business leaders that provided emotional support and on occasion were useful for business dealings. As a consequence of these networks and support groups, business leaders and employees sometimes reported that their faith and work were better integrated than in other contexts where they experienced tension between being true to their faith and effective in their work. For the wealthy, the studies suggested that "integration" meant feeling better about the privileges wealth provided. An integration of faith and work meant that divine guidance was present when difficult decisions had to be made. Some business leaders found that an integration of faith and work affirmed their belief, as Max Weber had observed for an earlier generation of capitalists, that being successful was a mark of divine favor.[67]

Unlike Weber's eighteenth-century capitalists, though, the wealthy included in recent studies of faith-friendly leadership were embedded in a fully formed late twentieth- or early twenty-first-century cultural milieu that powerfully shaped how they thought about success and the wealth that resulted from success. Although variations existed, the wealthy business leaders who sought to integrate their faith and work lived and worked in enclaves that often gave them considerable advantages in accomplishing whatever they wanted to do. "The wealthy construct businesses, establish foundations, initiate social and political campaigns, build hospital wings, endow university professorships," Paul Schervish observed in his study of the wealthy in the 1980s, and "have their clothes tailor-made, their offices distinctively decorated, and their homes personally designed." Schervish termed this expectation of getting things done "hyper agency." It was an affirmation of the wealthy's power as individuals. As one real estate magnate explained to Schervish, "I can pick up the phone and call a congressman who's heard my name and I can have the impact of one million votes on the issue with a phone call. You always have the upper hand in negotiating."[68]

Hyper agency was reinforced, studies of faith-friendly leadership found, by the fact that wealthy CEOs rarely participated in religious congregations where they interacted with ordinary people. Being a person of faith meant participating in a small group composed of a few other wealthy individuals or meeting individually with a trusted member of the clergy. Otherwise, layers of gatekeepers protected wealthy persons of faith from unwanted intrusions that might conflict with their sense of how the world worked. Protected as they were, they gave lectures about themselves, wrote autobiographies, and told their stories to inquiring journalists and scholars, and these stories often drew on or resembled moral tales of struggle and triumph and character and redemption, all of which reinforced their understanding that the wealth at their disposal was well deserved.[69]

None of the wealth ministry programs paid much attention to the possible negative consequences of wealth inequality for democracy. A common feature of these ministries was the personalization of faith and wealth. Faith's consequences—to the extent that they could be imagined—were in individual acts of generosity and good works and in the hope, peace, and sometimes material progress that could be identified in individual lives. In the extreme, when personalized faith was wedded with neoliberal economics, as a study of Walmart's founders suggested, "no such thing as society or community" existed, "only individuals."[70] If instances in which the wealth gap was addressed did occur, therefore, the way in which they were to be handled was through individuals at the top being more thoughtful about their wealth and individuals at the bottom becoming more confident about their prospects for financial improvement. Wealth ministries in these ways fit well with the popular conception of democracy as a system of government that provided maximum freedom for individuals to pursue their personal destinies.

Faith-Based Community Organizing

Faith-based community organizing contrasted sharply with the prosperity gospel and the various other wealth ministries. Originating in Saul Alinsky's community organizing movement of the 1960s, this approach evolved into some of the twenty-first century's most active advocates against wealth inequality. The emphasis on community meant two things: that participants would be from the community or integrated into it and that the results worked for would be enacted at the community level. Leadership in local communities typically included clergy and laity in local congregations. Influencing the community implied laws and regulations at the local and regional levels rather than at the federal level. Community organizing was thus a method of mobilizing grassroots democracy. Community organizers trained participants who met in churches and town halls in how to convene meetings, speak to legislators, monitor the submission and passage of bills, and run for office. Although its activities were local, community organizing's local groups were loosely integrated into regional and national networks.

In the 1990s the "living wage movement" became one of the most extensive efforts to address economic inequality through community organizing. The movement preceded the publicity that would focus a decade or so later on the wealth gap as such. Its focus nevertheless was on reducing the gap by elevating the incomes of those at the bottom. The movement was a response to the evidence that incomes at the bottom had remained stagnant despite increasing productivity while incomes at the top had risen substantially. Its aim was to secure legislation increasing the minimum wage for workers in particular occupations in certain cities by targeting locations in which progressive lawmakers were in power. The Association of Community Organizations for Reform Now (ACORN) was the group through which the participants in these local efforts received and passed along ideas. ACORN had been founded in 1970 and in the intervening years had been active in advocating among low-income families for affordable housing, healthcare, neighborhood safety, and voter registration.

Clergy and Laity United for Economic Justice (CLUE) was an example illustrating how the living wage movement evolved at the local level. In 1973, Reverend Jim Conn, a young pastor with experience in antiwar protests and the farm workers' movement, took a position at a Methodist church in Santa Monica, California, and became active in the denomination's urban community development programs. Conn was elected to the Santa Monica City Council in 1981 as a representative of a renters' rights coalition, and from 1986 to 1988 he served as the mayor of Santa Monica. A few years later CLUE was organized with Conn as its director.[71]

CLUE originated through another grassroots organization, the Los Angeles Alliance for a New Economy (LAANE). Founded in 1993, LAANE became the city's principal advocate for living wage legislation. LAANE's organizers included a coalition of Black clergy, among whom the most prominent was Reverend James M. Lawson Jr., pastor of the large Holman United Methodist Church in the predominantly Black and Hispanic neighborhood of Jefferson Park. Lawson had been expelled from Vanderbilt Divinity School in 1960 for civil rights activism, finished his training in theology at Boston University, and in 1962 became the pastor of a Methodist church in Memphis. In 1968 when Dr. Martin Luther King Jr. was assassinated in Memphis, Lawson, as chair of the city's sanitation strike, was the one whose invitation King had accepted. After moving to Los Angeles in 1974, Lawson led protests against antibusing measures and police violence, headed the regional Southern Christian Leadership Council, and provided sanctuary at his church during and after the 1992 riots for families whose homes had been burned and for undocumented Salvadorans and Guatemalans.[72] Lawson's prominence as one of the city's best-known civil rights leaders, his connections with the city's churches, and his involvement with health workers' unions contributed to the living wage movement's success in passing minimum wage legislation. In 1996 Lawson and his colleagues organized CLUE and Reverend Conn, who had worked with Lawson on the Methodist Board of Church and Society and collaborated with him during the 1992 unrest, was named its director.[73]

Over the following decade CLUE grew into a large coalition of pastors, congregations, labor activists, and unions collecting information about poverty and wages, holding seminars about economic justice, and working for living wage legislation.[74] CLUE's efforts drew the attention of journalists, economists, and sociologists who conducted interviews with its leaders and monitored its activities. Several features stood out among the reasons for its effectiveness. Among other things, CLUE enlisted support from unions as well as from churches. It attracted Christian, Jewish, and Muslim clergy whose theological convictions emphasized economic justice and the alleviation of human suffering and whose activities reached beyond their local congregations to include participation in protests and lobbying. CLUE also benefited from its leaders' experience in civil rights activism and the networks they had formed through church committees. These networks facilitated CLUE's expansion and gave it the credibility it needed to solicit contributions and apply for grants. Through its clergy networks, CLUE also connected with national and regional advocacy organizations such as ACORN and the Asset-Based Community Development Institute.[75] These wider connections notwithstanding, CLUE's leadership strategically limited its efforts to local issues on which it could make a difference. A study of the Coastal Zone Minimum Wage legislation that CLUE worked to pass in Santa Monica, for example, concluded that the effort was successful because it was geographically focused and targeted a relatively small sector of the labor force.[76]

Assessments of the living wage movement's accomplishments nationally were mixed but generally positive. Between 1995 and 2002 the movement succeeded in securing passage of living wage laws in more than one hundred cities and counties. Although the details varied, the common aim of these initiatives was to reduce the income gap by increasing the wages and benefits of low-income workers. Nearly all the ordinances were directed at city and county employees and service contract workers, usually with certain exemptions and additional restrictions. The Los Angeles ordinance, for example, set a minimum wage that exempted contractors under $25,000 but also prohibited the use of part-time employees on county contracts under most conditions.

Favorable assessments pointed to the fact that wages did increase for some workers and that the ordinances covered not only municipal employees and union members but also the growing number of workers employed by private contractors. The movement also succeeded in mobilizing coalitions similar to CLUE that brought activists interested in economic justice together in other communities. Many of these coalitions were interfaith and multiethnic.

Critical assessments of the living wage movement noted, as the Santa Monica study did, that living wage ordinances affected relatively small numbers of low-wage workers, often helped medium-wage workers more than low-wage workers, and usually failed to increase wages to sustainable levels. Assessments of the impact on unemployment and tax rates varied.[77] The movement was successful enough that by 2006 a growing number of states passed preemption laws against local reforms, and in 2010 pressure against ACORN resulted in its demise. Meanwhile, CLUE remained active, receiving more than $500,000 a year in contributions and grants, diversifying its focus, expanding to new locations, participating in the New Sanctuary Movement, organizing against family separation, and advocating for immigrant rights, gun control legislation, voter registration, and decent wages for low-income workers.[78]

The living wage movement was but one of several initiatives based on the principles of community organizing. The best known of these initiatives was Communities Organized for Public Service (COPS), founded in San Antonio in 1974 by Industrial Areas Foundation (IAF) regional director Ernesto Cortés Jr. Preceding the national debate about the wealth gap as it did, COPS organized projects in Texas and across the Southwest, South, and Midwest involving churches, schools, labor unions, and neighborhood groups to educate participants about economic justice, build community infrastructure, and advocate for jobs and sustainable wages. In one of the many articles and books about COPS, religion scholar Jeffrey Stout wrote that the organization was as much about grassroots democracy as about economic redress. Although the focus of COPS and other community organizing groups was not in most cases on the wealth gap per se, community organizing activities often contested corporate and government decisions that impeded the rights and freedoms of ordinary citizens. Community organizing pursued these aims by bringing people together, organizing them into diverse citizens' groups, and insisting on their right to speak and be heard at public meetings.[79]

Wealth and Democracy

Taken together, religious groups' approaches toward wealth inequality in the late twentieth and early twenty-first centuries demonstrate considerable interest in the topic. Leaders implicitly agreed that economic inequality was something about which religious institutions could do relatively little, much as they might wish to do more. But their actions showed that some ways of challenging economic inequality were possible. Wealth could be channeled in small ways toward good works, it could be justified and its pursuit could be encouraged, and it could be the focus of proxy resolutions and political pressure. The successes religious groups and their allies achieved were small: a corporation feeling the pressure to support sustainable energy, a wealthy person feeling better about wealth and doing more to help others, a faith-in-action network lobbying for a fiduciary responsibility measure, and perhaps a candidate for elected office arguing for solidarity across the income divide. If the gap was as wide as ever, religious advocacy helped keep it from being completely taken for granted.

The wealth gap's relevance to democracy was more implicit than explicit. And, unlike many other issues, religious advocacy concerning wealth focused less on politics and more on private sector initiatives. Still, democracy was never absent from these activities. Shareholder resolutions engaged people in democratic procedures through proxies and board meetings. Wealth ministries encouraged congregants to pursue wealth on their own and if they had wealth to start philanthrocapitalist ventures that did not require government action. The living wage movement was an engagement in local democracy. The exceptions were trickle-down movements like the one in Kansas that depended on legislation. Religious organizations played enough of a role in these activities that the divisions separating them theologically kept them motivated to form coalitions and prevented any of the coalitions from impinging heavily on the separation of church and state.

Of course religious participation sometimes distracted participants from policies meant to reduce economic inequality. This was most evident in research showing that clergy and laity were focused on social issues such as abortion and homosexuality to the point of supporting candidates and policies that consistently favored the wealthy, providing tax breaks and resisting regulations, while voting against candidates and policies that benefited the poor by raising the minimum wage and expanding access to healthcare. Despite proclaiming themselves in defense of the poor theologically, the result was thus to facilitate inequality. Fortunately, other religious groups mobilized around different options. For example, as conservative policies in Kansas widened economic inequality, progressive groups formed coalitions of clergy and laity, union leaders, teachers, and civil rights activists through the ACLU, Council on American Islamic Relations, Dignity, Groundswell, Indivisible, Kansas Interfaith Action, and Solidarity Sundays, all contributing to the election of a Democratic governor in 2018.[80]

Religion's role in mobilizing constituents to reduce the wealth gap or to perpetuate it was constrained—appropriately so—by religion's diversity and by the constitutional barriers that kept it from intervening directly in affairs of governance. Despite religion's exceptional prominence, and notwithstanding the historic teachings about economic justice of its major traditions, the wealth gap was wider in the early twenty-first century than it had been for many decades. Serious questions remained about the outsized influence of the few at the top and about the economic reforms needed to distribute the benefits of economic growth more equally. Addressing the wealth gap would depend at least on major tax reforms and corporate finance regulations in addition to spiritual and moral inspiration.

Religious advocacy groups nevertheless found ways to encourage people of faith from their various perspectives—and in cooperation with leaders in other sectors—to acknowledge the power of wealth and to act in thoughtful ways on the basis of that awareness. Policy makers who favored trickle-down economics found enough support from religious conservatives that opponents of these measures worried about religious groups playing too active a role in public affairs. And yet, other religious groups strenuously challenged religious conservatives' views. Indeed, religion's diversity prompted debate and mobilized advocacy for a wide range of ideas. Shareholder resolutions to promote corporate social responsibility, philanthrocapitalism, faith-friendly leadership networks, and living wage movements—these were among the many ways of motivating citizens' interest and of facilitating grassroots activities that strengthened democracy.

7

Health and Wellness

FAITH COMMUNITIES AND COVID-19

THIS CHAPTER TAKES UP the debate about health, wellness, and vaccinations that accompanied the COVID-19 pandemic as it spread across the United States and around the world in 2020. Public health is a common good that an effective system of democratic government seeks to ensure. COVID-19 posed an unprecedented challenge. In the absence of a vaccine and with contagion and deaths rising at an exponential rate, social distancing was the best means of limiting its spread. Within two weeks of the first documented COVID-19 death, nonessential businesses were closed, in-person meetings were canceled, and evidence collected through cell phone tracking showed that the vast majority of Americans were leaving their homes less often. The response was an example of democracy working best when individuals and families took responsibility for protecting themselves and their neighbors. But democracy is meant to uphold disagreement as well as to embrace agreement. Although there was widespread agreement that COVID-19 required the public to exercise civic responsibility, there was far less agreement about what else should be done. Much of the disagreement centered on questions about leadership: the division of power between the federal government and the states, responsibility for testing and protective equipment, funding for hospitals and medical research, transparency of public information, and weighing the relative costs of death and economic disaster. In addition, disagreement about the response was profoundly influenced by the different effects the pandemic had on different segments of the population. People in sparsely populated rural areas were initially less affected than people in densely populated cities, governors of some states were responding more aggressively than in other states, older Americans were more at risk than younger Americans, and exceptionally high rates of contagion and death were being reported in low-income communities and among African Americans and Hispanics.[1]

Religion was involved from the start. Some of the first documented cases of community contagion involved people exposed by attending religious services. Congregations whose identity was closely connected with ideals of community, fellowship, and caring almost immediately closed their doors. The ones with means to do so replaced in-person services with livestreaming. Support groups in homes and conference rooms shifted to online meetings. Religion was part of the consensual response in these ways. But religion was also part of the dissensus the pandemic generated. A few religious leaders made headlines by refusing to abide by social distancing mandates. Some held in-person worship services in violation of public health regulations. Some voiced doubts about the role of science and the efficacy of vaccines.

A case can be made that the naysayers whose opposition to reasonable public health mandates was based on religion were the kind of folks a good democracy should push as far to the margins as possible. It might be one thing to put one's own health at risk but quite another to become a hub from which contagion can spread throughout the community. Religious freedom—how far it should be protected under such conditions—was part of the debate. However, it misses the larger relationship among religion, public health, and democracy to focus only on that part. The more accurate approach requires considering how the broader diversity of American religion influenced its response to the COVID-19 crisis. That diversity contributed by responding to the fact that the pandemic affected different segments of the population differently and needed to be addressed in multiple ways. In the following sections I divide these responses into three broad categories: resistance, adaptation, and advocacy. After discussing each, I offer some thoughts

about how these responses show religious diversity's contribution to
democracy.

Resistance

Religion-based resistance to measures designed to combat the spread
of COVID-19 took two principal forms. One was resistance to executive
orders closing houses of worship. The other was resistance to the idea
that vaccinations were the best hope for stopping the pandemic. The
two were related to the extent that both expressed mistrust of government. But in other respects their origins and the concerns they represented were quite different.

Resistance to church closings was rare but highly publicized. The
most notable opponent of church closings was Baton Rouge pastor
Tony Spell, whose Life Tabernacle Church held services with more than
1,200 people attending in violation of Louisiana restrictions. Spell seized
the opportunity to declare, "We feel we are being persecuted for the
faith by being told to close our doors. There is a real virus, but we're not
closing Planned Parenthood where babies are being murdered. If they
close those doors today, we'd save more lives than will be taken by the
coronavirus." The pastor of a large independent charismatic church in
Florida also made headlines for defying social distancing restrictions
but a week later conceded to holding worship services online. A pastor
at an evangelical church in Virginia defied the restrictions only to die
after contracting the virus.[2]

The reason these instances were rare was theological as well as practical. Besides credible warnings from public health officials about the
importance of social distancing, the Christian scriptures taught believers obedience to civil authorities. The definitive text was Romans 13:1:
"Let every soul be subject unto the higher powers. For there is no power
but of God: the powers that be are ordained of God." The teaching,
theologian Bruce Worthington wrote in a 2015 essay, was a "nasty hang-
nail" to free-thinking biblical interpreters. It was a theology of submission based on the teaching, as the verses in Romans explained, that
rulers are ordained by God and that whoever resists their authority will

be punished. In practical terms, the scripture meant obeying the law, paying taxes, and demonstrating deference to elected officials. For some religious leaders, it implied praying for the authorities; for other believers, it suggested actively supporting them; and for still other interpreters, it was a useful defense of particular policies, as it was in 2018 when then Attorney General Jeff Sessions defended harsh family separation policies at the US border, stating, "Illegal entry into the United States is a crime—as it should be. Persons who violate the law of our nation are subject to prosecution. I would cite you to the apostle Paul and his clear and wise command in Romans 13 to obey the laws of the government because God has ordained them for the purpose of order."[3]

These teachings notwithstanding, Christian leaders had always acknowledged the possibility of exceptions. Righteous rebellion, dissent, disobedience, and resistance were permissible when civil authorities deviated from their own responsibility to obey the laws of God. Christians could decide when it was warranted to engage in holy resistance, as they did under Nero when Christians were martyred and in later centuries when they rebelled against medieval kings. A more recent example was the 1989 United Mine Workers strike against the Pittston coal company in which dozens of Christian activists were arrested for engaging in civil resistance.[4] Another example was Indianapolis pastor Greg Dixon, who became a hero among conservative antigovernment Protestants for defying a 1993 subpoena for church financial documents and in 1999 refused to pay millions of dollars in back taxes, which led to a three-month standoff between church members and the police.[5]

Thus, when executive orders announced that churches should not hold in-person meetings, the orders symbolized something to some religious groups other than a reasonable public health decision. The pastor in Florida called his arrest an example of "tyrannical government" persecuting religious dissidents just as it had done to Baptists and Quakers in the past. The pastor in Virginia who died was quoted as saying, "I firmly believe that God is larger than this dreaded virus." For others, it was less about God than about the democratic process. A pastor in California who felt left out of the state's decision-making process said, "We're an essential part of this whole journey and we've been bypassed, kicked to the curb and deemed nonessential." Others argued variously that churches were being treated unfairly compared with restaurants and beauty parlors, that scientists were misrepresenting the severity of the crisis, and that churches needed to remain open because crime would increase if they were closed.

Resistance to social distancing measures also played into partisan politics. Seeking to divert criticism of its failure to respond more quickly to the pandemic, the Trump administration seized occasions to criticize Democratic governors' executive orders. Upholding religious freedom was an issue that played well with the administration's conservative evangelical supporters. Some of their most vocal evangelical leaders had supported Trump in his 2016 victory against Democratic candidate Hillary Clinton because they considered the Affordable Care Act passed under the Democratic administration of Barack Obama a violation of their religious freedom. They hoped the Trump administration would end the Affordable Care Act or at least ensure that it did not in any way support abortion or require religious organizations to pay for health insurance covering the costs of contraception. Thus some pastors were primed to resist closing their churches on grounds that doing so abridged their religious freedom. When local authorities charged the pastor of a conservative nondenominational church in Virginia for holding in-person services in violation of the state's coronavirus restrictions, for example, the church sued the state with the support of the US Department of Justice on grounds that its freedom of religion was at stake.[6]

Religious freedom came up in yet another way for a few religious leaders. In their view COVID-19 was God's punishment on America for tolerating homosexuality—which they regarded as a sin that the US government under Democratic administrations had protected instead of defending religious organizations' convictions about heterosexual marriage and the right to avoid employing or doing business with homosexuals. Reverend Ralph Drollinger, an evangelical pastor who led a Bible study group attended by several members of the Trump administration's cabinet, was one of the religious leaders who held this view. The nation was suffering enormous consequences, he believed, because of its "disobedience to God's laws in terms of same-sex marriage."

Drollinger was not alone in voicing these views; however, the idea that COVID-19 was God's punishment for homosexuality and government policy was rarely expressed by other leaders who worried about restrictions on religious freedom.[7]

Although some of the clergy who opposed social distancing hosted in-person worship services in clear violation of government restrictions, others sought relief in the courts. When the US Supreme Court ruled five to four in their favor against a restriction on religious service attendance in New York state, the plaintiffs were the Roman Catholic Diocese of Brooklyn and Agudath Israel of Kew Garden Hills, an Orthodox Jewish community. As it had in other cases concerning religion, the court weighed arguments about harm to religion, the public interest, and fairness.[8]

Opposition to vaccinations bore some of the same concerns that prompted resistance to church closings. The similarity was dissent from being told what to do by government officials. The difference was that antivaccination sentiment was also entangled with concerns about family values, safety, health, science, and the economy. These concerns waxed and waned, converged and diverged, and varied in the constituencies to whom they appealed. Religion was central on some of the occasions when people had mobilized against vaccinations in the past and absent on other occasions.

Although the Vaccination Act of 1898 in Great Britain included a "conscientious objection" provision (the first time the phrase was used), the possibility of exemption on moral or religious grounds was not tested in the United States until several years later.[9] The landmark case concerning vaccinations that came to the US Supreme Court in 1905 as *Jacobson v. Massachusetts* involved a pastor named Henning Jacobson, who had been ordained in Kansas by the Sweden Mission Board and, at the time of being charged with refusing a smallpox inoculation, was serving the Swedish Augustana Evangelical Lutheran Church in Cambridge, Massachusetts. Jacobson's refusal was based not on his religious beliefs per se, but on having been subjected to mandatory vaccination while living in Sweden, from which he claimed he and one of his sons had suffered adverse effects. Jacobson believed democracy in the United

States should protect his freedom better than the government had done in Sweden. The court ruled that the state could force people to be vaccinated in order to protect the safety of the general public but allowed that certain individuals could be given an exemption for medical reasons.[10]

The Jacobson decision provided an opening for subsequent groups wishing to resist vaccinations to assert their claims. By the 1930s an organization calling itself the Committee for Medical Freedom regularly organized meetings petitioning the Massachusetts legislature for repeal of the mandatory vaccination law. Its principal arguments were that the notable decline in smallpox fatalities since the 1890s was the result of better hygiene rather than vaccinations and that religious groups, especially Christian Scientists, of whom there were many in the Boston area, should be given the right to refuse being inoculated. Some of the more vocal opponents said vaccinations were dangerous, caused blood poisoning, and led to death.[11]

In the 1960s, as the period's counterculture inspired thinking about spirituality less in terms of organized religion and more in terms of individuals' self-defined beliefs and practices, antivaccination sentiment gained adherents who defended their views on these more personalistic grounds. For example, in 1966 a family in Baltimore became a short-term media sensation when the mother, Delores Sprague, a forty-five-year-old back-to-land farm woman who had graduated from Oberlin College, was sued along with her husband for refusing to have their three school-age children vaccinated against smallpox. Sprague's refusal, she said, was based not on formal membership in any religious organization but on "a personal belief in the supremacy of nature and the sanctity of the body." She held that the body is the temple of the soul and regarded any but nonviolent treatments of disease morally objectionable. An oral homeopathic vaccine would have been acceptable according to her beliefs, but not an injection.[12]

The most common grounds for refusing vaccinations, however, were explicitly religious. Based on claims similar to the ones faith healers used in calling for divine healing or on which Jehovah's Witnesses based opposition to blood transfusions, opponents argued that vaccinations violated their religious convictions. A well-publicized example occurred in 1991 as the national incidence of measles climbed to twenty-six thousand, up from an annual average of only three thousand during the previous decade. After seven children in Philadelphia died—five from families practicing faith healing—the city mandated that all school-age children be vaccinated. A family affiliated with the Faith Tabernacle Church, a congregation that espoused faith healing, refused, citing the Bible as their reason: "Is any sick among you? Let him call for the elders of the church, and let them pray over him, anointing him with oil in the name of the Lord; and the prayer of faith shall save the sick" (James 5:14–15). The family was charged and convicted in a lower court but appealed on grounds that their religious freedom was being violated. The case went to the Pennsylvania Supreme Court, which upheld the lower court's decision.[13]

This and other cases led to most states providing for religious as well as medical exemptions in laws mandating vaccinations. By the early twenty-first century, all but two states (Mississippi and West Virginia) provided for exemptions on medical and religious grounds. New Jersey, for example, approved a statute in 2013 exempting students from vaccination on condition that a written statement was submitted to school officials by a licensed physician indicating that the vaccine was medically contraindicated for a specific period for specific medical reasons. Alternatively, a statement by the student, student's parent, or guardian was required explaining that the vaccine "conflicts with the bona fide religious tenets or practices of the student, or the parent or guardian." But "a general philosophical or moral objection to the vaccination shall not be sufficient for an exemption on religious grounds." Two years later the statute was revised to indicate that "in the event of an actual or threatened outbreak of meningitis at a public or private institution of higher education in this state, the institution may exclude from attendance a student who has been exempted from the vaccination." The exclusion from attendance applied to students whose exception was based on medical grounds if determined as such by the commissioner of Health and Senior Services. It was silent as to whether students exempt on religious grounds could be excluded from attendance.[14]

Connecticut was one of several states that dealt with the issue in greater detail. Its statute authorized the governor to declare a public health emergency under which individuals within a geographic area were to be vaccinated, but officials were required to explain the benefits and risks of the vaccine, explain the individual's "option to refuse to be vaccinated for any reason, including, but not limited to, health, religious or conscientious objections," and administer the vaccination only with the individual's, parent's, or guardian's written consent. The possibility that individuals would refuse to be vaccinated was dealt with by authorizing the health commissioner to quarantine those individuals if they posed a reasonable threat to public health. In addition, individuals could appeal a vaccination or quarantine order to the probate court, where a hearing was required to be held within seventy-two hours of receiving the request, at which the individual had a right to be present and have access to all relevant records and testimony.[15]

The impetus for further revision of statutes governing vaccinations was an outbreak of measles in 2015 involving more than one hundred cases presumed to have spread among visitors at Disneyland and exacerbated by low vaccination rates in California. In response to the outbreak, Democratic governor Jerry Brown signed into law a measure eliminating religious and other personal vaccination exemptions. The measure drew widespread opposition, much of it from parents claiming that childhood vaccinations caused autism—a claim that scientists said was untrue. Conservative religious groups also opposed the law, claiming it was a violation of religious freedom. The law and the opposition it generated drew media attention less because of the religious angle, which was not new, but because of the number of well-educated liberal parents who were apparently becoming mistrustful of vaccinations. As it happened, that mistrust seemed to diminish when reports circulated of new or anticipated outbreaks of measles, whooping cough, and other communicable diseases. Nevertheless, the opposition received sympathetic treatment in conservative media that considered the law to be an example of Democratic intrusion on individual freedom and called for "vaccine hesitancy" to be regarded as a broad-minded approach based on questions about the credibility of science.[16]

In 2019 a measles outbreak in New York City with high incidence among Orthodox Jews who had refused vaccinations prompted the state to end all religious exemptions for vaccines, just as California had done four years earlier. When New Jersey debated and then passed a similar law, hundreds of protesters demonstrated at the state capitol in Trenton. Over the preceding four years, the "antivaxxer" movement had grown, attracting support from wealthy donors and celebrities, extending its reach through social media and a National Vaccine Information Center, and broadening its arguments to include claims that mandatory vaccinations amounted to anti-Semitism, resembled Nazi Germany, violated parental choice, endangered children with risks of autism, resembled environmental pollution, were either ineffective or unnecessary, and abused religious freedom. "Even when the lives of infants, children, pregnant women, and the elderly are at risk," First Amendment scholar Marci Hamilton observed in criticizing the antivaccination movement, "we live in an era of extreme religious liberty that preaches that one's faith is to be protected at all costs, including when third parties are harmed."[17]

These various strands of antivaccination sentiment—religious freedom, fear of personal injury, mistrust of science, conservative politics, and conservative media—formed the background for protests against the possibility of a vaccine to combat COVID-19. At rallies in Chicago, Los Angeles, Sacramento, and several other large cities, for example, demonstrators marched carrying signs calling for "medical freedom," questioning the deadliness of the virus, and challenging plans for producing a vaccine as well as calling for social distancing restrictions to be lifted and businesses reopened.[18]

The majority of religious organizations that had long since made peace with vaccinations and other medical treatments said little in terms of public statements to counter the antivaccination arguments. The counternarratives came almost exclusively from the media, scientists, legal experts, and public health specialists. However, a few attempts were made to supply alternatives to antivaccination arguments from a faith perspective. For example, National Institutes of Health director Francis Collins, who was an active church member and widely known as a scientist who spoke frankly about his faith, gave interviews urging the public and clergy to be wary of false information on social media and advising faith leaders to pay attention to statements from scientists and public health officials. Publications geared to religious groups also played a role in countering the publicity generated by church-closing resisters and vaccination opponents. *America, Baptist News,* and *Christianity Today,* for example, published numerous essays debunking conspiracy theories and reminding readers about responsibilities toward neighbors. Less noticeable but perhaps more significant, many congregations provided reminders on their websites about the value of vaccinations against previous epidemics, included information in church bulletins and on websites about when and where to receive regular childhood vaccinations, and in some communities provided venues for free administrations of vaccines, all of which reinforced positive attitudes toward the newly developed coronavirus vaccines.[19]

Adaptation

Most religious organizations adapted to the COVID-19 crisis by doing what they could to provide information and services to all who were affected, given the reality that everyone was in many ways affected and yet some were affected far more deeply than others. The forms in which information and services were provided therefore differed. One form consisted primarily of support at the level of local congregations. Another reflected religion's larger presence in the healthcare industry. Both reflected the fact that religious groups were among the most widespread and diverse of all community organizations. As voluntary associations that thrived on in-person gatherings and depended on charitable contributions, these groups found that their resources were nevertheless diminished by social distancing requirements and the economic crisis.[20]

Congregational support consisted in the first instance of information encouraging members to stay home, engage in social distancing, and take advantage of livestreamed worship services and yet maintain a sense of ritual familiarity and cohesion through web-based social gatherings. Catholic, Methodist, and Episcopal bishops, for example, canceled or called on congregations to cancel in-person worship services and meetings and offered assistance in setting up livestreaming and in the case of Catholics receiving spiritual communion and baptism by desire. Synagogues, mosques, and temples responded similarly. A national poll found that only 3 percent of typical churchgoers planned to attend in-person services. Cell phone location tracking data confirmed that in-person attendance plummeted. Practitioners who likely would not have attended in-person gatherings anyway were discouraged from doing so by decisions from the highest denominational levels to the most authoritative in local communities. In Salt Lake City all meetings and activities of the Church of Jesus Christ of Latter-day Saints were canceled worldwide. In Dallas at the First Baptist Church, where Reverend Robert Jeffress was known for praising President Trump and conservative Republican officeholders and preaching about abortion and Muslims, in-person services were held the first two Sundays of the nationwide pandemic but livestreamed the following Sunday, the first time the church had not met collectively for worship in its 152-year history. "People should not confuse faith with foolishness," Jeffress told a reporter. "God expects us to certainly exercise faith, but common sense as well."[21]

Within days of mandated restrictions, many congregations began updating health and wellness information and services already available to members and the wider community. These resources reflected congregations' increasing interest in health and wellness ministries during the last quarter of the twentieth century. An outgrowth of early twentieth-century projects involving churches constructing gyms, organizing baseball teams and bowling leagues, and encouraging nutritious diets, the late twentieth-century health and wellness ministries included fitness regimens, yoga, lectures and conferences about weight control, blood drives, vaccinations, wellness checkups, support groups for persons with addictions, and care for the elderly. Large congregations sponsored congregation-based nursing programs that visited members' homes as well as rehabilitation and hospice facilities, and smaller congregations participated in community networks that included meetings with county health officials, visiting public health nurses, and senior citizen centers. Synagogues, mosques, Hindu temples, and Buddhist meditation centers provided information about sources of appropriate food and linkages to healthcare providers familiar with the various religious and ethnic traditions. Several incentives oriented congregations in these directions: imitation across congregations, competition to provide services that ministered to a growing cultural interest in "wholeness," greater availability of health professionals within congregations, an increase in the number of large well-funded congregations, an aging population among the most active members of congregations, and an emphasis in schools, the medical community, and the media on the need to combat obesity and related sources of illness. One discernible strand was what historian Marie Griffith termed Americans' "doctrine of the perfectible body," which had long inspired religious communities to promote fasting, temperance, and chastity; another strand was the ethic of service found in all religious traditions that encouraged assistance in the well-being of persons physically as well as spiritually.[22]

Many congregations were in a position to respond almost immediately to the pandemic by updating websites already staffed by health and wellness committees with blogs, advice, and links to physical and mental health resources. For example, a Congregational church in Winchester, Massachusetts, had initiated a Health and Wellness Ministry in 2001 to promote healthy lifestyle choices, mindfulness, emotional support, and reliance on medical science, which included a committee that organized workshops, retreats, health consultations, and website information. This facilitated the immediate formation of a COVID-19 community resource hub to provide information about food assistance, pharmacies, telemedicine, and emergency contacts. The congregation also set up a COVID-19 financial response fund to which families in the congregation and the wider community could apply for assistance with household expenses, medical expenses, and other virus-related needs. Similarly, a Methodist church in Northern Virginia that had an active health and wellness care team in place composed of health professionals and lay volunteers posted a "health and wellness" blog with weekly updates offering coronavirus-related safety tips for opening mail and packages, information from national public health agencies, and links to local resources.[23]

A resource that congregations of all sizes had at their disposal was health and wellness information assembled and made available to them by denominational agencies. The United States Conference of Catholic Bishops, for example, supplied resources to parishes about medical treatments, patient rights, and access to emergency funds. The National Baptist Convention posted information on its website about the impact of the coronavirus on Black churches, resources available through the NAACP, and links to government health and service agencies. At the regional level, Lutheran Health and Wellness Ministry staff hosted on-line lectures for families and churches. Separate from denominational sponsorship, the urban coalitions that had developed in the late twentieth century to promote interchurch cooperation for housing and economic development engaged in COVID-19 responses. The Congregational Wellness Program, initiated in 1997 in New Orleans, for example, was a coalition of nearly one hundred inner-city churches that trained and supported nurses and lay health leaders and responded to COVID-19 by providing $500,000 in additional support for its participants to work with families affected by the crisis. Other coalitions focused on specific constituencies with which they had worked in the past and which were now particularly affected. For example, the Virginia Interfaith Center assisted low-income and minority families in obtaining unemployment compensation and helped with applications for health insurance, childcare needs, and eviction avoidance. Dallas's Project Unity, an interfaith movement of Black, White, and multiracial churches principally concerned with policing and race relations, became a hub for free coronavirus testing in sections of the city where few other sites were available. And, taking a different approach, the Boise Interfaith Sanctuary in Idaho was one of many faith-based organizations that provided housing for homeless persons who were COVID-19 positive.[24]

Unlike religious organizations in which a charismatic leader unilaterally decided when to shut down or reopen in-person services, most denominational religious organizations formed working groups to collect information and put together detailed plans about how to respond. These working groups originated in single congregations, among congregations within districts or regions, and within denominational administrative bodies. The groups typically included health professionals as well as clergy. Some of the groups sent notices to congregations with relatively straightforward warnings about social distancing and wearing face masks. Others provided detailed instruction about how to conduct in-person communion services safely and when it might be appropriate to offer drive-in services. Still others described the reporting procedures to be undertaken if someone in the congregation tested positive. Many religious organizations posted these and other guidelines on websites and circulated them by email. Methodist churches in North Georgia, for example, received regular updates on coronavirus response resources including guidelines on making and wearing masks, information about livestreaming music, sample questions for surveying members about needs and attitudes, and webinars with infectious disease experts.[25]

Religious organizations' extensive involvement in the healthcare industry gave them an additional role in responding to the crisis. The Catholic healthcare system was the largest, including more than 2,200 hospitals, nursing homes, and long-term care facilities. An estimated one in six patients in the United States was cared for each day at one of the nation's Catholic hospitals, staffed by more than five hundred thousand full-time employees. The system underwent a severe financial shortfall as a result of the pandemic. Within the first six weeks of the COVID-19 outbreak, the Catholic Health Association reported a 30 percent drop in revenue from canceled elective surgical procedures, outpatient treatments, and primary care visits. Several hospitals were reporting losses of $1 million to $2 million a day. The financial burden was no greater than that on other hospitals, but the burden demonstrated the significant extent to which Catholic organizations were on the front lines of healthcare provision. In one respect, Catholic healthcare provision was also at greater risk of financial losses because many of its agencies, including ones in Chicago, Cleveland, Detroit, Los Angeles, New Orleans, and New York, were in COVID-19 hot spots and were heavily involved in assisting low-income, uninsured, minority, and migrant families.[26]

Apart from its involvement in healthcare delivery, religion's traditional functions of providing spiritual support were in significant demand as well. Despite being restricted from visiting the sick in person or conducting funerals in the accustomed manner, priests, rabbis, pastors, imams, and interfaith chaplains offered as much assistance as they could through personal phone calls, emails, and social media. Many of the nation's nursing homes and care centers for the elderly—where large numbers of COVID-19 deaths occurred—were owned and operated by religious organizations or were populated by persons with long histories of involvement in congregations.

Workers in overcrowded, subsistence-wage meatpacking factories with substandard health and safety conditions were another population devastated by the pandemic. The employees' strenuous schedules, language barriers, and uncertain status as recent immigrants made it nearly impossible for them to establish firm supportive ties with local congregations. Chaplains were often the only resource available for spiritual care and consolation. Tyson Foods was one of the companies that prided itself on being a "faith friendly" workplace and reportedly employed more than ninety chaplains full or part time, including imams as well as pastors and priests. At a ratio of approximately one chaplain for every thousand workers, though, the chaplains were stretched thin even before the outbreak, yet they did what they could to provide solace. "I'm just trying to be a compassionate active presence," one of the chaplains explained, describing his days walking the plant floor, making himself available for conversations in the cafeteria, and taking employees' temperatures.[27]

The help religious groups could provide in any of these ways— through health and wellness programs in congregations, through denominational offices and hospitals, and through spiritual care in nursing homes and meat processing facilities—was of course limited. The war on the pandemic had to be fought in other ways, especially through public health agencies, government funding and supervision, and medical research. Nevertheless, religious groups could assist in small ways because they had ties in diverse local communities that varied across the full spectrum of socioeconomic, ethnic, racial, and religious identities. Because of these ties, religious groups could mediate between national sources of information and the local information that families often considered more trustworthy and that—albeit with notable exceptions—encouraged families to take the pandemic seriously. In addition to providing information, many religious organizations were experienced in helping people gain access to medical resources, and most religious organizations were experienced in assisting families coping with illness, bereavement, and death.

Advocacy

Religious groups' third response to the COVID-19 pandemic was advocacy. As a potential source of advocacy for public health funding and for an appropriate economic recovery response, some religious groups were well positioned because they were already engaged in advocacy on similar issues. They had an infrastructure in place from which to conduct advocacy and were familiar with the skills advocacy required. That infrastructure and those skills were a strength, but also a weakness. The strength was that staff, websites, money, and means of communicating with policy makers were easily adapted to making new appeals related specifically to the COVID-19 crisis. The weakness was that advocacy groups were already overtaxed with agendas they had agreed to pursue and, for this reason, sometimes piggybacked COVID-19 advocacy onto these existing agendas rather than responding more directly or creatively to the immediate crisis. A further limitation was that financial contributions declined as the economy struggled, in addition to which advocacy had to be mobilized and publicized online rather than in person.

The suddenness with which the pandemic's seriousness became known meant that religious advocacy organizations' initial response was to encourage Congress to increase support for activities that the organizations already regarded as priorities. This advocacy focused less on testing, healthcare, and research and more on the needs of the poor,

which was a long-standing priority for many of the religious organizations involved. The Action Center of the Evangelical Lutheran
Church in America, for example, encouraged the denomination's clergy
and members to contact lawmakers about support for hunger programs,
childcare, farmworkers, housing, and international aid. The Action Center appealed for Congress to increase funding for all of these programs
in view of the disproportionate effect of COVID-19 on low-income
communities. Similarly, the United Methodist Board of Church and
Society hosted a series of webinars under the heading "COVID 19: Pre-
Existing Disparities Exposed," which emphasized systemic racism, in-
carceration, food insecurity, peace, and economic justice.[28] Bishops of
the African Methodist Episcopal Church issued a statement deeply
critical of the Trump administration's mismanagement, misinformation,
and lack of leadership. The bishops called on Congress to expedite bills
seeking to help at-risk and underserved communities.[29]

Other religious groups resembled these denominations in emphasizing the pandemic's effects on the poor—sometimes in other countries
as well as in the United States. The Catholic Health Association was an
example. It was one of the most active religious organizations in advocating for executive branch leadership and congressional action to respond more effectively and generously to the outbreak. A Catholic
Health Association statement to Congress on behalf of more than a
hundred Benedictine, Dominican, Franciscan, Jesuit, and Marianist
orders and organizations appealed for legislation to include resources
specifically directed toward African American, Latino, and tribal communities. The statement called for a moratorium on shutoffs of water,
electricity, and heat to low-income households. It also took the occasion
to include reminders about energy efficiency, job training for clean energy employment, and investments in solar and wind energy as well as
redirecting excessive military expenditures toward public health
programs.[30]

Unlike the Catholic Health Association's advocacy for policies to
help native-born groups disproportionately affected by COVID-19
within the United States, the advocacy of a coalition organized by the

US Conference of Catholic Bishops' Justice for Immigrants was directed toward immigrants, migrant workers, and refugees. In a letter to the Department of Homeland Security's acting secretary, the heads of Catholic Charities, the Catholic Legal Immigration Network, and the Committee on Migration advocated for the DHS to remove barriers to healthcare for immigrants, ensure health safety during enforcement actions and at sensitive locations, distribute information in multiple languages about testing and preventive care, and review all enforcement activities and operations in view of negative implications from the pandemic. As the pandemic worsened, the coalition's partner organizations continued to engage in advocacy through press releases, webinars, and informational kits, including answers to questions about eligibility for assistance through the CARES Act.[31]

The Interfaith Immigration Coalition launched a similar campaign for immigrant rights in the face of threats worsened by the pandemic and the Trump administration's anti-immigrant policies. Speaking on behalf of its two hundred member organizations, which included Catholic, Jewish, Muslim, and Protestant groups as well as independent interest groups, the coalition put out press releases, sent letters to Congress, and provided tool kits to be used at places of worship to conduct litanies and host online meetings. In addition to these informational activities, the coalition participated in livestreamed meetings with House Democrats to protest immigration officials' failure to provide basic hygiene and sanitary measures before people began dying at detention centers. Coalition lawyers also challenged the legality of the administration's executive order canceling all immigration to the United States.[32]

Among responses to the pandemic from Jewish organizations, the Religious Action Center of Reform Judaism urged individuals and partner organizations to contact Congress to increase federal healthcare funding through Medicaid match programs, ensure stable funding for hospitals and community health centers, and strengthen the unemployment compensation system. The center also advocated for the inclusion in relief packages of special assistance for families needing food assistance, the homeless, incarcerated persons, and immigrants. Through its publications, the center also called on public officials as well as the public to avoid stereotyping and scapegoating.[33]

Reflecting a history of advocacy directed at the corporate sector, the Interfaith Center on Corporate Responsibility focused its efforts on the pandemic's economic consequences. Representing more than three hundred institutional investors and service providers, ICCR urged the management of these and related firms to make emergency paid leave available to employees including part-time and subcontracted workers, institute remote work and enhanced safety protections, provide health and safety training, and close locations when indicated for health reasons. At the same time, ICCR urged companies to retain workers, adhere to nondiscriminatory policies if layoffs were necessary, suspend share buybacks, and reduce senior management compensation. Additional statements released by ICCR to the media and in letters to CEOs urged pharmaceutical companies to develop a collaborative approach to health technologies for diagnostics and treatments.[34]

Convergence

The response to the COVID-19 pandemic, then, was a case in which religious diversity brought different ideas, interests, and services to bear on a national crisis. Although the public's response showed a great deal of uniformity, the response was not so consensual as to deny the value of differences of opinion and perspective. Whether the initial response might have happened sooner and been more effective under a more unified regime is a legitimate question. Democracy is often considered to be slow, cumbersome, and less than effective in addressing national emergencies. Yet it does well in most such instances at being attentive to the balance of freedom and collective well-being.

Although nearly all of America's religious organizations encouraged their members to abide by social distancing, which nearly all members heeded in their religious observances, religion's diversity meant that it was capable of reaching different segments of the population who heeded different authorities, were embedded in different social networks, and were affected differently by the pandemic. It wasn't that the public's responses were being guided primarily by religious organizations. Nor were people simply heeding what they heard directly from the White House via television and social media. Although there was legitimate concern about officials and conspiracy groups misleading the public, information about the serious practicalities of social distancing was being filtered through trusted local networks, community groups, and online meetings among families and neighbors and among members of religious organizations.

As well as the flow of informal information that passed through diverse social networks, religious organizations contributed to the spread of practical information about the various resources on which different segments of the population depended. For many this information consisted of resources posted on church websites about how to stay healthy and how to maintain emotional well-being while physically isolated from friends and family. For many it included resources for staying connected with spiritual habits and practices.

Religious organizations' contribution also consisted importantly of social services and advocacy. Religion's extensive involvement in hospitals, nursing homes, hospice care, and chaplaincies meant services to many of the populations most severely affected. That involvement motivated advocacy as well, especially for legislation and emergency measures taking account of the adverse effects among healthcare providers, the elderly, and members of low-income and minority communities.

Religious organizations were among the many kinds of organizations—universities, research facilities, businesses, labor unions, community groups—that together constituted the basis of civil society on which democracy always depends, especially during times of national crisis. The key to an effective civil society is that it not only assists citizens in supporting common societal goals but also reaches into the diverse niches of the population and mobilizes them to defend democracy when they believe it is threatened.

Conclusion

I HAVE ARGUED that diversity—the fact that Americans adhere to a wide variety of religious and secular traditions and further sort themselves into vastly different and often competing congregations and activist groups—is the reality that facilitates religion's contributions to democracy. Diversity provides the space for dissent to be expressed when the leaders of one religious tradition or faith community gain a level of power corrosive to the ethic of a democratic society. When this happens—whether at the local, regional, or national level—leaders of other faith communities and of secular groups organize against them, calling them out for making false arguments or for compromising church-state separation.

Diversity is not only a safeguard but also the condition under which basic values are debated and from which their implications are adapted to new situations. In making these adaptations, religious and secular groups borrow and reframe each other's ideas, advance alternatives, and on occasion find issues on which some of them can work together. James Madison called this "variety of sects" the reality that reduces the danger posed by an ascendancy of any one of them. Rephrasing Madison, George Will writes of the "saving multiplicity of factions" that prevents the majority's power from becoming entrenched.[1]

As religious groups have contended with one another, some have obviously been winners and others losers. Protestants during much of the nation's history won more often than Catholics, Christians won more often than Jews, and among Christians White mainline denominations exercised a dominant influence compared with Black churches and White evangelical groups well into the 1970s. To speak of White mainline Protestantism as a hegemonic influence, though, masks the divisions within it and how much those divisions affected what was done. Because Protestantism was as fragmented as it was, its leaders took sides against one another on almost every issue that came before them, whether it was about national defense, war, the economy, labor, or racial justice. The differences in opinion were even starker beyond White mainline Protestant elites, especially among the many small sects that counted as evangelical Protestants and the many ethnic groups of which American Catholicism was composed. More recently, White evangelical Protestants and conservative Catholics, working together in recent decades more than they would have imagined possible in earlier years, have of course waged and won battles in the courts and during elections on issues that many Black leaders and liberal White Protestants, Catholics, Jews, and leaders of secular organizations have opposed.

As well as the differences separating Protestants from Catholics and Christians from Jews, much of the past century's religious history has been dominated by the tension that ran through all the various traditions between upholding the distinctive rights and freedoms of religion, on the one hand, and, on the other hand, joining with nonreligious groups and government in the interest of making a difference in the wider world. Both these approaches were consistent with the teachings and interests of religious groups themselves. Religious leaders were concerned—correctly—that secularization, materialism, the government, antireligious groups, and even other religious groups could threaten what they held most dear. They wanted to protect their freedom to act in accordance with their religious beliefs—and for that matter to keep control of the finances, buildings, and service organizations they had worked hard to create. But it was also in keeping with religious teachings to serve the poor, feed the hungry, advocate for common decency, oppose racism, and work for peace and justice. Those objectives frequently coincided with the aims of groups representing other religious traditions as well as groups with no religious inclinations. Religious groups understood the basic fact that it is more effective to work through diverse coalitions and networks when pursuing a social or political goal than it is to work alone. The challenges that can arise from working in coalition—especially when the coalition partners are strange bedfellows—was part of the contention that prompted religious groups to hunker down at times and to reach out at others.

The religious practices that Americans have argued about in these diverging ways are different from the conception of religion that many depictions of it emphasize when connecting it with democracy. In those depictions religion is good for democracy—or should be—because it is a unifying cultural force providing the very suppositions on which democratic institutions are founded. More than any other social sector, this argument emphasizes, religion naturally imparts shared beliefs and values and a common understanding of morality. Moreover, the institution of the family—which is prized by religious groups across the spectrum—is the mechanism through which this shared morality becomes active and contributes to the common values and social bonds on which democracy depends. It follows that religion's contribution is weakened when it does not speak with one voice, when it consists of different traditions that have widely divergent beliefs and values, when internal disputes disturb what are assumed to be the beliefs and values that all should share, and when critics dispute religious claims. It is difficult from this perspective to contemplate the possibility that disagreements about religion, morality, and the family can be present without democracy being weakened. But democracy does not necessitate everyone believing the same thing. Democracy is strengthened more by citizens acknowledging and accepting diversity—and willingly contending for differing beliefs. Indeed, contending for differing beliefs is especially important when particular religious convictions are the grounds for claims that only the persons holding those convictions should be in power.

The genius of America's democratic framework is that it accords differing groups the freedom to contend for their beliefs. Justice William O. Douglas's famous assertion "We are a religious people whose institutions presuppose a Supreme Being" probably reads less convincingly today than it did in the middle of the last century. But Douglas's

emphasis on the nation's wide variety of beliefs and creeds must be remembered: "We sponsor an attitude on the part of government," he
wrote, "that shows no partiality to any one group and that lets each flour-
ish according to the zeal of its adherents and the appeal of its dogma."[2]

well.

Although a crucial benefit for democracy has been the willingness
of religious and secular groups to call foul on religious leaders' own
antidemocratic tendencies, this is by no means the only contribution
religious diversity makes—as I have tried to show in the foregoing
chapters. To review briefly, in the 1930s when the Great Depression
prompted an unprecedented expansion of the federal government, religious groups spoke and acted from diverse traditions, convictions,
and social locations, with advocacy that ranged from enthusiastically
supporting the New Deal, to arguing that it did not go far enough
toward helping the poor or addressing racial discrimination, to questioning the ideological notion of a "new world order." This advocacy
also included convening convocations of business and labor leaders,
hosting critics of the New Deal, and vigorously warning of the dangers
of authoritarianism—in sum, broadening the deliberations about how
best to uphold the values democracy was meant to preserve. In retrospect, Roosevelt's administration did more to preserve democracy than
to undermine it, but at the time, many Americans, even among Roosevelt's supporters, were worried about the possibilities of tyranny, and
they found venues in their religious organizations through which to
express their concerns.

The second crucial episode we considered occurred in the late 1930s
as America pondered the prospect of another war: religious groups'
divergent contributions to the discourse about what should be done
included concerted advocacy for pacifism and equally concerted advocacy for rearmament, and—also of great importance—a searching debate with practical consequences about freedom of conscience: its
meaning for persons conscientiously opposed to war, the grounds on
which conscientious objection to war might be based, how to verify the
sincerity of such convictions, and what it implied to disconnect the
basis for determining convictions' sincerity from religious affiliation. It
took the courts and special interest groups like the ACLU and

Fellowship of Reconciliation to work through the answers. Those answers necessitated a wide-ranging reexamination of how to think about
liberty of conscience—a rethinking that has continued to shape deliberations about the relationship of religious freedom to questions about
individual freedom and civil rights.

Along with freedom of conscience, freedom of assembly was another
fundamental aspect of democracy to which twentieth-century religious
debates contributed. The considerable extent to which local voluntary
associations were an integral feature of American civil society became
especially evident in the 1950s when the Cold War, on the one hand, and
mass culture, on the other hand, posed questions about White middle-
and working-class conformity becoming sufficiently prevalent to stul-
tify dissent, counterdissent, and creative adaptations to changing social
conditions. Along with other community organizations, religious
groups were the local spaces in which grassroots social networks
formed, reflecting differing ethnic, racial, regional, occupational, and
socioeconomic interests. Freedom of assembly was constituted not only
in practice but also as the NAACP, Black church coalitions, book clubs,
and campus groups sorted through how to protect and mobilize their
members. The dissent that broadened conceptions of civil rights depended in no small measure on the litigation to which both religious
and nonreligious groups contributed that specified the terms of privacy,
nondisclosure, property rights, and freedom of speech that freedom of
assembly implied.

Many of the groups that did in fact mobilize by the 1960s expanded,
spun off new groups, and, as we saw, played active roles through the end
of the century as advocates for differing views about human dignity,
public welfare provision, religious liberty, and the crafting of new ideas
about rights—such as the doctrines of "compelling government interest"
and "true private choice." Although much of the debate that separated
religious groups from one another focused on questions about private
charity versus government programs, religious groups with infrastructure and firsthand experience in working with the poor straddled partisan divides and contributed to the formation of public-private innova-
tions. Black churches, inner-city nonprofit coalitions, and interfaith

councils were especially important in traversing the complex territory that lay at the intersection of private and public welfare provision. Democracy was enhanced through deliberations that specified the implications of human dignity in terms of health, safety, privacy, and social responsibility.

The contributions of religious diversity to the debates about major twenty-first-century issues have demonstrated the limitations as well as the strengths of religious advocacy. On the one hand, partisan loyalties have sufficiently divided religious groups along ideological lines that much of the public debate about religion's role in upholding—or upending—democracy has revolved around these divisions. On the other hand, religious groups' prominence in national politics owes much to the fact that advocacy for particular issues that have resonance with religious and political conservatives is met with counteradvocacy by religious and secular groups holding alternative views. On questions of immigrant rights, the wealth gap, and the response to health and wellness issues raised by COVID-19, groups that favored differing policies organized coalitions, supported or opposed policy proposals, and when necessary worked around political impediments by engaging in private sector activities. Although the alignment of conservative religious groups with conservative partisan interests has dominated public discussion of these issues, the extent of countermobilization has been significant as well.

An important and perhaps underappreciated contribution of the various religious groups and coalitions has been their role in filtering, digesting, and in many instances countering the dominant national rhetoric—doing so through local networks and by focusing on practical concerns inadequately addressed through electoral politics. Although the outcomes of electoral politics were certainly consequential, local politics mattered too and were still possible to address through grassroots organizations. "Americans are hungry for opportunities to assemble, deliberate, and converse with one another," the American Academy of Arts and Sciences' Commission on the Practice of Democratic Citizenship concluded after conducting extensive research in communities across the nation. This was the role that houses of worship, book clubs, coffeehouses, and community associations had played in the past, the commission said, and surely could continue to play in strengthening democracy even in an era of social media and incipient political alienation.[3]

The challenge to democracy that religious diversity has contributed least to resolving is systemic racism. The reasons are many, including the taken-for-grantedness of White privilege by the majority White population, the subtle and not so subtle ways in which racial prejudice perpetuates itself, and the enduring effects of decades-long discrimination in housing policies, schooling, job opportunities, and healthcare. Religious groups populated by predominantly White memberships have in some cases worked for years to bring attention to systemic racism, but other groups have maintained nineteenth-century sectional identities and implicitly espoused ideas about the virtues of racial separation.[4] It is therefore of particular importance that Black churches and coalitions of African American civil rights and community service organizations have contributed significantly to all the major deliberations the nation has faced in deciding what it means to be a democracy that upholds liberty and justice for all.

I suggested at the outset that religious diversity's place in American democracy can be understood along the lines of the agonistic pluralism framework advanced by Chantal Mouffe.[5] This framework recognizes that deep and persistent clashes about basic values and epistemic principles are a prevalent feature of social life and that democracies are therefore not the means through which people achieve consensus but are the practices, as Mouffe writes, with which people "share a common allegiance to the democratic principles of 'liberty and equality for all' while disagreeing about their interpretation."[6]

We have seen in the cases considered several ways in which the agonistic pluralism approach applies and can also be extended. The various advocacy groups we have considered illustrate the formation of collective identities that contend with one another for legitimacy, power, and the strategic means of expressing their claims. They have done so by forming coalitions that enable collaboration and by engaging in conflict with groups advancing opposing views. The identities of these adversarial groups are constituted in the process, meaning that their salient features change as the environments in which they are constituted change.[7]

"Tradition," for example, is important as a legitimizing legacy of beliefs and values, but what counts as tradition is subject to redefinition and to varying strategies of deployment. Group identities moreover are asserted not in terms of rational arguments about shared values and common interests but as narrative manifestations of beliefs, values, and passions embedded in practices, and these practices are intertwined with the ethnic, racial, regional, and socioeconomic contexts in which they occur.[8] Religious commitment is thus for many people less of an ascribed identity than one they have chosen. As Peter Berger once observed, "Pluralism plunges individuals toward free decisions, a good in itself."[9]

Mouffe's understanding of agonistic pluralism suggests that it functions best when certain procedures are in place to regulate the conflict it entails.[10] However, this understanding seems inadequate when the conflict in question presents a challenge to the legitimacy and interpretation of the procedures themselves, as in cases questioning the applicability of certain interpretations of the US Constitution by religious conservatives. As we have seen, there are in fact numerous cases in which certain procedures are challenged, including those pertaining to children's health and safety, undocumented immigrants, wartime emergencies, and special exemptions for religious groups. These challenges have been manageable, however, because other foundational procedures remained unchallenged, especially the legitimacy of the courts and court procedures. In addition, religious diversity itself played a role in providing avenues for alternative proposals to be considered. Disagreements among religious groups reflect confessional, racial, and ethnic histories as well as geographic locations, but they are usually oriented toward specific issues. Instead of contesting procedural matters or government legitimacy, religious groups mobilize constituents to advocate for or against specific policies and candidates.

The criticism most often directed at pluralism is that it encourages incessant contestation, normalizing conflicts and interest group politics rather than facilitating harmony around the principles on which liberal democracy depends. This is a well-founded concern in the case of religion, where seemingly petty disputes over doctrinal interpretation and styles of worship are all too frequent. To some extent, infighting of this kind is to be expected when leaders and their adherents are free to practice according to the dictates of conscience. It is furthered by the history of confessional diversity and the local contexts in which American congregations exist. What we have seen, though, in considering the public issues toward which religious advocacy has been directed is that the necessity of mobilizing resources tends toward the formation of coalitions, working groups, and strategic networks.

The condition that Mouffe and her interlocutors specify in terms of agreement on basic democratic and constitutional procedures is one that must be emphasized even when the interpretation of those procedures is challenged.[11] The challenges to which religious groups have been a party include questions about the conditions governing liberty of conscience, freedom of assembly, and the meanings of human dignity. These challenges have taken place within an understanding that religious claims should be made lawfully and with an expectation of being challenged. There are, however, notable instances in which religion has motivated unproductive argumentation and even violence or extreme measures stopping just short of violence on grounds of resisting a supreme evil on the basis of divine authority. These instances violate the premises of civility and mutual respect on which agonistic pluralism is based. An agonistic ethos is one that is institutionalized and thus subject to constraints on antidemocratic tendencies even when it contests democratic norms. It consists of institutional forbearance, a willingness to disagree, and an acknowledgment that rivals have a right to exist and to compete for what they consider of value.[12]

What might be termed *agonistic religious practice*, then, is a collection of religious practices that are genuinely diverse insofar as they include differing values, theologies, traditions, groups, and styles of worship that conflict with one another, rather than merely coexisting as proponents of tolerance, and that at the same time accept the right of rivals to contend energetically for their beliefs and values. Faith communities' diverse constituencies form coalitions, collaborate, and distinguish themselves in "us" and "them" relationships. They mobilize resources and seek to be heard in the public arena. Their differing claims advocate for values that reflect their particular interests but also tend to be framed in terms of what they perceive to be the common good, whether that means values such as freedom of conscience and human dignity or adherence to particular expressions of value such as Christian love. The differing claims moreover include passionate contention about democratic procedures and constitutional interpretations. Agonistic religious practice, in these terms, is an apt description of how public religion in the United States functions much of the time. Agonistic pluralism describes the fact that religious groups hold to distinctive traditions and beliefs, not about which they are willing to engage in aggressive denunciations of those with whom they disagree, but on which they stake their claims to unique identities and practices. Agonistic pluralism can also be regarded normatively, as Mouffe does, in emphasizing that religious convictions contribute through adversarial politics, contestation, and passion, and not only through calls for unity and calm deliberation. Acknowledging contention requires reckoning with the side with which one disagrees as well as the side with which one agrees.

An important implication of regarding religious groups as agonistic practices is that their engagement in the political arena on behalf of particular causes is a legitimate expression of democracy. Although it is not appropriate for religious groups to exercise coercive power, they are not expected to function only in the private realm. Rather, democratic governance itself is understood to be a pluralistic enterprise in which religious groups have as much right as any other group to fight for what they believe to be good and true. Agonistic religious practice therefore is not simply a description of the division of American religion into a plurality of groups with diverging values. Additionally, this view includes certain normative assumptions about democracy: that society includes groups whose diverging values may be incommensurate, that constitutional guarantees of individual rights and freedoms must be upheld, and that these rights and freedoms are subject to negotiation. Within this understanding, religious groups are expected to disagree with one another, to advocate for their respective convictions, and to do so within constitutional limits.[13]

Although contention is a defining feature of agonistic religious practices, alliances and cooperative arrangements are integral to these practices as well. The earlier view of religion as a source of social cohesion is an ideal that continues in several modified forms: as common purpose among groups engaged in ecumenical agreements, as an implicit agreement about tolerance of differences, and as the conviction that diverse groups might aspire to share common beliefs even if in reality they do not. Much of the contention by which agonistic religious practice is characterized is constrained by one or more of these understandings. Moreover, the idea of agonistic religious practice expands the discussion of how religion can contribute to democracy beyond one of the standard arguments in the academic literature. That argument perceives the benefit from religion to lie in religious teachings and practices that are themselves democratic, such as deciding on congregational matters by holding elections among congregants. While there is much to be said for the value of such procedures, the difficulty is that this conception pits "good" (democratic) religion against "bad" (undemocratic) religion, implying that only the former is beneficial. However, as much as it may be desirable to favor democratic religion, the key to agonistic religious practice is its emphasis on the diversity of religious organizations and thus the checks and balances, contention and countermobilization that operate even when some of the contenders are not themselves governed by democratic procedures.

The idea of agonistic religious practice is in some respects consistent with the views expressed by recent writers who have advanced a pluralistic approach to religion and politics. For example, former Republican senator John C. Danforth writes in *The Relevance of Religion: How Faithful People Can Change Politics* that Americans too often treat those with whom they disagree as enemies, rather than as persons of moral worth, and in acknowledging that people of faith are not of one mind, he urges them to be open to these differences.[14] Columnist Michael Gerson, agreeing with Danforth, says the basic rule of political participation is anticipating that one's side may lose and accepting the verdict when defeat occurs.[15]

However, agonistic religious practice differs from these views in focusing less than they do on compromise. Danforth, for example, emphasizes not only openness to difference but also moderation, unity, inclusiveness, centrism, and building bridges. From his own faith perspective, he believes that Christians should especially be concerned with healing divisions—what he calls a "ministry of reconciliation." Although the idea of agonistic religious practice would affirm a similar aim, its focus is less on reconciliation and more on spirited advocacy. The difference is evident in Mouffe's distinction between deliberative democracy and agonistic democracy—the former seeking to resolve troublesome disagreements through reasoned discussion, the latter valuing disagreement itself. Concretely, agonistic religious practice would place greater emphasis on strong claims about justice, rights, and representation than on compromise.

The other difference between agonistic religious practice and the perspective taken in many discussions of religion and politics concerns what must be present among disputants for democracy to function effectively. Danforth, Gerson, and many others stress that common decency, civility, moral responsibility, and decorum contribute valuably— and are contributions that faith communities can reinforce. These contributions are no less important to the idea of agonistic religious practice. However, agonistic religious practice puts greater stock in the institutions through which these virtues are reinforced than in the ideals that individuals may embrace because of personal religious convictions. These institutions of course include houses of worship as places where moral responsibility is learned but also consist importantly of the laws, regulations, and constitutional norms that reinforce democratic principles.

The issue that surfaces repeatedly in considering religious diversity's relationship to democracy during the past century is how much it has confronted—and been confronted by—authoritarianism. As the size and scope of the federal government expanded, religious groups repeatedly expressed concern about these developments' implications for democracy. Diversity was evident in what they thought should be done. Some religious groups sided with critics who thought almost anything the federal government did was a threat. Other groups wanted the federal government to take an even more active role in controlling the economy and protecting human rights. So much of the debate in fact focused on human rights that it came to be viewed as the litmus test through which to argue that religious groups were or were not supporting democracy. In reality, the issue of authoritarianism was just as important.

These two issues—human rights and authoritarianism—have become more important again in recent years as autocratic tendencies have gained a foothold in American politics and in other Western democracies.[16] The concern is that authoritarian leaders are willing to exploit constituents' economic grievances and feelings of being left behind by articulating racist and anti-immigrant messages—and then use the political capital that accrues from such appeals to restrict civil liberties. Religious convictions are implicated in this scenario to the extent that large numbers of religious conservatives appear to be comfortable with these authoritarian tendencies.[17]

The divisions that have separated certain religious liberals or moderates from religious conservatives over the past century have in fact deepened. Although diversity is present, it is overshadowed by polarization. On the one side is a large population of conservative White Christians who are comfortable being defined by the label evangelical or traditional Catholic. On the other side is a less clearly defined population composed variously of nonevangelical Christians, adherents of Islam and Hinduism and Judaism, and persons unaffiliated with any religion. The conservative Christian population has puzzled most observers because much of its theology has opposed big government in the past and yet its recent inclinations appear to run against those traditions.

Polarization of this kind has not been healthy either for religious organizations or for democracy. Its effect on religious groups has been to favor leaders and organizations on the right capable of commanding large budgets, mailing lists, television audiences, and social media followings—and who can garnish their public images by appearing at rallies with right-wing public officials. That alignment makes it harder for people who hold conservative religious convictions to perceive, much less consider, moderate or liberal political views. The response on the left is easier to formulate in terms of antireligious sentiment than on alternative grounds that embrace religion. Hence, it is not surprising that many of the increasing numbers of Americans who disavow religion do so because religious conviction seems intractably associated with right-wing politics.[18] None of this is good for politics, either. The polarization of religious groups magnifies and reifies knee-jerk affinities with partisan divisions rather than promoting reasoned, reflective dialogue.[19]

Nevertheless, even today more religious diversity exists in the United States than meets the eye. Despite polls suggesting overwhelming support among White evangelical Protestants for conservative Republican candidates and policies, for example, a progressive faction within evangelicalism has maintained vocal advocacy for greater emphasis on inclusion, equality, acceptance of diversity, and social justice. On the left, secular humanists and atheists and the religiously indifferent hardly fall neatly into a category that also includes progressive Protestants, Catholics, Jews, Muslims, and Hindus. Further diversity manifests itself among advocacy groups that coalesce to inform themselves about current issues—from climate change to racial discrimination and from gun violence to voter suppression—and to formulate plans for taking action.

None of this emphasis on diverse advocacy implies neglecting the quiet character-building efforts that families and schools and neighborhoods have always pursued, often with the support of faith communities. Nearly everyone agrees that congregations should play a role in helping parents instill good values in their children and supporting adults in putting their own values into practice. But character building is not enough. It too easily becomes self-absorbed, focusing on personal meaning, happiness, and individual success and too little on the value of community. Attempts to build character falter even when children learn to be kind and to value helping the needy, especially if those children also learn that morality doesn't seem to matter—a lesson they see when prominent religious leaders behave immorally and when these leaders support corrupt politicians. When religious leaders become powerful by associating with questionable beliefs and practices, the best antidote has been other religious groups and nonreligious organizations standing up for different values. Democracy depends on these opposing groups making themselves heard—rather than timidly adopting a let's-all-be-friends attitude.

Of course the fact that religious advocacy and counteradvocacy often contribute in these ways is no reason to be confident about democracy's well-being. The challenges facing America today are far deeper than whether one religious faction or another has the upper hand: an entrenched partisan division in national politics that seems to favor power grabbing and greed more than it does service to the common good, a plutocratic political economy that vastly benefits the superrich rather than generating a more equitable distribution of income, a broken immigration policy, and pervasive systemic racism, to name a few. None of what we have considered in tracing the history of religious advocacy has by itself safeguarded democracy. Yet religious groups' participation has often contributed constructively to debates about fairness, freedom, conscience, dignity, justice, and compassion.

A few years ago, it would have seemed unnecessary to write about threats to American democracy other than from foreign powers and perhaps from domestic apathy. We have been awakened to the soft spots that autocrats can exploit to their advantage and to the danger of rampant repetition of untruth, disrespect for common decency, and disregard for the widening gap between the privileged few and the majority. Those matters need to be addressed through political activism, protests, legislation, and litigation—a process that would revitalize the institutions on which American democracy was built. Also needed is sober reflection about the constructive roles that diverse religious organizations can play when they contend vigorously with one another about the meanings, practices, and implications of democracy.

NOTES

Introduction

1. Chantal Mouffe, *Agonistics: Thinking the World Politically* (London: Verso, 2013); Chantal Mouffe, "Deliberative Democracy or Agonistic Pluralism?," *Social Research* 66, no. 3 (Fall 1999): 745–58; Chantal Mouffe, "Religion, Liberal Democracy, and Citizenship," in *Political Theologies: Public Religions in a Post-secular World*, ed. Hent De Vries and Lawrence E. Sullivan (New York: Fordham University Press, 2006), 318–26; and as discussed in Marie Paxton, *Agonistic Democracy: Rethinking Political Institutions in Pluralist Times* (New York: Routledge, 2020); and Mark Wenman, "'Agonistic Pluralism' and Three Archetypal Forms of Politics," *Contemporary Political Theory* 2 (2003): 165–86. The latter draws useful comparisons among the work of Mouffe, William Connolly, and James Tully.

2. Jason A. Springs, "On Giving Religious Intolerance Its Due: Prospects for Transforming Conflict in a Post-secular Society," *Journal of Religion* 92, no. 1 (January 2012): 1–30; Jason A. Springs, *Healthy Conflict in Contemporary American Society: From Enemy to Adversary* (New York: Cambridge University Press, 2018); Mark S. Cladis, "Painting Landscapes of Religion in America: Four Models of Religion in Democracy," *Journal of the American Academy of Religion* 76, no. 4 (December 2008): 874–904. Jill Lepore observes, with characteristic clarity, "It's a paradox of democracy that the best way to defend it is to attack it, to ask more of it, by way of criticism, protest, and dissent." "In Every Dark Hour," *New Yorker*, February 3, 2020, 21.

3. Michael Kazin, "Pluralism Is Hard Work—and the Work Is Never Done," in *Christianity and American Democracy*, ed. Hugh Heclo, Mary Jo Bane, Michael Kazin, and Alan Wolfe (Cambridge, MA: Harvard University Press, 2009), 168–84, quote on page 171.

4. James Bryce, *The American Commonwealth*, 3rd ed. (New York: Macmillan, 1899; originally published 1888), 2:278.

5. The classic formulation of this argument is Seymour M. Lipset and Stein Rokkan, "Cleavage Structures, Party Systems, and Voter Alignments: An Introduction," in *Party Systems and Voter Alignments: Cross-National Perspectives*, ed. Seymour M. Lipset and Stein Rokkan (New York: Free Press, 1967), 1–67; also of relevance is Jean Bethke Elshtain's Seymour Martin Lipset lecture, in which Elshtain emphasizes voting, competitive elections, human rights, and curbs on arbitrary state power. "Religion and Democracy," *Journal of Democracy* 20, no. 2 (April 2009): 5–17.

6. These are among the reasons it makes sense to observe, as Nancy Rosenblum does, that the political face of religious organizations is relatively moderate. "Faith in America: Political Theory's Logic of Autonomy and Logic of Congruence," in *Religion and Democracy in the United*

States: Danger or Opportunity, ed. Alan Wolfe and Ira Katznelson (Princeton, NJ: Princeton University Press, 2010), 382–410.

7. An authoritative source on the history of "religious nationalism" is Philip Gorski, *American Covenant: A History of Civil Religion from the Puritans to the Present* (Princeton, NJ: Princeton University Press, 2017). On recent manifestations, excellent sources are Andrew L. Whitehead and Samuel L. Perry, *Taking America Back for God: Christian Nationalism in the United States* (New York: Oxford University Press, 2020); and Philip S. Gorski, *American Babylon: Christianity and Democracy before and after Trump* (London: Routledge, 2020). The latter traces the relationship of Christian and democratic ideals over the centuries and argues that this relationship is breaking down.

Chapter 1: Against Tyranny

1. H. Richard Niebuhr, *The Social Sources of Denominationalism* (New York: Meridian Books, 1922).

2. US Bureau of the Census, *Religious Bodies, 1916: Part I, Summary and General Tables* (Washington, DC: Government Printing Office, 1919).

3. "Church Must Aid New Deal Because Taught by Christ," *Dallas Morning News*, May 24, 1934.

4. T. H. Watkins, *Righteous Pilgrim: The Life and Times of Harold L. Ickes, 1874–1952* (New York: Henry Holt, 1990); on Ickes's religious upbringing, see Graham White and John Maze, *Harold Ickes of the New Deal: His Private Life and Public Career* (Cambridge, MA: Harvard University Press, 1985), 21–25.

5. Harold L. Ickes, *The Secret Diary of Harold L. Ickes: The First Thousand Days, 1933–1936* (New York: Simon and Schuster, 1953), 165.

6. Raymond B. Walker, "Nation's Present Period of Trial One for Exercise of Courage and Optimism," *Sunday Oregonian* (Portland, OR), September 3, 1934.

7. "As Others See Us: Dictator Roosevelt," *Living Age* 344 (July 1933): 459–77.

8. George W. Truett, "Baptists and Religious Liberty," May 16, 1920; bjconline.org.

9. Walter Friar Dexter, *Herbert Hoover and American Individualism* (New York: Macmillan, 1932).

10. Herbert Hoover to Henry L. Stoddard, July 8, 1933, Gilder Lehrman Institute of American History, New York City, gilderlehrman.org.

11. Herbert Hoover, *The Challenge to Liberty* (New York: Charles Scribner's Sons, 1934).

12. "Presbyterians Hit Economic System," *New York Times*, May 21, 1932.

13. "Churches and Labor Hold Joint Meeting," *Daily Boston Globe*, September 5, 1932.

14. "Protestants, Catholics and Jews Demand Aid for Unemployed," *American Israelite*, January 14, 1932; "New Group Backs Economic Liberty," *New York Times*, December 20, 1937.

15. "Church Urged to Avoid New Deal 'Ballyhoo' Lest Mistakes of War Days Be Repeated," *New York Times*, August 7, 1933.

16. Jonathan Gruber and Daniel M. Hungerman estimate, with national data on charitable spending for six large Christian denominations, that New Deal spending reduced church benevolent spending by 30 percent between 1933 and 1939, controlling for other variables.

"Faith-Based Charity and Crowd-Out during the Great Depression," *Journal of Public Economics* 91, no. 5–6 (June 2007): 1043–69. Positive effects of New Deal spending are discussed in Price Fishback, "How Successful Was the New Deal? The Microeconomic Impact of New Deal Spending and Lending Policies in the 1930s," *Journal of Economic Literature* 55, no. 4 (2017): 1435–85.

17. Theodore C. Wallen, "'Nest Lining' of Rich Hit by Roosevelt," *New York Herald Tribune*, December 7, 1933.

18. Henry A. Wallace, "Spiritual Forces and the State," *Forum and Century* 91, no. 6 (June 1934): 352–56, quote on page 355; elaborated in Henry A. Wallace, *Statesmanship and Religion* (New York: Round Table Press, 1934).

19. Reverend Dr. Edgar Blake, quoted in "New Deal: Church Bodies Sound the Praise and Blame of NRA," *Newsweek* 4, no. 10 (September 8, 1934): 39.

20. "NRA Is Product of Lunatic Asylum Churchmen Told," *Hartford (CT) Courant*, April 19, 1935.

21. "Churches Hurl Influence into Political Field," *Christian Science Monitor*, February 4, 1935.

22. Jay G. Hayden, "Mormon Leaders against New Deal," *Boston Globe*, October 24, 1935.

23. Roscoe Dunjee, "Baptist Prexy Scores New Deal," *Philadelphia Tribune*, September 13, 1934; "Racial Leaders Tell Why They Flock to Landon," *Chicago Daily Tribune*, October 29, 1936; Lacy K. Williams, "The New Freedom," *Plain Dealer*, October 30, 1936.

24. "Clergy Reply to Roosevelt on New Deal," *Hartford (CT) Courant*, September 26, 1935.

25. Roberto Marie Ike, "Catholic Priests and Franklin D. Roosevelt: Analysis of Clergy Consensus on the New Deal" (PhD diss., Saint Louis University, 2000).

26. Matthew Pehl, "'Apostles of Fascism,' 'Communist Clergy,' and the UAW: Political Ideology and Working-Class Religion in Detroit, 1919–1945," *Journal of American History* 99, no. 2 (September 2012): 440–65.

27. Carl Hermann Voss, *Rabbi and Minister: The Friendship of Stephen S. Wise and John Haynes Holmes* (New York: World Publishing, 1964); Melvin I. Urofsky, *A Voice That Spoke for Justice: The Life and Times of Stephen S. Wise* (Albany: State University of New York Press, 1982), 239–60.

28. Joseph Kip Kosek, *Acts of Conscience: Christian Nonviolence and Modern American Democracy* (New York: Columbia University Press, 2009), 118–22; Erik S. Gellman and Jarod Roll, *The Gospel of the Working Class: Labor's Southern Prophets in New Deal America* (Urbana: University of Illinois Press, 2011), 41–72.

29. For example, the forums discussed in "New Deal to Be Discussed at East Point," *Atlanta Daily World*, June 30, 1934; "Churchmen Hold NRA Falls Short," *New York Times*, December 15, 1933; "Yonkers Group Lauds New Deal," *New York Amsterdam News*, March 14, 1936.

30. Benson Y. Landis, "Religion," *American Journal of Sociology* 37, no. 6 (May 1932): 970–75; Arthur E. Holt, "What the Council for Social Action Proposes," *Advance* 125 (September 20, 1934): 494; "Religious Leaders Queried on Support of Social Reform," *Christian Science Monitor*, January 14, 1935; "Church Unit Urges New Social Policy," *New York Times*, March 23, 1936.

31. Robert Shaffer, "'A Missionary from the East to Western Pagans': Kagawa Toyohiko's 1936 U.S. Tour," *Journal of World History* 24, no. 3 (September 2013): 577–621; *Farm Marketing, Supply and Service Cooperative Historical Statistics*, Cooperative Information Report 1, sec. 26

(Washington, DC: US Department of Agriculture, 2004); on rural cooperatives in the Midwest, see Robert Wuthnow, *Remaking the Heartland: Middle America since the 1950s* (Princeton, NJ: Princeton University Press, 2011), 171–212.

32. William Warren Sweet, *Virginia Methodism: A History* (Richmond, VA: Whittet and Shepperson, 1955), 389–91.

33. For example, Charles C. Webber, "Methodists Turn Socialistic," *The World Tomorrow* 16, no. 19 (July 1933): 442; Marion D. Shutter, "Churches and the 'Social Order,'" *Nation's Business* 24, no. 6 (June 1936): 25.

34. Lizabeth Cohen, *Making a New Deal: Industrial Workers in Chicago, 1919–1939* (New York: Cambridge University Press, 2014), 221–28.

35. Alda Rowley Teachout, *Changes in Program and Message Made by Protestant Churches during the Depression* (Los Angeles: University of Southern California, Department of Social Work, 1937).

36. Donald R. McCoy, "The Good Neighbor League and the Presidential Campaign of 1936," *Western Political Quarterly* 13 (1960): 1011–21; Roger Daniels, *Franklin D. Roosevelt: Road to the New Deal, 1882–1939* (Urbana: University of Illinois Press, 2015), 272–73; Stanley High, "A Republican Takes a Walk," *Forum and Century* 95, no. 5 (May 1936): 261–67. During the 1936 campaign Roosevelt's staff also sought to enlist the support of Baptist, Catholic, Methodist, and Presbyterian clergy directly. Robert Dallek, *Franklin D. Roosevelt: A Political Life* (New York: Viking Penguin, 2017), 257.

37. "Dr. Peale Finds New Deal Lacks Common Sense," *New York Herald Tribune*, February 20, 1936.

38. "Ex-Yale Dean Calls Roosevelt Playboy," *New York Times*, October 9, 1935.

39. H. T. Upshaw, "Think Twice!," *Iola (KS) Register*, November 2, 1936.

40. "Clergy Resents New Deal Plot to Dictate Vote," *Chicago Daily Tribune*, May 28, 1936.

41. "Negro Clergy Join Landon's Drive," *New York Herald Tribune*, September 25, 1936.

42. "New Deal Opposed by Clergy in Poll," *New York Times*, February 21, 1936.

43. George Gallup, "Roosevelt Is Strongest with Catholics, Jews," *Washington Post*, October 11, 1936. The information was drawn from more than one hundred thousand ballots distributed nationally by mail; other results indicated that 82 percent of Jews were for Roosevelt, Lutherans leaned toward Landon by a 54 percent margin, and Congregationalists favored Landon by 78 to 22 percent.

44. Peter Whiffin, "A Priest Warns the Church," *Forum and Century* 97, no. 4 (April 1937): 195–202, quote on page 201; Alan Brinkley, *Voices of Protest: Huey Long, Father Coughlin, and the Great Depression* (New York: Vintage, 1982).

45. "Sweep Away Filth, Methodists Asked," *Dallas Morning News*, October 27, 1939; *Annual of the Southern Baptist Convention, 1935*, 60; J. B. Cranfill, "They're in Clover Now," *Dallas Morning News*, June 9, 1940.

46. "New Deal Paves Way to Tyranny, Levinson Warns," *Chicago Daily Tribune*, October 31, 1936.

47. "New Deal's Folly Told," *Los Angeles Times*, May 9, 1935.

48. Henry S. Commager, "Regimentation: A New Bogy," *Current History* 40, no. 4 (July 1934): 385–92; "Clergy Accept Roosevelt Call for Criticism," *New York Herald Tribune*, September 26, 1935.

49. "Methodists Fearful of New Deal Results," *Hartford Courant*, June 17, 1934.

50. "NRA Reveals Moral Lapse, Catholics Hear," *New York Herald Tribune*, December 25, 1933.

51. S. J. Woolf, "Chronicler of Bad Old Days Looks at the New," *New York Times*, October 31, 1937. In her autobiography Tarbell wrote, "The gist of the Bible, as it had come to me, was what I later came to call the brotherhood of man. Practically it was that we should do nothing, say nothing, that injured another." *All in the Day's Work: An Autobiography* (New York: Macmillan, 1939), 28.

52. Alison Collis Greene, *No Depression in Heaven: Religion and the Great Depression in the Mississippi Delta* (New York: Oxford University Press, 2016), 132–33.

53. "4 Bishops Join in Opposition to a Third Term," *New York Herald Tribune*, April 4, 1938; "3d Term for Roosevelt Opposed by Leaders of Nation's Churches," *New York Herald Tribune*, March 28, 1938.

54. On Catholic concerns, see Dallek, *Franklin D. Roosevelt*, 303. Although no precise indication of religious leaders' influence exists, Gallup Polls found that 35 percent of the public surveyed believed the "policies and acts of the Roosevelt Administration may lead to dictatorship" (April 1938); 45 percent said Roosevelt "has concentrated too much power in his own hands" (May 1938).

55. Frederick Rudolph, "The American Liberty League, 1934–40," *American Historical Review* 56, no. 1 (October 1950): 19–33; S. Wells Utley, "The Duty of the Church to the Social Order," *American Liberty League*, June 1935, document no. 43.

56. "Full Text of Address of Ex-Gov. Alfred E. Smith," *Boston Globe*, January 26, 1936; David M. Kennedy, *Freedom from Fear: The American People in Depression and War, 1929–1945* (New York: Oxford University Press, 1999), 281.

57. Among the league's critics was Lyndon Johnson. "Johnson Will Tell Voters of Liberty League, *Austin Statesman*, March 29, 1937.

58. Roger Shaw, "Fascism and the New Deal," *North American Review* 238, no. 6 (December 1934): 559–61. Reports indicated that members of the DuPont family provided a quarter of the organization's receipts. "Liberty League, Foe of New Deal, Expends $389,973," *Dallas Morning News*, January 3, 1936.

59. Jared A. Goldstein, "The American Liberty League and the Rise of Constitutional Nationalism," *Temple Law Review* 86 (2014): 288–330. Comparisons of the Liberty League and the 2010 Tea Party movement are made in Frank Rich, "The Billionaires Bankrolling the Tea Party," *New York Times*, August 29, 2010.

60. Michelle M. Nickerson, *Mothers of Conservatism: Women and the Postwar Right* (Princeton, NJ: Princeton University Press, 2012), 36–37.

61. Reinhold Niebuhr, *Love and Justice: Selections from the Shorter Writings of Reinhold Niebuhr*, ed. D. B. Robertson (Louisville, KY: Westminster/John Knox Press, 1957), 113.

62. Kevin M. Kruse, *One Nation under God: How Corporate America Invented Christian America* (New York: Basic Books, 2015), 3–33.

63. Stetson Kennedy, *Southern Exposure: Making the South Safe for Democracy* (Tuscaloosa: University of Alabama Press, 1991), 254.

64. Richard Neil Sheldon, "Richard Pearson Hobson: The Military Hero as Reformer during the Progressive Era" (PhD diss., University of Arizona, 1970).

65. "Brownsville Visitor Gets in Spotlight," *Heraldo de Brownsville (TX)*, August 2, 1938; Robert Wuthnow, *Red State Religion: Faith and Politics in America's Heartland* (Princeton, NJ: Princeton University Press, 2012), 143–66.

66. "Text of Speech by John H. Kirby," *Atlanta Constitution*, January 30, 1936.

67. Quoted in "Talmadge Brings Church into Fresh New Deal Attack," *Baltimore Sun*, November 22, 1935.

68. Albert L. Warner, "Landon Is Put in Race by Kansas Republicans; Talmadge Nominated," *New York Herald Tribune*, January 30, 1936. In 1929, Reverend Smith had become the national organizer for Huey Long and served in that capacity until Long was assassinated in 1935. Later, opposing the nation's intervention in World War II, Smith organized the America First Party in 1944 and ran as its candidate for president the same year. In the 1950s, he devoted his energies to the Christian Nationalist Crusade, a mass movement organized around lectures and radio broadcasts that focused on the dangers of communism but also became notorious for its racism and anti-Semitism.

69. James T. Patterson, *Congressional Conservatism and the New Deal* (Knoxville: University Press of Kentucky, 1967), 29.

70. "Bailey Warns Uplifters to Keep Hands off South," *Baltimore Sun*, November 18, 1938.

71. Matthew Avery Sutton, "Was FDR the Antichrist? The Birth of Fundamentalist Antiliberalism in a Global Age," *Journal of American History* 98, no. 4 (March 2012): 1052–74.

72. Fundamentalists were more likely than moderate evangelicals or theological conservatives within mainstream Protestant denominations to regard the New Deal in terms of prophecies about the end times. Joel A. Carpenter, *Revive Us Again: The Reawakening of American Fundamentalism* (New York: Oxford University Press, 1999), 94–95.

73. W.E.B. DuBois, *Black Reconstruction in America: An Essay toward a History of the Part Which Black Folk Played in the Attempt to Reconstruct Democracy in America, 1860–1880* (New York: Free Press, 1935); W.E.B. DuBois, "Voluntary Segregation," *Pittsburgh Courier*, May 29, 1937; on antilynching efforts, see Robert Wuthnow, *Rough Country: How Texas Became America's Most Powerful Bible-Belt State* (Princeton, NJ: Princeton University Press, 2014); on Southern resistance, see Ira Katznelson, *The New Deal and the Origins of Our Time* (New York: Liveright Publishing, 2013).

74. Allan Nevins, "A Decade Ends: A New Spirit Rises," *New York Times*, December 31, 1939.

Chapter 2: Liberty of Conscience

1. The convergence among Protestants between pacifists and realists is described in David A. Hollinger, *After Cloven Tongues of Fire: Protestant Liberalism in Modern American History* (Princeton, NJ: Princeton University Press, 2013), 56–81.

2. Horace M. Kallen, "Why Democratic Elections?," *Jewish Exponent*, May 27, 1938; on Kallen's thinking about religion and democracy, including his emphasis on discursive exchanges among diverse cultural groups, see Matthew J. Kaufman, *Horace Kallen Confronts America: Jewish Identity, Science, and Secularism* (Syracuse, NY: Syracuse University Press, 2019), 169–89.

3. C. Roland Marchand, *The American Peace Movement and Social Reform, 1889–1918* (Princeton, NJ: Princeton University Press, 1972), 323–80; William R. Marty, "A New Political Pacifism:

Churches in the Wake of the Great War," *Journal of Interdisciplinary Studies* 30, no. 1 (2018): 63–77.

4. "Sees World Peace Achieved by Churches," *New York Times,* June 28, 1929; "Peace Conference Begins Tomorrow," *Washington Post,* April 16, 1933; "Roosevelt Lauded on Peace Efforts by Baptist Parley," *Washington Post,* May 20, 1933; "Church Council Opposes U.S. Naval Building," *New York Herald Tribune,* October 9, 1933.

5. *World Tomorrow* survey conducted in 1934; summarized in Hornell Hart, "Religion," *American Journal of Sociology* 47, no. 6 (May 1942): 888–97. A 1936 poll of clergy found 56 percent opposed to sanctioning any future war. Donald B. Meyer, *The Protestant Search for Political Realism, 1919–1941* (Berkeley: University of California Press, 1960), 354.

6. Stanley High, "Churches Found Building Strong Public Opinion to Oppose War," *New York Herald Tribune,* January 28, 1933.

7. Harold Fraser, "War Called Sin by Methodists," *Boston Globe,* May 4, 1935.

8. "Church Group's Vote on Peace Is Laid to Reds," *Washington Post,* August 5, 1933; "Church Vote Gives Blow to Pacifism," *Hartford (CT) Courant,* November 18, 1935; J. Raymond Henderson, "Church Troubles Pointed Out by Atlanta Minister," *Pittsburgh Courier,* March 18, 1933.

9. "Baptists Demand Body to Ban Wars," *New York Times,* August 10, 1934.

10. "Church Union Demands End of Armaments," *New York Herald Tribune,* November 9, 1934.

11. "Seeking, Rather Desperately, to Draw a Parallel between Disarmament and Prohibition," *Baltimore Sun,* November 3, 1933.

12. World Peaceways Collected Records, 1931–1946, Swarthmore College Peace Collection.

13. John Evans, "Peace Campaign by Churchmen Grows Rapidly," *Chicago Daily Tribune,* June 12, 1941.

14. US Secretary of War, *Statement concerning the Treatment of Conscientious Objectors in the Army* (Washington, DC: Government Printing Office, 1919), 9, 16; Edward Needles Wright, *Conscientious Objectors in the Civil War* (Philadelphia: University of Pennsylvania Press, 1931).

15. Henry Cooprider Oral History Interview, Kansas State Historical Society, Kansas Memory Collection, 1970, www.kansasmemory.org.

16. Nicholas A. Krehbiel, *General Lewis B. Hershey and Conscientious Objection during World War II* (Columbia: University of Missouri Press, 2012), 50–79.

17. In fact, the Office of the Adjutant General of the Army issued a memorandum on December 19, 1917, advising that "'personal scruples against war' should be considered as constituting 'conscientious objections' and such persons should be treated in the same manner as other 'conscientious objectors.'" Furthermore, "under no circumstances should these instructions be communicated to the newspapers" because, as was stated later, "had they been made public at the time they would undoubtedly have been the means of creating a large number of insincere objectors." US Secretary of War, *Statement concerning the Treatment of Conscientious Objectors,* 17, 37.

18. John Chalberg, *Emma Goldman: American Individualist* (New York: HarperCollins, 1991). Berkman had spent fourteen years in prison from 1892 to 1906 for the attempted assassination of Henry Clay Frick.

19. *Goldman v. United States*, 245 US 474 (1918), 595.

20. Emma Goldman, *Trial and Speeches of Alexander Berkman and Emma Goldman in the United States District Court in the City of New York, July 1917* (New York: Mother Earth Publishing Association, 1917), 56–66, quote on page 64.

21. David Waldstreicher, "Radicalism, Religion, Jewishness: The Case of Emma Goldman," *American Jewish History* 80, no. 1 (Autumn 1990): 74–92, quote on page 92.

22. *Schenck v. United States*, 249 US 47 (1919).

23. *Abrams v. United States*, 316 US 616 (1919).

24. Thomas Healy, *The Great Dissent: How Oliver Wendell Holmes Changed His Mind—and Changed the History of Free Speech in America* (New York: Metropolitan Books, 2013), 194–95.

25. Senate Committee on Military Affairs, *Compulsory Military Training Service: Hearings before the Committee on Military Affairs*, 76th Cong., 1st sess. (1940), 160–61.

26. Senate Committee on Military Affairs, *Compulsory Military Training Service*, 148–49.

27. Senate Committee on Military Affairs, *Compulsory Military Training Service*, 202.

28. James F. Childress, "Reinhold Niebuhr's Critique of Pacifism," *Review of Politics* 36, no. 4 (October 1974): 467–91.

29. "Arming Shunned by Methodists," *Los Angeles Times*, June 28, 1940; "Conscience and Duty," *Washington Post*, June 12, 1939; "Urges Liberty of Conscience," *New York Herald Tribune*, May 28, 1941; "Churches and War," in *Editorial Research Reports* (Washington, DC: Congressional Quarterly Press, 1942), library.cqpress.com.

30. House Committee on Military Affairs, *Selective Compulsory Military Training and Service: Hearings, July 10 through August 14, 1940*, 76th Cong., 3rd sess. (1940), quotes on pages 184–85, 191; *United States Code*, Selective Training and Service Act of 1940, 50a U.S.C. 301–318 (1940); David M. Kennedy, *Freedom from Fear: The American People in Depression and War, 1929–1945* (New York: Oxford University Press, 1999), 633; US Selective Service System, *Conscientious Objection*, Special Monograph no. 11, vol. 1 (Washington, DC: Government Printing Office, 1950), 24–27, 318–20. The latter includes details of the relevant legislation, regulations, and service work performed by conscientious objectors.

31. *United States v. Kauten*, 133 F.2d 703 (2d Cir. 1943).

32. US Selective Service System, *Conscientious Objection*, 145. Of approximately twelve thousand cases handled by the Department of Justice, 50 percent were classified as being based on references to specific or general religious training and belief while the other 50 percent were based on personal convictions that included Bible study, beliefs about war, and moral, philosophical, and political beliefs.

33. Gilbert Ryle, "Conscience and Moral Convictions," *Analysis* 7, no. 2 (June 1940): 31–39, quotes on page 33.

34. Quoted in US Selective Service System, *Conscientious Objection*, 144.

35. Daniel R. Ernst, "State, Party, and Harold M. Stephens: The Utahn Origins of an Anti-New Dealer," *Western Legal History* 14, no. 2 (2001): 123–58, quote on page 153; *Berman v. United States*, 156 F.2d 377 (9th Cir. 1946).

36. *Berman v. United States*, 380, 384.

37. Cynthia Eller, *Conscientious Objectors and the Second World War: Moral and Religious Arguments in Support of Pacifism* (New York: Praeger, 1991).

38. Robert C. Clothier, "Destroy War's Causes," *New York Herald Tribune*, June 4, 1934.

39. Quoted in "To a War Objector," *New York Herald Tribune*, June 21, 1942.

40. "Methodists Debate War," *Baltimore Sun*, May 3, 1944.

41. John K. Ryan, "Of Pacifists," *Washington Post*, May 6, 1941.

42. Meredith Ashby Jones, "Text and Pretext: The Conscientious Objector," *Atlanta Constitution*, October 20, 1940.

43. Bertrand Russell, "The Future of Pacifism," *American Scholar* 13, no. 1 (Winter 1943–44): 7–13, quote on page 13.

44. *West Virginia State Board of Education v. Barnette*, as discussed in Harrop A. Freeman, "The Constitutionality of Peacetime Conscription," *Virginia Law Review* 31, no. 1 (December 1944): 40–82, quote on page 46.

45. Dean K. Thompson, "World War II, Interventionism, and Henry Pitney Van Dusen," *Journal of Presbyterian History* 55, no. 4 (Winter 1977): 327–45; Mark Edwards, "The 'Ecumenical Statesman': Henry Pitney Van Dusen," *Princeton University Library Chronicle* 71, no. 1 (Autumn 2009): 37–44; Henry Hemming, *Agents of Influence: A British Campaign, a Canadian Spy, and the Secret Plot to Bring America into World War II* (New York: Public Affairs, 2019), 57–60; Lynne Olson, *Those Angry Days: Roosevelt, Lindbergh, and America's Fight over World War II, 1939–1941* (New York: Random House, 2013), 161–68; Henry Van Dusen, *Life's Meaning: The Why and How of Christian Living* (New York: Association Press, 1951), 27.

46. Charles Clayton Morrison, *The Christian and the War* (Chicago: Willett and Clark, 1942); quote in "The 'Dilemma of Conscience' Presented to the Christian by War," *Christian Science Monitor*, October 31, 1942.

47. Inez Robb, "Sergeant York Tells Why He's Ready to Fight Again," *American Weekly*, May 24, 1942.

48. "That Inner Voice," *Christian Endeavor World* 58, no. 5 (November 1, 1942): 22.

49. *United States Code*, 1964 ed., title 50, *War and National Defense*, appendix, chap. 9, Universal Military Training and Service Act, 50a U.S.C. 456(j), 9566.

50. "Man in the News; Agnostic Pacifist Daniel Andrew Seeger," *New York Times*, January 21, 1964.

51. Quoted in *United States v. Seeger*, 380 US 163 (1965), 28.

52. Leo Pfeffer, Brief for the American Jewish Congress, Amicus Curiae, *United States v. Seeger*, quotes on page 13.

53. Quoted in *United States v. Seeger*, 35–36.

54. *United States v. Seeger*; also see "Constitutionality of Requiring Belief in Supreme Being for Draft Exemption as Conscientious Objector," *Columbia Law Review* 64, no. 5 (May 1964): 938–50; Robert L. Rabin, "When Is a Religious Belief Religious: *United States v. Seeger* and the Scope of Free Exercise," *Cornell Law Review* 51, no. 2 (Winter 1966): 231–49.

55. Harvard Law Review Association, "Toward a Constitutional Definition of Religion," *Harvard Law Review* 91, no. 5 (March 1978): 1056–89.

56. *Welsh v. United States*, 398 US 333 (1970). The proportion of conscientious objectors who were members of the historic peace churches fell from 51.5 percent in 1968 to 40 percent in 1970. Catholics increased from 2 percent to 8 percent, mainline Protestants from 9 percent to 19 percent, and those with no religious affiliation from 2 percent to 20 percent. "Religious

Affiliations of 1-Ws," *Reporter for Conscience' Sake* 26 (December 1970): 2; see also Jean Anne Mansavage, *"A Sincere and Meaningful Belief": Legal Conscientious Objection during the Vietnam War* (College Station: Texas A&M University Press, 2000); Andrew Koppelman, "The Story of *Welsh v. United States*: Elliott Welsh's Two Religious Tests," in *First Amendment Stories*, ed. Richard W. Garnett and Andrew Koppelman (Eagan, MN: West Group, 2011), 293–318.

57. "Local Board Memorandum No. 107," Selective Service System, July 6, 1970, included as appendix A in "Conscientious Objection and the Constitution," Congressional Research Service (1970), no. 70–212.

58. David John Frank and John W. Meyer, "The Profusion of Individual Roles and Identities in the Postwar Period," *Sociological Theory* 20, no. 1 (March 2002): 86–105.

59. Jocelyn Maclure and Charles Taylor, *Secularism and Freedom of Conscience* (Cambridge, MA: Harvard University Press, 2011), 81–84.

60. Wade Clark Roof, *Spiritual Marketplace: Baby Boomers and the Remaking of American Religion* (Princeton, NJ: Princeton University Press, 1999); Courtney Bender, *The New Metaphysicals: Spirituality and the American Religious Imagination* (Chicago: University of Chicago Press, 2010); Gerardo Marti and Gladys Ganiel, *The Deconstructed Church: Understanding Emerging Christianity* (New York: Oxford University Press, 2014).

61. Kent Greenawalt, *From the Bottom Up: Selected Essays* (New York: Oxford University Press, 2016), 438–78; Ronit Y. Stahl, "Conscience," in *Religion, Law, USA*, ed. Joshua Dubler and Isaac Weiner (New York: New York University Press, 2019), 40–58; the latter discusses similarities and differences between the Seeger case and *Burwell v. Hobby Lobby*, 573 US (2014). For a recent discussion of varying interpretations of conscience, see Lorenzo Zucca, "Conscience, Truth, and Action," *Daedalus* 149, no. 3 (Summer 2020): 135–47.

Chapter 3: Freedom of Assembly

1. Arthur M. Schlesinger, "Biography of a Nation of Joiners," *American Historical Review* 50, no. 1 (October 1944): 1–25, quote on page 23.

2. Schlesinger, "Biography of a Nation," 23.

3. Sydney E. Ahlstrom, "The Radical Turn in Theology and Ethics: Why It Occurred in the 1960s," *Annals of the American Academy of Political and Social Science* 387 (January 1970): 1–13, quote on page 1.

4. John D. Inazu, *Liberty's Refuge: The Forgotten Freedom of Assembly* (New Haven, CT: Yale University Press, 2012), 23–25.

5. Fred I. Greenstein, *The Hidden-Hand Presidency: Eisenhower as Leader* (New York: Basic Books, 1982).

6. James T. Sparrow, *Warfare State: World War II Americans and the Age of Big Government* (New York: Oxford University Press, 2011), 113–17, 242–60.

7. William I. Hitchcock, *The Age of Eisenhower: America and the World in the 1950s* (New York: Simon and Schuster, 2018).

8. George Cornell, "American Churches Pulling Together on Scale Unprecedented in History," *Austin Statesman*, January 31, 1951; Reinhold Niebuhr, "Is There a Revival of Religion?," *New York Times*, November 19, 1950.

9. Michael Hout and Andrew M. Greeley, "The Center Doesn't Hold: Church Attendance in the United States, 1940–1984," *American Sociological Review* 52, no. 3 (June 1987): 325–45. Weekly attendance was higher in 1959 than in 1950 for each of the categories examined (Protestants, Catholics, Jews, "other," and "none").

10. George Gallup, "U.S., British Polls Differ on Religion's Influence," *New York Herald Tribune*, April 21, 1957. The question about religion solving problems forced respondents to choose between that option and saying that religion was "old-fashioned and out of date." But an alternative view based on nonpolling data is given in Seymour M. Lipset, "Religion in America: What Religious Revival?," *Review of Religious Research* 1, no. 1 (Summer 1959): 17–24.

11. Robert Nisbet, *The Quest for Community: A Study in the Ethics of Order and Freedom* (New York: Oxford University Press, 1953), 46.

12. "Truman Calls on All Faiths to Fight Bigotry," *New York Herald Tribune*, November 17, 1952; "Truman Calls Religion Basis for Democracy," *New York Herald Tribune*, November 24, 1952; "Bigotry Issue Laid to Truman by Eisenhower," *Los Angeles Times*, October 24, 1952.

13. "Inter-faith Tracts Tell 'Why We Fight,'" *Hartford (CT) Courant*, May 2, 1951.

14. Kevin M. Kruse, *One Nation under God: How Corporate America Invented Christian America* (New York: Basic Books, 2015), xii. Eisenhower also proclaimed a national day of penance and prayer each year of his presidency. Gary Scott Smith, *Faith and the Presidency: From George Washington to George W. Bush* (New York: Oxford University Press, 2006), 229.

15. "Ike Approves Evangelicals' Freedom Aim," *Washington Post*, July 3, 1953.

16. "National Conference on the Spiritual Foundations of American Democracy," Central Intelligence Agency, cia.gov; "Spiritual Foundations Meeting," Presbyterian Historical Society, Pearl Digital Collections; K. Healan Gaston, "The Cold War Romance of Religious Authenticity: Will Herberg, William F. Buckley Jr., and the Rise of the New Right," *Journal of American History* 99, no. 4 (March 2013): 1133–58.

17. Harry C. Kenney, "Industrial Success Hinged to Golden Rule," *Christian Science Monitor*, February 25, 1952.

18. Conrad N. Hilton, "We Were Molded by the Spiritual," *Detroit Free Press*, June 14, 1953.

19. Frederick L. Hovde, "The Vector Factor: Our Christian Ethic," *Detroit Free Press*, June 14, 1953.

20. "Text of Address by Dulles on Foreign Policy," *New York Herald Tribune*, January 13, 1954.

21. Josephine Ripley, "The Bible in These Times," *Christian Science Monitor*, August 20, 1952.

22. Wendy Wall, *Inventing the 'American Way': The Politics of Consensus from the New Deal to the Civil Rights Movement* (New York: Oxford University Press, 2008). Wall cites a number of examples such as the Rockefeller Brothers Fund's Special Studies Project Report and President Eisenhower's Commission on National Goals.

23. "Text of Statement by Catholic Bishops on Secularism and Schools," *New York Times*, November 16, 1952.

24. "Luther Held Maker of Our Democracy," *Los Angeles Times*, October 27, 1952.

25. Canon Howard Harper, "Calvin 'Fathered' Modern Democracy," *Austin Statesman*, July 5, 1952.

26. "Rabbi Says Decalogue Ranks First," *New York Herald Tribune*, October 4, 1953.

27. Will Herberg, *Protestant-Catholic-Jew: An Essay in American Religious Sociology* (Chicago: University of Chicago Press, 1955).

28. "Hearings on Religion Called Off in Dispute," *Washington Post*, October 6, 1955. For other examples of diversity and disagreement, see Robert S. Ellwood, *The Fifties Spiritual Marketplace: American Religion in a Decade of Conflict* (New Brunswick, NJ: Rutgers University Press, 1997).

29. Gaston, "Cold War Romance," 1144–50.

30. Max Lerner, "Christian Culture and American Democracy," *American Quarterly* 6, no. 2 (Summer 1954): 126–36; "Preacher Links US Political Conformity to Religion That Ignores a Dynamic God," *New York Times*, June 28, 1954.

31. Charles R. Wright and Herbert H. Hyman, "Voluntary Association Memberships of American Adults: Evidence from National Surveys," *American Sociological Review* 23, no. 3 (June 1958): 284–94.

32. Herbert H. Hyman and Charles R. Wright, "Trends in Voluntary Association Memberships of American Adults: Replication Based on Secondary Analysis of National Sample Surveys," *American Sociological Review* 36, no. 2 (April 1971): 191–206; see also Frank R. Baumgartner and Jack L. Walker, "Survey Research and Membership in Voluntary Associations," *American Journal of Political Science* 32, no. 4 (November 1988): 908–28, who argue that the earlier studies significantly underestimated membership in voluntary associations; and Tom W. Smith, "Trends in Voluntary Group Membership: Comments on Baumgartner and Walker," *American Journal of Political Science* 34, no. 3 (August 1990): 646–61, who observes that in a 1952 survey active membership was 42 percent but simple membership was 66 percent.

33. US Department of Commerce, Bureau of the Census, *Statistical Abstract of the United States* (Washington, DC: Government Printing Office, 1954), 59–60.

34. US Department of Commerce, Bureau of the Census, *Statistical Abstract of the United States* (Washington, DC: Government Printing Office, 1962), 46–47.

35. Robert D. Putnam, *Bowling Alone: The Collapse and Revival of American Community* (New York: Simon and Schuster, 2000), 48–60.

36. Arnold M. Rose, *Theory and Method in the Social Sciences* (Minneapolis: University of Minnesota Press, 1954), 50–71.

37. William J. Novak, "The American Law of Association: The Legal-Political Construction of Civil Society," *Studies in American Political Development* 15 (Fall 2001): 163–88. Novak makes the case for the role of laws in the development of voluntary associations; this role should not be overemphasized in the case of religious organizations, though. For instance, Novak lists approximately 300 churches that were the subject of statutes in New York State prior to 1866, yet the US Census identified a total of 5,625 churches in the state in 1870; of the statutes at issue, the vast majority referred to authorizations to sell land and other real estate or to remove, repair, or build a meetinghouse. See also Alpha J. Kynett, *The Religion of the Republic and Laws of Religious Corporations: A Treatise on the American Social Structure, Civil and Religious* (Cincinnati: Cranston and Curts, 1895); and Frank Way, "Religious Disputation and the Civil Courts: Quasi-Establishment and Secular Principles," *Western Political Quarterly* 42, no. 4 (December 1989): 523–43.

38. Carl Zollman, *American Civil Church Law* (New York: Columbia University, Studies in History, Economics and Public Law, 1917), quote on page 305.

39. "Oust Rev. J. L. Horace from Chicago Church," *Chicago Defender*, August 9, 1952; "Police Boys' Club Splits with Church," *Washington Post*, November 15, 1954.

40. "The Rocky Mount Case: A History-Making Decision," *Review and Expositor*, 1954, 364–81; *Reid v. Johnston* 85 S.E. 2d 114 (1954).

41. *State v. Fowler* 83 A.2d 67 (1951); *State v. Fowler* 91 A.2d 27 (1952); Virginia Law Review Association, "Constitutional Law: Municipal Ordinance Prohibiting Political and Religious Speeches in Public Parks Held Constitutional," *Virginia Law Review* 38, no. 8 (December 1952): 1075–76; S. I. Shuman, "Freedom of Assembly: Equal Protection of the Law," *Michigan Law Review* 51, no. 8 (June 1953): 1234–36; Harvard Law Review Association, "Freedom of Speech: City Ordinance Prohibiting Political or Religious Speeches in Public Park Held Constitutional," *Harvard Law Review* 65, no. 4 (February 1952): 690–91; Slater Trust Company, "Pawtucket Past and Present," in *Rhode Island History*, book 1 (1917), Providence College Digital Commons, digitalcommons.providence.edu.

42. *Niemotko v. Maryland* 340 US 268 (1951).

43. *State v. Derrickson* 97 NH 91 (1951).

44. "Church's Plea Turned Down by Zone Board," *Chicago Daily Tribune*, July 5, 1953; "Protest Plan for Synagogue in Shop Area," *Chicago Daily Tribune*, January 19, 1958.

45. In *American Communications Association v. Douds* 339 US 382 (1950), the court noted that "indirect 'discouragements' undoubtedly have the same coercive effects upon the exercise of First Amendment rights as imprisonment, fines, injunctions or taxes. A requirement that adherents of particular religious faiths or political parties wear identifying arm-bands, for example, is obviously of this nature."

46. *DeJonge v. Oregon* 299 US 353 (1937).

47. *NAACP v. Alabama* 360 US 240 (1959); *NAACP v. Patterson* 357 US 449 (1958). The right to withhold names of members was also upheld in *Bates v. Little Rock* 361 US 516 (1960), in which the city claimed it was requesting names only to determine the tax status of the local chapter; however, as Inazu emphasizes (*Liberty's Refuge*, 85), the decision in *NAACP v. Alabama* left unclear "the source or scope of the new right of association." In other instances, non-NAACP-affiliated White antisegregation activist church groups were intimidated by their license plate numbers being recorded and their names, addresses, and businesses harassed, for example as discussed in Andrew M. Manis, "'City Mothers': Dorothy Tilly, Georgia Methodist Women, and Black Civil Rights," in *Politics and Religion in the White South*, ed. Glenn Feldman (Knoxville: University Press of Kentucky, 2005), 125–56.

48. Commission on Law and Social Action, *Assault upon Freedom of Association: A Study of the Southern Attack on the National Association for the Advancement of Colored People* (New York: American Jewish Congress, 1957).

49. See "Texas Church Council Condemns NAACP Bill," *Presbyterian Outlook* 140, no. 17 (April 28, 1958): 10, regarding a related bill under consideration by the Texas state legislature.

50. "Motion of Amici Curiae," *NAACP v. Alabama*, quotes on pages 2, 10, 11. On the disposition of the brief, see Leo Pfeffer, "Amici in Church-State Litigation," *Law and Contemporary Problems* 44, no. 2 (Spring 1981): 83–110; see also US Supreme Court, *Records and Briefs of the United States Supreme Court*, no. 91 (Washington, DC: Government Printing Office, 1957).

51. Leo Pfeffer, "What Hath God Wrought to Caesar: The Church as a Self-Interest Interest Group," *Journal of Church and State* 13, no. 1 (Winter 1971): 97–112.

52. Richard Kluger, *Simple Justice: The History of* Brown v. Board of Education *and Black America's Struggle for Equality* (New York: Vintage Books, 1977), 395; Peter B. Levy, "The Black Freedom Struggle and White Resistance: A Case Study of the Civil Rights Movement in Cambridge, Maryland," in *New Left Revisited,* ed. John McMillian and Paul Buhle (Philadelphia: Temple University Press, 2003), 67–91; Ronald Walters, "The Great Plains Sit-In Movement, 1958–60," *Great Plains Quarterly* 16 (1996): 85–94.

53. Obie McCollum, "Virginia Prayer Pilgrims," *New Journal and Guide,* January 10, 1959; letter from Wyatt Tee Walker to Dr. Martin L. King Jr., January 16, 1959, Martin Luther King, Jr. Research and Education Institute, Stanford University. Examples of subsequent activities are discussed in Simon Hall, "Civil Rights Activism in 1960s Virginia," *Journal of Black Studies* 38, no. 2 (November 2007): 251–67.

54. Elizabeth Gillespie McRae, *Mothers of Massive Resistance: White Women and the Politics of White Supremacy* (New York: Oxford University Press, 2018), 172–76; Waltraut Stein, "The White Citizens' Councils," *Negro History Bulletin* 20, no. 1 (October 1956): 2, 21–23; Charles C. Bolton, *William F. Winter and the New Mississippi: A Biography* (Jackson: University Press of Mississippi, 2013), 121–22.

55. Thomas J. Sugrue, "Crabgrass-Roots Politics: Race, Rights, and the Reaction against Liberalism in the Urban North, 1940–1964," *Journal of American History* 82, no. 2 (September 1995): 551–75; Katie J. Wells, "Saving the Neighborhood: Racially Restrictive Covenants, Law, and Social Norms," *Journal of Race and Policy* 11, no. 1 (Spring/Summer 2015): 71–75.

56. A prominent spokesperson for the right not to associate was a Virginian named Leon Dure; see Ray Niblack, "The Virginia 'Freedom of Choice' School Plan: Interview with Leon Dure," American Archive of Public Broadcasting, April 10, 1961; Leon Dure, "Letter: For Freedom of Assembly," *New York Times,* November 23, 1961; and Leon Dure, "Individual Freedom versus 'State Action,'" *Virginia Quarterly Review* 38, no. 3 (Summer 1962): 400–409. The argument against Dure's views included Hardy Cross Dillard, "Freedom of Choice and Democratic Values," *Virginia Quarterly Review* 38, no. 3 (Summer 1962): 410–35. Goldwater's remarks are quoted in "Goldwater," *St. Louis Post-Dispatch,* October 17, 1964; "Right 'Not to Associate,'" *New York Times,* October 27, 1964, and "Goldwater Touches on Civil Rights," *Christian Science Monitor,* October 20, 1964.

57. Robert T. Handy, *A History of Union Theological Seminary in New York* (New York: Columbia University Press, 1987), 252–53; Mark Wild, *Renewal: Liberal Protestants and the American City after World War II* (Chicago: University of Chicago Press, 2019).

58. Phillip E. Hammond and Robert E. Mitchell, "Segmentation of Radicalism: The Case of the Protestant Campus Minister," *American Journal of Sociology* 71, no. 2 (September 1965): 133–43.

59. "Guide to the Rev. William A. Lawson Papers, 1955–2008," Woodson Research Center, Rice University.

60. John G. Turner, *Bill Bright and Campus Crusade for Christ: The Renewal of Evangelicalism in Postwar America* (Chapel Hill: University of North Carolina Press, 2008), 93–117.

61. Howard Merry, "Tenderloin Ministry: A 'Secularized' Church Pursues Its Mission in Unorthodox Causes," *Wall Street Journal,* March 13, 1967.

62. Daniel Vaca, *Evangelicals Incorporated: Books and the Business of Religion in America* (Cambridge, MA: Harvard University Press, 2019), 147–48.

63. Robert E. Hooper, *A Distinct People: A History of the Churches of Christ in the 20ᵗʰ Century* (West Monroe, LA: Howard, 1993), 250–51.

64. Michelle M. Nickerson, *Mothers of Conservatism: Women and the Postwar Right* (Princeton, NJ: Princeton University Press, 2012), 32–68.

65. Walter W. Ruch, "End of Intolerances Everywhere Urged by Baptist World Alliance," *New York Times*, July 26, 1950; "Rights and Covenants," *Christian Science Monitor*, July 18, 1952; "Council of Churches Approves Group Aid," *Atlanta Daily World*, September 3, 1952; Walter W. Van Kirk, "Negotiations for Peace with Russia Favored by Methodist Conference," *Christian Science Monitor*, May 8, 1952; "Catholics Propose U.N. Rights Draft," *New York Times*, March 26, 1950.

66. Megan Brand, "Neighbors on the Southern Border: Republican Refugee Policy the Eisenhower Way," August 19, 2019, Berkley Center for Religion, Peace, and World Affairs, berkleycenter.georgetown.edu; Tracy Voorhees, "The Freedom Fighters: Hungarian Refugee Relief, 1956–57," Tracy Voorhees Papers, 1961, Rutgers University Libraries; Peter Pastor, "The American Reception and Settlement of Hungarian Refugees in 1956–1957," *Hungarian Cultural Studies* 9 (2016): 197–205; "Eisenhower Welcomes 12 Hungarian Refugees," *Christian Science Monitor*, November 27, 1956.

67. Gabriel Almond and Sidney Verba, *The Civic Culture: Political Attitudes and Democracy in Five Nations* (Princeton, NJ: Princeton University Press, 1963), 313.

Chapter 4: Human Dignity

1. Josiah Ober, "Democracy's Dignity," *American Political Science Review* 106, no. 4 (November 2012): 827–46; Yechiel Michael Barilan, *Human Dignity, Human Rights, and Responsibility* (Cambridge, MA: MIT Press, 2012), 93–148.

2. Jean Bethke Elshtain, "Democracy and Human Dignity," *Soundings* 87, no. 1–2 (Spring/Summer 2004): 15–26; Alan Mittleman, "Dignity and Democracy: Defending the Principle of the Sanctity of Human Life," in *Is Judaism Democratic? Reflections from Theory and Practice throughout the Ages*, ed. Leonard J. Greenspoon (West Lafayette, IN: Purdue University Press, 2018), 197–218.

3. George Kateb, *Human Dignity* (Cambridge, MA: Harvard University Press, 2011), 28–112.

4. "Text of President Truman's Foreign Policy Speech," *Washington Post*, October 18, 1950; Eleanor Roosevelt, "Transcript of Speech on Human Rights," 1951, Franklin D. Roosevelt Presidential Library and Museum, fdrlibrary.org; "The Dignity of Man," *Furrow* 5, no. 3 (March 1954): 172–79; "Church Youth Hear President," *Christian Science Monitor*, July 26, 1954.

5. Jean-Paul Sartre, *Existentialism Is a Humanism* (New York: Philosophical Library, 1946); Harold Lasswell, "Educational Broadcasters as Social Scientists," *Quarterly of Film, Radio, and Television* 7, no. 2 (Winter 1952): 150–62; Mary Ann Glendon, *A World Made: Eleanor Roosevelt and the Universal Declaration of Human Rights* (New York: Basic Books, 2001); Mark P. Lagon and Anthony Clark Arend, "Introduction: Human Dignity in a Neomedieval World," in *Human Dignity and the Future of Global Institutions*, ed. Mark P. Lagon and Anthony Clark Arend (Washington, DC: Georgetown University Press, 2014), 16.

6. Ronald Reagan, "Remarks at the New York City Partnership Luncheon in New York, January 14, 1982," Ronald Reagan Presidential Library and Museum, reaganlibrary.gov.

7. "Church League of America Presents Ronald Reagan on the Welfare State," Church League of America, n.d., Rare Book and Manuscript Library, Columbia University, Box 403.

8. Ronald Reagan, "A Time for Choosing," October 27, 1964, Ronald Reagan Presidential Library and Museum, reaganlibrary.gov.

9. Barry Goldwater, *The Conscience of a Conservative* (Shepherdsville, KY: Victor, 1960), 13.

10. Dan L. Thrapp, "Communism Fight Held Church Duty," *Los Angeles Times*, January 21, 1962; James W. Fifield Jr., "Dr. Fifield on Radio," *Los Angeles Times*, February 28, 1965. Fifield saw Auguste Comte's "positivism" as an antidote to negativism (of course badly misunderstanding Comte). "Evangelist Gives Talk on Shore," *Baltimore Sun*, September 26, 1964.

11. William F. Buckley Jr., "Churches out of Their Proper Sphere Entering Rights Battle," *Los Angeles Times*, May 25, 1964.

12. "War on Poverty Lauded by Council of Churches," *Washington Post*, May 23, 1964.

13. National Conference of Catholic Bishops, "Pastoral Statement on Race Relations and Poverty, November 19, 1966," in *Pastoral Letters of the United States Catholic Bishops*, vol. 3, *1962–1974* (Washington, DC: United States Catholic Conference, 1975), 83–90, quotes on pages 84–86.

14. Edward Farley, letter to Senator Joseph Clark, Congressional Record, Senate, July 23, 1968; Testimony of Rev. Arthur M. Brazier, in *Hearings, Reports and Prints of the Senate Committee on Government Operations* (1968), 2560–62.

15. "Welfare Leader Calls for Charity Practice," *Chicago Daily Defender*, August 25, 1965.

16. Congressional Record: Proceedings and Debates of the 89th Cong., 1st sess. (Washington, DC: Government Printing Office, 1965), 14228.

17. Helen Dewar, "Anguished Search for Help Ends with Death of Mother in Hospital," *Washington Post*, April 16, 1965.

18. Douglas Watson, "Etheridge Children Still Await City Welfare Aid," *Washington Post*, June 12, 1965.

19. Howard Gillette Jr., *Between Justice and Beauty: Race, Planning, and the Failure of Urban Policy in Washington, D.C.* (Philadelphia: University of Pennsylvania Press, 1995), 173–88; Faye P. Haskins, "The Art of D.C. Politics: Broadsides, Banners, and Bumper Stickers," *Washington History* 12, no. 2 (Fall/Winter 2000/2001): 46–63.

20. David Corbin, *The Last Great Senator: Robert C. Byrd's Encounters with Eleven U.S. Presidents* (Dulles, VA: Potomac Books, 2012).

21. Rima Vesely-Flad, *Racial Purity and Dangerous Bodies: Moral Pollution, Black Lives, and the Struggle for Justice* (Minneapolis: Fortress Press, 2017); Isabel Wilkerson, *Caste: The Origins of Our Discontents* (New York: Random House, 2020).

22. Congressional Record: Proceedings and Debates of the 89th Cong., 1st sess., 14228–43.

23. Charles A. Reich, "The New Property," *Yale Law Journal* 73, no. 5 (April 1964): 733–87, quote on page 758.

24. A 1960 study conducted in Cook County, Illinois; cited in Reich, "New Property," 762.

25. Reagan, "Remarks at the New York City Partnership Luncheon." A transcript of the lecture included in the White House Private Sector Initiatives file at the Ronald Reagan

Presidential Library and Museum shows slightly different wording: "He didn't look, then hurry on to the nearest town to find an official to help."

26. *Allgood v. Bradford* 473 So. 2d 402 (1985); Joseph L. Maxwell III, "Funding Our Children's Future: The Interplay of Funding and Regulatory Philosophies on Private Children's Homes," in *Rethinking Orphanages for the 21st Century*, ed. Richard B. McKenzie (Thousand Oaks, CA: Sage, 1999), 247–68, quote on page 262.

27. "Catholic Bishops Plead for Dignity," *New York Times*, November 22, 1953; Pope Paul VI, "Declaration on Religious Freedom," December 7, 1965; "Pope's Message Urges Respect for Dignity of Child," *Los Angeles Times*, December 26, 1979.

28. Amy L. Stone, *Gay Rights at the Ballot Box* (Minneapolis: University of Minnesota Press, 2012); Gillian Frank, "'The Civil Rights of Parents': Race and Conservative Politics in Anita Bryant's Campaign against Gay Rights in 1970s Florida," *Journal of the History of Sexuality* 22, no. 1 (January 2013): 126–60.

29. John Dart, "Churches Review Attitude on 'Gays,'" *Los Angeles Times*, July 7, 1975; Laura R. Olson and Wendy Cadge, "Talking about Homosexuality: The Views of Mainline Protestant Clergy," *Journal for the Scientific Study of Religion* 41, no. 1 (March 2002): 153–67; Wendy Cadge, "Vital Conflicts: The Mainline Denominations Debate Homosexuality," in *The Quiet Hand of God: Faith-Based Activism and the Public Role of Mainline Protestantism*, ed. Robert Wuthnow and John H. Evans (Berkeley: University of California Press, 2002), 265–86.

30. Robert Wuthnow, "Restructuring of American Religion: Further Evidence," *Sociological Inquiry* 66, no. 3 (August 1996): 303–29; Sharon Bailey, "Falwell: U.S. Creates Generation of Bums," *Atlanta Constitution*, March 14, 1981; George W. Cornell, "Religious Groups Protest Reagan's Welfare Cuts," *Washington Post*, March 6, 1982.

31. J. Zamgba Browne, "Solidarity," *New York Amsterdam News*, November 7, 1981.

32. David E. Anderson, "Church Can Help Blacks in Current Crisis," *Los Angeles Times*, February 6, 1982.

33. *The Black Leadership Family Plan for the Unity, Survival, and Progress of Black People*, February 1982, 6, blackinformationhighway.com.

34. Claudia MacLachlan and E. F. Porter Jr., "Child-Abuse Case Is Closed," *St. Louis Post-Dispatch*, December 11, 1981.

35. E. F. Porter Jr. and Claudia MacLachlan, "Agency Role in Case Is Under Study," *St. Louis Post-Dispatch*, December 13, 1981; Roger Signor, "3 Cases Daily Said to Need Medical Aid," *St. Louis Post-Dispatch*, December 13, 1981; Claudia MacLachlan and E. F. Porter Jr., "Mother Cited in Death of Son Regains Family," *St. Louis Post-Dispatch*, July 16, 1982.

36. Lewis D. Solomon, *In God We Trust? Faith-Based Organizations and the Quest to Solve America's Social Ills* (New York: Lexington Books, 2003), 133–36.

37. Sally Bixby Defty, "How 'Ordinary Folks' Can Help," *St. Louis Post-Dispatch*, March 10, 1982.

38. *Morales v. Turman*, 364 F. Supp. 166, 173 (E.D. Tex.1973); *Corpus Christi, etc. v. Tex. Dept. of Human Resources*, 481 F. Supp. 1101 (S.D. Tex. 1979); Wolfgang Saxon, "Lester Roloff, Radio Preacher, 68, Dies as His Plane Crashes in Texas," *New York Times*, November 4, 1982; John M. Crewdson, "Texas Demands That Preacher Shut Girls Home," *New York Times*, May 22, 1979; "Children in Roloff Homes Are Moved out of State," *Houston Chronicle*, December 31, 1985.

39. Confirmation Hearing on the Nomination of John Ashcroft to Be Attorney General of the United States: Hearing before the Committee of the Judiciary (Serial J-107-1), 107th Cong., 269, 467 (January 16–19, 2001) (testimony of Harriet Woods, testimony of James M. Dunn); Karen L. Koman, "Teen Homes Moving to State to Avoid Tougher Texas Rules," *St. Louis Post-Dispatch*, January 4, 1986.

40. Personal Responsibility and Work Opportunity Reconciliation Act of 1996, H.R. 3734, 104th Cong. (1995–1996).

41. Rebecca Sager, *Faith, Politics, and Power: The Politics of Faith-Based Initiatives* (New York: Oxford University Press, 2009), 52–92.

42. "Rights Group Seeking Changes in East Orange Police Structure," *New York Times*, December 19, 1975; Tom Groenfeldt, "For Minister, Civil Rights Is Not the Issue," *New York Times*, May 17, 1992; Iver Peterson, "Firebrand Considers the Post-Whitman Era," *New York Times*, December 8, 2000.

43. Rev. Dr. DeForest Soaries, "Breaking Free from Financial Slavery," Princeton University, Center for the Study of Religion, March 12, 2013, csr.princeton.edu.

44. Joel A. Carpenter, *Revive Us Again: The Remaking of American Fundamentalism* (New York: Oxford University Press, 1997); James Davison Hunter, *American Evangelicalism: Conservative Religion and the Quandary of Modernity* (New Brunswick, NJ: Rutgers University Press, 1983).

45. Marvin Olasky, *The Tragedy of American Compassion* (Wheaton, IL: Crossway, 1992), 220–21; Herb Kutchins, "Neither Alms nor a Friend: The Tragedy of Compassionate Conservatism," *Social Justice* 28, no. 1 (Spring 2001): 14–34.

46. Newt Gingrich, foreword to *Renewing American Compassion: A Citizen's Guide*, by Marvin Olasky (Washington, DC: Regnery, 1996), xiii.

47. Confirmation Hearing on the Nomination of John Ashcroft (quoted in testimony of Robert L. Woodson Sr.).

48. Confirmation Hearing on the Nomination of John Ashcroft (testimony of James M. Dunn).

49. Faith-based rehabilitation ministries were among the cases in which these constitutional issues frequently occurred, as discussed in Winnifred Fallers Sullivan, *Prison Religion: Faith-Based Reform and the Constitution* (Princeton, NJ: Princeton University Press, 2009).

50. *State ex rel. Pringle v. Heritage Baptist Temple, Inc.*, 236 Kan. 544, 693 P.2d 1163 (1985).

51. *Teen Ranch, Inc., Matthew Koch, and Mitchell Koster, Plaintiffs-appellants, v. Marianne Udow, Musette Michael, and Debora Buchanan, Defendants-appellees*, 479 F.3d 403 (6th Cir. 2007).

52. *Zelman v. Simmons-Harris*, 536 US 639 (2002).

53. *Freedom From Religion Foundation, Inc. v. McCallum*, 214 F. Supp. 2d 905 (W.D. Wis. 2002); *Winn, et al v. Garriott, et al*, no. 05-15754 (9th Cir. 2009).

54. *Zelman v. Simmons-Harris* (brief for Christian Legal Society et al.; brief for Council on Religious Freedom et al.)

55. Daniel Bennett traces the origin and significance of these organizations in *Defending Faith: The Politics of the Christian Conservative Legal Movement* (Lawrence: University Press of Kansas, 2017).

56. *John Doe, et al. v. The Boone County Prosecutor, et al.*, 06A01–1612-PL-02741 (2017); *Beth Bryant, Atascocita United Methodist Church and the Weekday Learning Center v. S.A.S. and L.O.S.,*

No. 01-12-00189–CV (2013); *Wiener v. Southcoast Childcare Centers*, 107 Cal.App.4th 1429 (2003).

57. *DSS v. Emmanuel Baptist Preschool*, 434 Mich. 380 (1990).

58. *Pedreira, et al. v. Kentucky Baptist Homes for Children, et al.*, no. 08–5538 (2009); *Pedreira, et al v. Sunrise Children's Services, et al.*, no. 3:2000cv00210—Document 505 (W.D. Ky. 2013).

59. *Williams v. Strickland*, 837 F. Supp. 1049 (N.D. Cal. 1993).

60. *United States v. Carr*, 202 F. Supp.2d 467 (E.D.N.C. 2002).

61. *Ryan v. Holy Trinity Evangelical Lutheran Church*, A-116/117–01 (2003).

62. *People v. Hodges*, no. 121292 (1992); *Westminster Presbyterian Church of Muncie v. Yonghong Cheng and Hongjun Niu*, no. 18A02–1210-CT-791 (2013).

63. Sullivan, *Prison Religion*, 18.

Chapter 5: Inclusion

1. *2002 Yearbook of Immigration Statistics* (Washington, DC: Office of Immigration Statistics, US Department of Homeland Security, 2003); *2010 Yearbook of Immigration Statistics* (Washington, DC: Office of Immigration Statistics, US Department of Homeland Security, 2011).

2. "The Foreign-Born Population in the United States: 2010," *American Community Survey Reports* (Washington, DC: US Census Bureau, 2012).

3. "The Religious Affiliation of U.S. Immigrants: Majority Christian, Rising Share of Other Faiths," Pew Research Center, May 17, 2013. A study that was not limited to legal permanent residents found that a fifth of new immigrants identified with a faith other than Christianity. Douglas S. Massey and Monica Espinoza Higgins, "The Effect of Immigration on Religious Belief and Practice: A Theologizing or Alienating Experience?," *Social Science Research* 40, no. 5 (September 2011): 1371–89.

4. Bryan Baker and Nancy Rytina, "Estimates of the Unauthorized Immigrant Population Residing in the United States: January 2012," *Population Estimates*, March 2013, 3.

5. Bradley Jones, "Majority of Americans Continue to Say Immigrants Strengthen the U.S.," Pew Research Center, January 31, 2019.

6. "Religion and Politics: Contention and Consensus," Pew Research Center, July 24, 2003.

7. Christopher Smith, "Anti-Islamic Sentiment and Media Framing during the 9/11 Decade," *Journal of Religion and Society* 15 (2013): 1–15; Yvonne Haddad and Nazir Harb, "Post-9/11: Making Islam an American Religion," *Religions* 5, no. 2 (2014): 477–501.

8. Bradley Jones, "Americans' View of Immigrants Marked by Widening Partisan, Generational Divides," Pew Research Center, April 15, 2016.

9. Rachel L. Swarns, "Senate, in Bipartisan Act, Passes Immigration Bill," *New York Times*, May 26, 2006.

10. Oscar Handlin, *The Uprooted: The Epic Story of the Great Migrations That Made the American People* (Boston: Little, Brown, 1951), 185.

11. Milton Gordon, *Assimilation in American Life: The Role of Race, Religion, and National Origins* (New York: Oxford University Press, 1964); Will Herberg, *Protestant, Catholic, Jew: An Essay in Religious Sociology* (Garden City, NY: Doubleday, 1960); Jay P. Dolan, *The American Catholic Experience* (Garden City, NY: Doubleday, 1985); Marshall Sklare, *America's Jews* (New

York: Random House, 1971); Herbert J. Gans, "Symbolic Ethnicity: The Future of Ethnic Groups and Cultures in America," *Ethnic and Racial Studies* 2, no. 1 (1979): 1–20.

12. Alejandro Portes and Rubén G. Rumbaut, *Immigrant America: A Portrait*, 4th ed. (Berkeley: University of California Press, 2014), 306–70; Alejandro Portes and Min Zhou, "The New Second Generation: Segmented Assimilation and Its Variants," *Annals of the American Academy of Political and Social Science* 530 (November 1993): 74–96; Peggy Levitt and B. Nadya Jaworsky, "Transnational Migration Studies: Past Developments and Future Trends," *Annual Review of Sociology* 33 (2007): 129–56.

13. Sarah Song, *Immigration and Democracy* (New York: Oxford University Press, 2019); Lea M. Klarenbeek and Marjukka Weide, "The Participation Paradox: Demand for and Fear of Immigrant Participation," *Critical Policy Studies* 1 (2019): 1–19.

14. Massey and Higgins, "Effect of Immigration on Religious Belief and Practice."

15. Charles Hirschman, "The Role of Religion in the Origins and Adaptation of Immigrant Groups in the United States," *International Migration Review* 28 (2004): 1206–34; J. Benjamin Taylor, Sarah Allen Gershon, and Adrian D. Pantoja, "Christian America? Understanding the Link between Churches, Attitudes, and 'Being American' among Latino Immigrants," *Politics and Religion* 7, no. 2 (2014): 339–65; Mae M. Ngai, "Brokering Inclusion: Education, Language, and the Immigrant Middle Class," in *Citizenship, Borders, and Human Needs*, ed. Rogers M. Smith (Philadelphia: University of Pennsylvania Press, 2011), 135–56.

16. Faiqa Mahmood, "Understanding Effective Civic Engagement: The Muslim Community Association of the San Francisco Bay Area," Institute for Social Policy and Understanding, 2016, ispu.org.

17. Margarita Mooney, "The Catholic Church's Institutional Responses to Immigration: From Supranational to Local Engagement," in *Religion and Social Justice for Immigrants*, ed. Pierrette Hondagneu-Sotelo (New Brunswick, NJ: Rutgers University Press, 2007), 157–71.

18. Nancy Foner and Richard Alba, "Immigrant Religion in the U.S. and Western Europe: Bridge or Barrier to Inclusion?," *International Migration Review* 42, no. 2 (2008): 360–92; Robert Wuthnow and Conrad Hackett, "The Social Integration of Practitioners of Non-western Religions in the United States," *Journal for the Scientific Study of Religion* 42, no. 4 (December 2003): 651–67. Phillip Connor and Matthias Koenig emphasize the relatively more religious climate overall in the United States than in Europe in "Bridges and Barriers: Religion and Immigrant Occupational Attainment across Integration Contexts," *International Migration Review* 47, no. 1 (Spring 2013): 3–38. See also Phillip Connor, *Immigrant Faith: Patterns of Immigrant Religion in the United States, Canada, and Western Europe* (New York: New York University Press, 2014). On language skills, see Mona M. Abo-Zena and Meenal Rana, "Religion," in *Transitions: The Development of Children of Immigrants*, ed. Carola Suárez-Orozco, Mona M. Abo-Zena, and Amy K. Marks (New York: New York University Press, 2015), 80–96.

19. Elaine Howard Ecklund, *Korean American Evangelicals: New Models for Civic Life* (New York: Oxford University Press, 2006), 52–74; Michael A. Stoll and Janelle S. Wong, "Immigration and Civic Participation in a Multiracial and Multiethnic Context," *International Migration Review* 41, no. 4 (Winter 2007): 880–908; Young-joo Lee and Seong-Gin Moon, "Mainstream and Ethnic Volunteering by Korean Immigrants in the United States," *Voluntas* 22 (2011): 811–30.

20. Robert Wuthnow, *America and the Challenges of Religious Diversity* (Princeton, NJ: Princeton University Press, 2005), 188–229; see also Pazit Ben-Nun Bloom, Gizen Arikan, and Marie Courtemanche, "Religious Social Identity, Religious Belief, and Anti-immigration Sentiment," *American Political Science Review* 109, no. 2 (May 2015): 203–21; Stephen M. Merino, "Religious Diversity in a 'Christian Nation': The Effects of Theological Exclusivity and Interreligious Contact on the Acceptance of Religious Diversity," *Journal for the Scientific Study of Religion* 49, no. 2 (June 2010): 231–46.

21. Wuthnow, *America and the Challenges of Religious Diversity*.

22. R. Stephen Warner, *A Church of Our Own: Disestablishment and Diversity in American Religion* (New Brunswick, NJ: Rutgers University Press, 2005); Christian Smith, *American Evangelicalism: Embattled and Thriving* (Chicago: University of Chicago Press, 1998).

23. Ruth Braunstein, "Muslims as Outsiders, Enemies, and Others: The 2016 Presidential Election and the Politics of Religious Exclusion," *American Journal of Cultural Sociology* 5, no. 3 (2017): 355–72; Jessamin Birdsall, "White Evangelicals for Trump," *Books and Ideas*, November 3, 2016; Cary Beckwith, "Of Mosques and Men," *New Republic*, January 31, 2016; Robert Wuthnow, *The Left Behind: Decline and Rage in Small-Town America* (Princeton, NJ: Princeton University Press, 2018).

24. Sharon Cornelissen, "National Politics, Neighborly Politics: How Trump's Election Impacted a Black and White Detroit Community," *Sociological Forum* 35, no. 1 (March 2020): 1–20.

25. Susanna Snyder, Holly Bell, and Noel Busch-Armendariz, "Immigration Detention and Faith-Based Organizations," *Social Work* 60, no. 2 (2015): 165–73; Donald Kerwin and Mike Nicholson, "The Effects of Immigration Enforcement on Faith-Based Organizations: An Analysis of the FEER Survey," *Journal on Migration and Human Security* 7, no. 2 (2019): 42–51; Laurie Goodstein, "Christian Leaders Denounce Trump's Plan to Favor Christian Refugees," *New York Times*, January 29, 2017.

26. Irene Bloemraad, Kim Voss, and Taeku Lee, "The Protests of 2006: What Were They, How Do We Understand Them, Where Do We Go?," in *Rallying for Immigrant Rights: The Fight for Inclusion in 21ˢᵗ Century America*, ed. Kim Voss and Irene Bloemraad (Berkeley: University of California Press, 2011), 3–43.

27. Robert Wuthnow, *Rough Country: How Texas Became America's Most Powerful Bible-Belt State* (Princeton, NJ: Princeton University Press, 2014), 430.

28. Luisa Heredia, "From Prayer to Protest: The Immigrant Rights Movement and the Catholic Church," in *Rallying for Immigrant Rights: The Fight for Inclusion in 21ˢᵗ Century America*, ed. Kim Voss and Irene Bloemraad (Berkeley: University of California Press, 2011), 101–22.

29. Kraig Beyerlein, David Sikkink, and Edwin Hernandez, "Citizenship, Religion, and Protest: Explaining Latinos' Differential Participation in the 2006 Immigrant Rights Marches," *Social Problems* 66 (2019): 163–93. The study also found additional variations in protest participation that were associated with levels of religious involvement and differences between first- or second- and third-generation Latinos.

30. Robert Pear, "A Million Faxes Later, a Little-Known Group Claims a Victory on Immigration," *New York Times*, July 15, 2007; Roy Beck, "Americans of All Religions Join NumbersUSA in Pushing a Moral Policy of Lower Immigration Numbers," NumbersUSA, May 19, 2009.

31. Wuthnow, *Rough Country*, 431. Biblical literalism apparently emphasized "law and order" and thus hindered protest involvement among Latino noncitizens. Beyerlein, Sikkink, and Hernandez, "Citizenship, Religion, and Protest."

32. Samuel Freedman, "Church Expands Mission to Immigration Advocacy," *New York Times*, September 8, 2007.

33. Julia Preston, "Latino Leaders Use Churches in Census Bid," *New York Times*, December 23, 2009.

34. Paul E. Ceruzzi, *Internet Alley: High Technology in Tysons Corner, 1945–2005* (Cambridge, MA: MIT Press, 2008), 53–68.

35. Samuel G. Freedman, "Delays in Muslims' Cases Spur Interfaith Call to Action," *New York Times*, September 5, 2009; Voice for Justice, Virginians Organized for Interfaith Community Engagement, January 2020, voice-iaf.org.

36. Amanda Kolson Hurley, *Radical Suburbs: Experimental Living on the Fringes of the American City* (Cleveland, OH: Belt Publishing, 2019); Michael Freedman-Schnapp, "Reston, We Have a Problem," Greater Greater Washington, May 8, 2019; ggwash.org.

37. "Reston Master Plan Report," March 10, 1962, George Mason University, Planned Community Archives.

38. Herbert Gans, "Some Assumptions and Predictions," June 22, 1963, George Mason University, Planned Community Archives.

39. "The Voice of Reason: Reston Citizens Association," 1994, George Mason University, Planned Community Archives.

40. John T. Dockery, "Tactical Considerations for 'New Town' Citizens Groups: An Urban Guerrilla Warfare Manual," 1967, George Mason University, Planned Community Archives; Carlos Marighella, *Mini-Manual of the Urban Guerrilla* (Chico, CA: Abraham Guillen Press, 1970); see also Nicholas Dagen Bloom, *Suburban Alchemy: 1960s New Towns and the Transformation of the American Dream* (Columbus: Ohio State University Press, 2001), 94.

41. United Christian Parish's founding denominations were United Methodist, Disciples of Christ, United Church of Christ, United Presbyterian, and Presbyterian Church (USA); its mission statement included "building justice beyond charity"; between 1964 and 1981 its membership grew from 500 to 1,300. "United Christian Church: A Simple, Logical Approach," *Washington Post*, August 1, 1981.

42. Sylvia F. Fava, "Diversity in Reston at 20: Is the Glass Half-Empty or Half-Full," May 1985, George Mason University, Planned Community Archives.

43. "Herndon, Va.'s Labors," *New York Times*, August 18, 2007; Marie Price and Audrey Singer, "Edge Gateways: Immigrants, Suburbs, and the Politics of Reception in Metropolitan Washington," in *Twenty-First Century Gateways: Immigrant Incorporation in Suburban America*, ed. Audrey Singer, Susan W. Hardwick, and Caroline B. Brettell (Washington, DC: Brookings Institution Press, 2008), 137–68.

44. Abel Valenzuela Jr., Nik Theodore, Edwin Melendez, and Ana Luz Gonzalez, *On the Corner: Day Labor in the United States* (Los Angeles: University of California, Los Angeles, Center for the Study of Urban Poverty, 2006).

45. James Barron, "Churches to Offer Sanctuary," *New York Times*, May 9, 2007.

46. Wendy Cole, "Elvira Arellano," *Time*, December 25, 2006; Gretchen Ruethling, "Chicago Woman's Stand Stirs Immigration Debate," *New York Times*, August 19, 2006; Pepe Lozano, "Born in the USA, Don't Take Our Parents Away," *People's Weekly World*, September 21, 2007.

47. Pepe Lozano, "In Sanctuary, Mexican Mother Fights for Dignity," *People's Weekly World*, February 9, 2008; Laura Carlsen, "Under NAFTA, Mexico Suffered, and the United States Felt Its Pain," *New York Times*, November 24, 2013.

48. Grace Yukich, *One Family under God: Immigration Politics and Progressive Religion in America* (New York: Oxford University Press, 2013), 219.

49. Manya Brachear Pashman, "Pro-immigrant Rights Pilsen Church Vandalized Twice," *Chicago Tribune*, March 30, 2016; Walter L. Coleman, *Elvira's Faith: The Grassroots Struggle for the Rights of Undocumented Families* (Chicago: Wrightwood Press, 2017); Esther Morales Guzman, "Imprisonment, Deportation, and Family Separation: My American Nightmare," *Social Justice* 36, no. 2 (2009–10): 106–9.

50. Julia C. Mead, "4 Are Held in Attack on Mexican Immigrants," *New York Times*, June 15, 2006; Robin Rinn, "Immigrants Say Slaying Brings Bias to the Fore," *New York Times*, November 23, 2008; "FBI Releases 2011 Hate Crime Statistics," FBI National Press Office, December 10, 2012; Altaf Husain and Stephenie Howard, "Religious Microaggressions: A Case Study of Muslim Americans," *Journal of Ethnic and Cultural Diversity in Social Work* 26, no. 1–2 (2017): 139–52.

51. Tom Rosentiel, "Attitudes toward Immigration: In the Pulpit and the Pew," Pew Research Center, April 25, 2006.

52. "Understanding the Muslim Ban," June 2019, National Immigrant Law Center, nilc.org.

53. Polled in 2017, 78 percent of White evangelicals approved of the way Trump was handling his job as president and 51 percent thought there was a great deal or fair amount of extremism among US Muslims. Michael Lipka, "Muslims and Islam," Pew Research Center, August 9, 2017; Philip Schwadel and Gregory A. Smith, "Evangelical Approval of Trump Remains High," Pew Research Center, March 18, 2019.

54. Josh Nathan-Kazis, "At Interfaith Rally against Trump's Muslim Ban, Prayers for Resistance," *Forward*, January 27, 2017; Josh Nathan-Kazis, "At JFK Protest against Muslim Ban, Cries of 'Never Again,'" *Forward*, January 28, 2017; Bob Allen, "Baptists Weigh in on Muslim Travel Ban," *Baptist News Global*, January 30, 2017; "US Bishops, Others Oppose Trump Executive Order Addressing Refugee Admissions," *Nation*, January 30, 2017; "Trump's Action Banning Refugees Brings Outcry from US Church Leaders," Catholic News Service, January 30, 2017.

55. Emily K. Alhadeff, "*JFS v. Trump*," *Jewish in Seattle Magazine*, February 14, 2018; Martha Bellisle, "Judge Considers Lifting Travel Ban on Entry of Refugees, Families," Associated Press, December 21, 2017.

56. *Jewish Family Service of Seattle, et al. v. Donald Trump, et al.* 18–35026 (January 11, 2018); *Jewish Family Services, et al. v Donald Trump, et al.* C17–1707JLR (December 23, 2017), 21; "Understanding the Muslim Ban."

57. Nina Totenberg, "In Big Win for White House, Supreme Court Upholds President Trump's Travel Ban," National Public Radio, June 26, 2018.

286 NOTES TO CHAPTER 6

58. Ruth Braunstein, "Muslims as Outsiders, Enemies, and Others: The 2016 Presidential Election and the Politics of Religious Exclusion," *American Journal of Cultural Sociology* 5 (2017): 355–72.

59. Jack Jenkins, "Faith Groups Overwhelmingly Condemn Trump's Decision to Phase Out DACA," *Think Progress*, September 5, 2017.

60. Julie Hirschfeld Davis and Michael D. Shear, "How Trump Came to Enforce a Practice of Separating Migrant Families," *New York Times*, June 18, 2018; Phillip Pullella, "Pope Francis Slams Trump's Family Separation Policy as 'Immoral,'" Reuters, June 20, 2018; Mary Alice Parks, "Religious Leaders Implore Trump White House: Stop Separating Immigrant Families," *ABC News*, June 14, 2018.

61. See the excellent treatment of political theory on these questions in Sarah Song, *Immigration and Democracy* (New York: Oxford University Press, 2018).

62. Heide Castaneda contrasts deservingness criteria in Germany and the United States in "Deportation Deferred: 'Illegality,' Visibility, and Recognition in Contemporary Germany," in *The Deportation Regime: Sovereignty, Space, and the Freedom of Movement*, ed. Nicholas De Genova and Nathalie Peutz (Durham, NC: Duke University Press, 2010), 245–61.

63. Engin Isin, "Performative Citizenship," in *The Oxford Handbook of Citizenship*, ed. Ayelet Shachar, Rainer Bauböck, Irene Bloemraad, and Maarten Vink (New York: Oxford University Press, 2017), 500–25; Charles Tilly, *Contentious Performances* (New York: Cambridge University Press, 2008).

Chapter 6: The Wealth Gap

1. Thomas Jefferson to James Madison, October 28, 1785, in *The Papers of Thomas Jefferson Digital Edition*, ed. James P. McClure and J. Jefferson Looney (Charlottesville: University of Virginia Press, 2020), Main Series, 8: 682–83.

2. Noah Webster, *A Collection of Essays and Fugitiv Writings on Moral, Historical, Political and Literary Subjects* (Boston, 1790), 328–32, reprinted in *The Founders' Constitution*, ed. Philip B. Kurland and Ralph Lerner (Chicago: University of Chicago Press, 1987), vol. 1, chap. 15, doc. 44.

3. Alexis de Tocqueville, *Democracy in America* (New York: Harper and Row, 1988), vol. 2, chap. 8.

4. Nathan O. Hatch, *The Democratization of American Christianity* (New Haven, CT: Yale University Press, 1989). On the growing criticism of wealth concentration in the 1870s and 1880s, see Robert R. Roberts, "The Social Gospel and the Trust Busters," *Church History* 25, no. 3 (1956): 239–57.

5. Francis Asbury, *The Journal and Letters of Francis Asbury*, ed. Elmer C. Clark, J. Manning Potts, and Jacob S. Payton (Nashville: Asbury Press, 1958), 3:475–76.

6. John Errett Lankford, *Protestant Stewardship and Benevolence, 1900–1941: A Study in Religious Philanthropy* (PhD diss., University of Wisconsin, 1962); Merle Curti, Judith Green, and Roderick Nash, "Anatomy of Giving: Millionaires in the Late 19th Century," *American Quarterly* 15 (1963): 416–35; Bruce J. Evensen, *God's Man for the Gilded Age: D. L. Moody and the Rise of Modern Mass Evangelism* (New York: Oxford University Press, 2003); Robert P. Wilder, *The*

Student Volunteer Movement: Its Origins and Early History (New York: Student Volunteer Movement, 1935).

7. Kevin M. Kruse, *One Nation under God: How Corporate America Invented Christian America* (New York: Basic Books, 2015), 3–34; Grant Wacker, *America's Pastor: Billy Graham and the Shaping of a Nation* (Cambridge, MA: Harvard University Press, 2014), 154–56; Darren Dochuk, *Anointed with Oil: How Christianity and Crude Made Modern America* (New York: Basic Books, 2019), 353–63.

8. Walter Rauschenbusch, *Christianity and the Social Crisis* (New York: Macmillan, 1907), 218; Christopher H. Evans, *The Social Gospel in American Religion: A History* (New York: New York University Press, 2017), 79–83; Christopher H. Evans, "Ties That Bind: Walter Rauschenbusch, Reinhold Niebuhr, and the Quest for Economic Justice," *Soundings* 95, no. 4 (2012): 351–69.

9. Richard P. Poethig, "Charles Stelzle and the Roots of Presbyterian Industrial Mission," *Journal of Presbyterian History* 77, no. 1 (Spring 1999): 29–36.

10. "Rerum Novarum," *The Tablet*, May 23, 1891; John A. Ryan, *Distributive Justice: The Right and Wrong of Our Present Distribution of Wealth* (New York: Macmillan, 1916), 256–57.

11. Robert H. Wiebe, *The Search for Social Order, 1877–1920* (New York: Hill and Wang, 1967); Ronald C. White, *The Social Gospel: Religion and Reform in Changing America* (Philadelphia: Temple University Press, 1976).

12. Walter Rauschenbusch, "The New Evangelism," *The Independent* 56 (May 12, 1904): 1055–56; Evans, *Social Gospel in American Religion*, 84.

13. Charles Stelzle, "Rockefeller, Jr. Scores Employers for Ignorance of Great Labor Problems," *Rockford (IL) Morning Star*, March 25, 1917.

14. Quoted in Aaron I. Abell, "Monsignor John A. Ryan: An Historical Appreciation," *Review of Politics* 8, no. 1 (1946): 128–34, quote on page 132.

15. B. M. Pietsch, "Lyman Stewart and Early Fundamentalism," *Church History* 82, no. 3 (September 2013): 617–46.

16. Melissa J. Wilde and Sabrina Danielsen, "Fewer and Better Children: Race, Class, Religion, and Birth Control Reform in America," *American Journal of Sociology* 119, no. 6 (May 2014): 1710–60; Evans, *Social Gospel in American Religion*, 135–92; June Hopkins, *Harry Hopkins: Sudden Hero, Brash Reformer* (New York: St. Martin's Press, 1999), 17; George Dugan, "Liberal Sermons Split Church," *New York Times*, April 13, 1953.

17. Thomas Piketty and Emmanuel Saez, "Income Inequality in the United States, 1913–1998," *Quarterly Journal of Economics* 108, no. 1 (February 2003): 1–39; Emmanuel Saez and Gabriel Zucman, "Wealth Inequality in the United States since 1913: Evidence from Capitalized Income Tax Data," National Bureau of Economic Research Working Paper 20625, October 2014; Chad Stone, Danilo Trisi, Arloc Sherman, and Jennifer Beltran, "A Guide to Statistics on Historical Trends in Income Inequality," Center on Budget and Policy Priorities, January 13, 2020; Walter Scheidel and Steven J. Friesen, "The Size of the Economy and the Distribution of Income in the Roman Empire," *Journal of Roman Studies* 99 (November 2009): 61–91.

18. Congressional Budget Office, *Trends in the Distribution of Household Income between 1979 and 2007*, October 2011; Congressional Budget Office, *The Role of Immigrants in the U.S. Labor Market*, November 2005; David Card, *Immigration and Inequality*, National Bureau of Economic

Research Working Paper 14683 (Cambridge, MA: National Bureau of Economic Research, January 2009), estimated that immigration accounted for approximately 5 percent of the increase in US wage inequality between 1980 and 2000; Ping Xu, James C. Garand, and Ling Zhu, "Imported Inequality? Immigration and Income Inequality in the American States," *State Politics and Policy Quarterly* 16, no. 2 (June 2016): 147–71.

19. Fabrizio Perri, "Inequality, Recessions and Recoveries," 2013 Annual Report Essay, Federal Reserve Bank of Minneapolis, 2013.

20. "US Income and Wealth Inequality," Deutsche Bank Research, January 2018; "Distribution of Aggregate Household Wealth," Deutsche Bank Research, November 2019; Sylvia A. Allegretto, "The State of Working America's Wealth, 2011," Economic Policy Institute Briefing Paper, March 2011.

21. Martin Gilens, *Affluence and Influence: Economic Inequality and Political Power in America* (Princeton, NJ: Princeton University Press, 2012); Larry M. Bartels, *Unequal Democracy: The Political Economy of the New Gilded Age*, 2nd ed. (Princeton, NJ: Princeton University Press, 2016); Kenneth Scheve and David Stasavage, *Taxing the Rich: A History of Fiscal Fairness in the United States and Europe* (Princeton, NJ: Princeton University Press, 2016); Kenneth Scheve and David Stasavage, "Wealth Inequality and Democracy," *Annual Review of Political Science* 20 (2017): 451–68; Jeffrey A. Winters, "Oligarchy in the United States?," *Perspectives on Politics* 7, no. 4 (2009): 731–51; Jeffrey A. Winters, *Oligarchy* (New York: Cambridge University Press, 2011); *World Social Report 2020: Inequality in a Rapidly Changing World* (New York: United Nations, Department of Economic and Social Affairs, 2020); Alon Yakter, "The Heterogeneous Effect of Diversity: Ascriptive Identities, Class, and Redistribution in Developed Democracies," *European Journal of Political Research* 58, no. 1 (2019): 315–40.

22. Jeffrey A. Winters, "Democracy and Oligarchy," *American Interest*, November/December 2011, 1–27; Paul Starr, *Entrenchment: Wealth, Power, and the Constitution of Democratic Societies* (New Haven, CT: Yale University Press, 2019), 191–92.

23. Angela Farizo McCarthy, Nicholas T. Davis, and James C. Garand, "Religion and Attitudes toward Redistributive Policies among Americans," *Political Research Quarterly* 69, no. 1 (2016): 121–33, although age and race explain significantly more variation than religious attendance and conservatism; Vivekinan Ashok, Ilyana Kuziemko, and Ebonya Washington, "Support for Redistribution in an Age of Rising Inequality," *Brookings Papers on Economic Activity*, Spring 2015, 367–433. A modification of the usual relationship, though, is noted in Robert A. Thomson and Paul Froese, "God, Party, and the Poor: How Politics and Religion Interact to Affect Economic Justice Attitudes," *Sociological Forum* 33, no. 2 (2018): 334–53.

24. Ceyhun Elgin, Turkmen Goksel, Mehmet Y. Gurdal, and Cuneyt Orman, "Religion, Income Inequality and the Size of the Government," *Economic Modelling* 30 (2013): 225–34; Oguzhan C. Dincer and Michael J. Hotard, "Ethnic and Religious Diversity and Income Inequality," *Eastern Economic Journal* 37 (2011): 417–30; Oguzhan C. Dincer and Peter J. Lambert, "Taking Care of Your Own: Ethnic and Religious Heterogeneity and Income Inequality," *Journal of Economic Studies* 39, no. 3 (2012): 290–313; Amjad Naveed and Cong Wang, "Can Religion Explain Cross-Country Differences in Inequality? A Global Perspective," *Social Choice and Welfare* 50 (2018): 481–518; Lisa A. Keister, *Faith and Money: How Religion Contributes to Wealth and Poverty* (New York: Cambridge University Press, 2013); Sedefka V. Beck and Donka Mirtcheva

Brodersen, "The Great Recession and Wealth in the United States: Differentials by Religious Affiliation," *International Journal of Social Economics* 45, no. 9 (2018): 1335–54.

25. Mark Chaves, "Religious Congregations," in *The State of Nonprofit America*, ed. Lester M. Salamon (Washington, DC: Brookings Institution Press, 2012), 362–93.

26. Robert Wuthnow, *Saving America? Faith-Based Services and the Future of Civil Society* (Princeton, NJ: Princeton University Press, 2004), 25–62.

27. "History of ICCR," Interfaith Center on Corporate Responsibility, May 2020; iccr.org.

28. Robert J. Regan, "Big Business Feels Impact of Church Wealth," *Chicago Tribune*, August 13, 1967; George W. Cornell, "Equality Pushed by Church Buyers," *Austin Statesman*, June 16, 1967.

29. Clergy and Laity Concerned Records, 1965–1983, Swarthmore College Peace Collection; Richard Gibson, "Militants, Pacifists Demand End of Honeywell's War Production," *Minneapolis Star*, April 28, 1970; Dick Youngblood, "Honeywell Critics Remain in Minority," *Minneapolis Tribune*, April 26, 1973; Russell Chandler, "Church Leaders Ask End to Salvador Aid," *Los Angeles Times*, February 23, 1982.

30. Chris Whitcraft, "Private, Non-profit Council Seeks Social Responsibility," *Austin Statesman*, May 5, 1970; Marylin Bender, "Investments: For Good or Gold?," *New York Times*, March 19, 1972.

31. Martin Skala, "Firms Start to Tackle 'Social Responsibility,'" *Christian Science Monitor*, October 6, 1970; Milton Friedman, "The Social Responsibility of Business Is to Increase Its Profits," *New York Times*, September 13, 1970; Archie B. Carroll, "A History of Corporate Social Responsibility: Concepts and Practices," in *The Oxford Handbook of Corporate Social Responsibility*, ed. Andrew Crane, Dirk Matten, Abagail McWilliams, Jeremy Moon, and Donald S. Siegel (New York: Oxford University Press, 2008), 20–48.

32. Jarol B. Manheim, *The Death of a Thousand Cuts: Corporate Campaigns and the Attack on the Corporation* (Mahwah, NJ: Lawrence Erlbaum, 2001), 48; Lynn Robinson, "Doing Good and Doing Well: Shareholder Activism, Responsible Investment, and Mainline Protestantism," in *The Quiet Hand of God: Faith-Based Activism and the Public Role of Mainline Protestantism*, ed. Robert Wuthnow and John H. Evans (Berkeley: University of California Press, 2002), 343–63.

33. Dan Crosby, "Inspired by Faith, Committed to Action," Marquette University, October 16, 2018, Capuchin Franciscan Province of St. Joseph, thecapuchins.org; Ginger K. Hedstrom, "Investing to Make a Difference," *Justice Matters*, October 8, 2013; Dorothy Pagosa, "Investment Aligned with Our Values," Global Sisters Report, December 6, 2018, globalsistersreport.org.

34. Lynn Adler and Jim Mayer, "Faith, Hope, and Capital: Interviews with Sister Marie Lucy and Doris Gromley," Public Broadcasting Service, March 31, 2000, pbs.org.

35. The African Activist Archive at Michigan State University, africanactivist.msu.edu, provides lists of organizations and copies of documents.

36. Fred Dycus Miller Jr., *Out of the Mouths of Babes: The Infant Formula Controversy* (Bowling Green, OH: Bowling Green State University, Social Philosophy and Policy Center, 1983). Crosby's role based on a 1982 interview is described in M. David Ermann and William H. Clements II, "The Interfaith Center on Corporate Responsibility and Its Campaign against Marketing Infant Formula in the Third World," *Social Problems* 32, no. 2 (December 1984): 195–96.

37. Michael H. Crosby, "Socially Responsible Investing Is No 'Sell Out,'" *Tobacco Control* 18, no. 5 (October 2009): 338–39.

38. Taavi Tillman, Jonny Currie, Alistair Wardrope, and David McCoy, "Fossil Fuel Companies and Climate Change: The Case for Divestment," *British Medical Journal* 350 (June 25, 2015): 1–2; but see Brian Roewe, "ExxonMobil Shareholders Push through Climate Resolution," *National Catholic Reporter*, June 13, 2017.

39. Yonca Ertimur, Fabrizio Ferri, and Volkan Muslu, "Shareholder Activism and CEO Pay," *Review of Financial Studies* 24, no. 2 (February 2011): 535–92.

40. Miguel Rojas, Bouchra M'zali, Marie-France Turcotte, and Philip Merrigan, "Bringing about Changes to Corporate Social Policy through Shareholder Activism: Filers, Issues, Targets, and Success," *Business and Society Review* 114, no. 2 (2009): 217–52; W. Trexler Proffitt Jr. and Andrew Spicer, "Shaping the Shareholder Activism Agenda: Institutional Investors and Global Social Issues," *Strategic Organization* 4, no. 2 (2006): 165–90.

41. Rojas et al., "Bringing about Changes"; Kathleen Rehbein, Jeanne M. Logsdon, and Harry J. Van Buren III, "Corporate Responses to Shareholder Activists: Considering the Dialogue Alternative," *Journal of Business Ethics* 112, no. 1 (January 2013): 137–54; Randall S. Thomas and James F. Cotter, "Shareholder Proposals in the New Millennium: Shareholder Support, Board Response, and Market Reaction," *Journal of Corporate Finance* 13, no. 2–3 (2007): 368–91.

42. Pamela Paxton, "Social Capital and Democracy: An Interdependent Relationship," *American Sociological Review* 67, no. 2 (April 2002): 254–77; Kai Schafft and David Brown, "Social Capital, Social Networks, and Social Power," *Social Epistemology* 17, no. 4 (2003): 329–42; Robert D. Putnam, *Making Democracy Work: Civic Traditions in Modern Italy* (Princeton, NJ: Princeton University Press, 1993).

43. Pope John Paul II, "Day of Peace Statement, January 1, 1980," *The Wanderer*, January 3, 1980, quoted in Michael H. Crosby, "Corporate Law Violations and Executive Liability," Corporate Criminal Liability, Hearings before the Subcommittee on Crime of the Committee on the Judiciary, House of Representatives (Washington, DC: Government Printing Office, 1981), 223–24.

44. "Faith and Finance: Finding Common Ground to Protect the Common Good," Interfaith Center on Corporate Responsibility, 2010; "Ranking the Banks: A Survey of Seven U.S. Banks Conducted by Members of the Interfaith Center on Corporate Responsibility and Sustainalytics," Interfaith Center on Corporate Responsibility, 2013; Theo Anderson, "Storming the Corporate Castle: Does Shareholder Activism Work?," *In These Times*, March 23, 2015.

45. "Tea Party and Views of Government Overreach," Pew Research Center, April 18, 2010.

46. Scott Clement and John C. Green, "The Tea Party and Religion," Pew Research Center, February 23, 2011; Wuthnow, *Rough Country*, 437.

47. David E. Campbell and Robert D. Putnam, "Crashing the Tea Party," *New York Times*, August 16, 2011; Ruth Braunstein and Malaena Taylor, "Is the Tea Party a 'Religious' Movement? Religiosity in the Tea Party versus the Religious Right," *Sociology of Religion* 78, no. 1 (2017): 33–59; Ruth Braunstein, *Prophets and Patriots: Faith in Democracy across the Political Divide* (Berkeley: University of California Press, 2017), 82–117.

48. Wuthnow, *Rough Country*, 438–39.

49. Hans Bader, "Obama Administration Attacks Religious Freedom and Separation of Church and State," Competitive Enterprise Institute, September 26, 2011, cei.org; Robert P. Jones, Daniel Cox, and Juhem Navarro-Rivera, "Economic Insecurity, Rising Inequality, and Doubts about the Future," Public Religion Research Institute, 2014, prri.org.

50. "Pulling Apart: A State-by-State Analysis of Income Trends," Center on Budget and Policy Priorities, November 2012; Michael Leachman, "Kansas' Economic Growth Continues to Lag, Despite Tax Cuts," Center on Budget and Policy Priorities, November 2015; "Income Inequality in Kansas: A Snapshot," Center on Budget and Policy Priorities, June 2016, cbpp.org; Josh Barro, "Yes, If You Cut Taxes, You Get Less Revenue," New York Times, June 27, 2014.

51. Thomas Frank, What's the Matter with Kansas? How Conservatives Won the Heart of America (New York: Holt, 2004), 7. However, Larry M. Bartels showed with national data that economic as well as social issues mattered to religious people. "What's the Matter with What's the Matter with Kansas?," Quarterly Journal of Political Science 1, no. 2 (2006): 201–26.

52. On the Fellowship, see D. Michael Lindsay, "Organizational Liminality and Interstitial Creativity: The Fellowship of Power," Social Forces 89, no. 1 (September 2010): 163–84; Jeff Sharlet, The Family: The Secret Fundamentalism at the Heart of American Power (New York: Harper, 2008). On inequality, see Jim Tankersley, "Kansas Tried a Tax Plan Similar to Trump's," New York Times, October 10, 2017. A survey of likely voters prior to the 2010 election showed 68 percent of regular religious service attenders planning to vote for Brownback compared with 54 percent of occasional attenders and 39 percent of those almost never attending. SurveyUSA, September 17, 2010.

53. Pope Francis, Evangelii Gaudium: Apostolic Exhortation (Vatican: Vatican Press, 2013), vatican.va; Katie Glueck, "Pope's Economic Ideas Rattle GOP," Politico, December 25, 2013; Bill Glauber, "Paul Ryan Signals Support for Kenosha Casino," Milwaukee Journal Sentinel, December 19, 2013.

54. Arlie Russell Hochschild, Strangers in Their Own Land: Anger and Mourning on the American Right (New York: New Press, 2016), 8; Theda Skocpol and Vanessa Williamson, The Tea Party and the Remaking of Republican Conservatism (New York: Oxford University Press, 2012), 198.

55. Kate Bowler, Blessed: A History of the American Prosperity Gospel (New York: Oxford University Press, 2013); Ebenezer Obadare, "'Raising Righteous Billionaires': The Prosperity Gospel Reconsidered," Hervormde Teologiese Studies 72, no. 4 (2016): 1–8. Scott Schieman and Jong Hyun Jung found prosperity gospel beliefs more common among low-income respondents in a study of US Pentecostals; see "'Practical Divine Influence': Socioeconomic Status and Belief in the Prosperity Gospel," Journal for the Scientific Study of Religion 51, no. 4 (December 2012): 738–56. Kevin D. Dougherty, Mitchell J. Neubert, and Jerry Z. Park showed that beliefs about God promising financial success and success in business being evidence of God's blessing were associated with perceptions of oneself as successful and capable, creative and curious, and willing to explore new ways or to take risks to get ahead; see "Prosperity Beliefs and Value Orientations: Fueling or Suppressing Entrepreneurial Activity," Journal for the Scientific Study of Religion 58, no. 2 (2019): 475–93.

56. Mary V. Wrenn, "Consecrating Capitalism: The United States Prosperity Gospel and Neoliberalism," Journal of Economic Issues 53, no. 2 (2019): 425–32; Peter Mundey, "The

Prosperity Gospel and the Spirit of Consumerism According to Joel Osteen," *Pneuma* 39, no. 3 (January 2017): 318–41; Jeremy W. Peters and Elizabeth Dias, "Paula White, Newest White House Aide, Is a Uniquely Trumpian Pastor," *New York Times*, November 5, 2019.

57. Michael Edwards, *Small Change: Why Business Won't Save the World* (San Francisco: Berrett-Koehler, 2010).

58. Linsey McGoey and Darren Thiel, "Charismatic Violence and the Sanctification of the Super-Rich," *Economy and Society* 47, no. 1 (2018): 111–34; Linsey McGoey, "Philanthrocapitalism and Its Critics," *Poetics* 40 (2012): 185–99.

59. Darrell M. West, *Billionaires: Reflections on the Upper Crust* (Washington, DC: Brookings Institution Press, 2014), 81; Garry W. Jenkins, "Who's Afraid of Philanthrocapitalism?," *Case Western Law Review* 61, no. 3 (2011): 753–821. This concern was also compounded by tax reform policies that gave only the largest donors a tax incentive to give.

60. Nicolas J. Duquette, "Inequality and Philanthropy: High-Income Giving in the United States 1917–2012," *Explorations in Economic History* 70 (2018): 25–41.

61. Angela M. Eikenberry and Roseanne Marie Mirabella, "Extreme Philanthropy: Philanthrocapitalism, Effective Altruism, and the Discourse of Neoliberalism," *PS: Political Science and Politics* 51, no. 1 (January 2018): 43–47; Bill Gates, "Why Inequality Matters," *GatesNotes*, October 13, 2014, gatesnotes.com.

62. D. Michael Lindsay, *Faith in the Halls of Power: How Evangelicals Joined the American Elite* (New York: Oxford University Press, 2007), 176–80.

63. Vincci Li, "'Shopping for Change': World Vision Canada and Consumption-Oriented Philanthropy in the Age of Philanthrocapitalism," *Voluntas* 28 (2017): 455–71; Marcia Pally, "Non-market Motives at Work in the Market: 'New Evangelicals' in Civil Society in the United States and Overseas," *Telos* 157 (Winter 2011): 165–84; Becky Yang Hsu, *Borrowing Together: Microfinance and Cultivating Social Ties* (New York: Columbia University Press, 2017).

64. Robert L. Payton and Michael P. Moody, *Understanding Philanthropy: Its Meaning and Mission* (Bloomington: Indiana University Press, 2008).

65. Allison Schnable, "What Religion Affords Grassroots NGOs: Frames, Networks, Modes of Action," *Journal for the Scientific Study of Religion* 55, no. 2 (2016): 216–32; Allison Schnable, "New American Relief and Development Organizations: Predictors at the U.S. County Level," *Social Problems* 62, no. 2 (2015): 309–29.

66. David W. Miller, *God at Work: The History and Promise of the Faith at Work Movement* (New York: Oxford University Press, 2007); Lake Lambert III, *Spirituality, Inc.: Religion in the Workplace* (New York: New York University Press, 2009); James Dennis LoRusso, *Spirituality, Corporate Culture, and American Business: The Neoliberal Ethic and the Spirit of Global Capital* (London: Bloomsbury Academic, 2017).

67. Max Weber, *The Protestant Ethic and the Spirit of Capitalism* (Los Angeles: Roxbury, 2002; originally published 1920); Lindsay, *Faith in the Halls of Power*, 230–21; Bradley C. Smith, *Baptizing Business: Evangelical Executives and the Sacred Pursuit of Profit* (New York: Oxford University Press, 2020).

68. Paul G. Schervish, "The Moral Biographies of the Wealthy and the Cultural Scripture of Wealth," in *Wealth in Western Thought: The Case for and against Riches*, ed. Paul G. Schervish (Westport, CT: Praeger, 1994), 167–208, quotes on page 202.

69. Examples of elite networks are given in D. Michael Lindsay, "Evangelicals in the Power Elite: Elite Cohesion Advancing a Movement," *American Sociological Review* 73, no. 1 (February 2008): 60–82. On character and personality traits in wealth narratives, see Lambert, *Spirituality, Inc.*, 93–98.

70. Bethany Moreton, *To Serve God and Wal-Mart: The Making of Christian Free Enterprise* (Cambridge, MA: Harvard University Press, 2009), 126.

71. "A Former Mayor Looks Back," *Santa Monica Mirror*, July 13, 2006.

72. Diane Lefer, "An Interview with Rev. James Lawson," *Believer Magazine*, March 1, 2013.

73. Jim Conn, "James Lawson, Conscience of History," *Capital and Main*, August 15, 2012, capitalandmain.com; Diane Lefer, "Making Our Country a Better Country: The Fellowship of Reconciliation Interview with James Lawson," Satyagraha Foundation for Nonviolence Studies, January 12, 2017, satyagrahafoundation.org.

74. C. Melissa Snarr, *All You That Labor: Religion and Ethics in the Living Wage Movement* (New York: New York University Press, 2011), 129–33; Grace Yukich, *One Family under God: Immigration Politics and Progressive Religion in America* (New York: Oxford University Press, 2013), 17–18.

75. Pierrette Hondagneu-Sotelo, *God's Heart Has No Borders: How Religious Activists Are Working for Immigrant Rights* (Berkeley: University of California Press, 2008), 104–29; Dan Clawson, *The Next Upsurge: Labor and the New Social Movements* (Ithaca, NY: Cornell University Press, 2003), 171; Stephanie Luce, *Fighting for a Living Wage* (Ithaca, NY: Cornell University Press, 2004), 201; John P. Kretzmann and John L. McKnight, "Asset-Based Strategies for Faith Communities," Asset-Based Community Development Institute, 2002.

76. Richard H. Sander, E. Douglass Williams, and Joseph Doherty, "The Economic and Distributional Consequences of the Santa Monica Minimum Wage Ordinance," Employment Policies Institute, University of California, Los Angeles, October 2002; Stephanie Luce, "Living Wage Movement: An Update," *Solidarity*, April 2001.

77. Jared Bernstein, "The Living Wage Movement: What Is It, Why Is It, and What's Known about Its Impact?," in *Emerging Labor Market Institutions for the Twenty-First Century*, ed. Richard B. Freeman, Joni Hersch, and Lawrence Mishel (Chicago: University of Chicago Press, 2004), 99–140.

78. Laura Huizar and Yannet Lathrop, "Fighting Wage Preemption: How Workers Have Lost Billions in Wages and How We Can Restore Local Democracy," National Employment Law Project, 2019, nelp.org; Clergy and Laity United for Economic Justice, IRS Form 990, 2017; Ismael Parra, "L.A. Labor Rallies to Build Unity with Grocery Workers, Stop Neighborhood Disruption," *People's World*, July 11, 2019.

79. Jeffrey Stout, *Blessed Are the Organized: Grassroots Democracy in America* (Princeton, NJ: Princeton University Press, 2010). As a religion scholar, Stout noted that in many of the meetings he observed, the language appealed to the sacred. In particular, it profaned the power of the privileged by replacing it with sacred stories of divine care and intervention on behalf of the poor, the enslaved, and the oppressed.

80. Self-identified "conservative Christians" were the largest bloc of Republican voters in 2018, but even among this group only 52 percent held favorable views toward the Republican candidate in 2018 compared with 74 percent of self-identified Tea Party supporters. Remington

Research Group, "Kansas Governor Republican Primary Election," August 2018, RealClear Politics, realclearpolitics.com.

Chapter 7: Health and Wellness

1. Sara Frueh, "COVID-19 and Black Communities," National Academies of Sciences, Engineering and Medicine, July 9, 2020, nationalacademies.org; Clarence Gravlee, "Racism, Not Genetics, Explains Why Black Americans Are Dying of COVID-19," *Scientific American*, June 7, 2020; "COVID-19 Hospitalization and Death by Race/Ethnicity," Centers for Disease Control and Prevention, November 30, 2020, cdc.gov.

2. Michelle Boorstein, "The Church That Won't Close Its Doors over the Coronavirus," *Washington Post*, March 20, 2020; Corky Siemaszko, "Florida Megachurch Pastor Caves after Defying Coronavirus Rules," *NBC News*, April 10, 2020; Neil Vigdor, "Pastor Who Defied Social Distancing Dies after Contracting COVID-19," *New York Times*, April 15, 2020.

3. Bruce Worthington, "Romans 13:1–7 with an Eye to Global Capital," in *Reading the Bible in an Age of Crisis: Political Exegesis for a New Day*, ed. Bruce Worthington (Minneapolis: Augsburg Fortress, 2015), 245–64, quote on page 245; Julie Zauzmer and Keith McMillan, "Sessions Cites Bible Passage Used to Defend Slavery in Defense of Separating Immigrant Families," *Washington Post*, June 15, 2018.

4. Andrew W. McThenia Jr., "Civil Resistance or Holy Obedience? Reflections from within a Community of Resistance," *Washington and Lee Law Review* 48, no. 15 (1991): 15–40.

5. Vic Ryckaert, "Greg J. Dixon, the Indianapolis Pastor Who Defied the Federal Government, Died Sunday," *Indianapolis Star*, October 22, 2019.

6. "Virginia Defends Coronavirus Restrictions in Church Lawsuit," *New York Times*, May 7, 2020. On partisan responses, 33 percent of Republicans but only 7 percent of Democrats in one poll favored allowing houses of worship greater flexibility with social distancing rules than other organizations. "Americans Oppose Religious Exemptions from Coronavirus-Related Restrictions," Pew Research Center, August 17, 2020. Variation in attitudes attributable to religio-political views, as well as background literature, is discussed in Samuel L. Perry, Andrew L. Whitehead, and Joshua B. Grubbs, "Save the Economy, Liberty, and Yourself: Christian Nationalism and Americans' Views on Government COVID-19 Restrictions," *Sociology of Religion*, December 29, 2020, academic.oup.com.

7. Brooke Sopelsa, "Trump Cabinet's Bible Teacher Says Gays Cause 'God's Wrath' in COVID-19 Blog Post," *NBC News*, March 25, 2020; for a counterargument, see Todd Mangum, "The Pandemic as God's Judgment," *Christianity Today*, May 15, 2020; and as background, see Anthony M. Petro, *After the Wrath of God: AIDS, Sexuality, and American Religion* (New York: Oxford University Press, 2015).

8. Roman Catholic Diocese of Brooklyn, *New York v. Andrew M. Cuomo*, Governor of New York, US Supreme Court, 592 US _____ (2020).

9. On the role of religion in these discussions, see Nadja Durbach, *Bodily Matters: The Anti-vaccination Movement in England, 1853–1907* (Durham, NC: Duke University Press, 2005), 173–78.

10. *Jacobson v. Massachusetts*, 197 US 11 (1905). In a subsequent case, *Zucht v. King*, 260 US 174 (1922), the US Supreme Court rendered a decision that had the effect of upholding a law

prohibiting children from attending school without having been vaccinated. Karen L. Walloch, *The Antivaccine Heresy: Jacobson v. Massachusetts and the Troubled History of Compulsory Vaccination in the United States* (Rochester, NY: University of Rochester Press, 2015).

11. "Anti-vaccination Forces Open Fight for Repeal of Law," *Christian Science Monitor*, March 23, 1937; "Anti-vaccination Bill Faces Defeat," *Christian Science Monitor*, April 19, 1939.

12. Dewitt Bliss, "Anti-vaccination Belief Defended," *Baltimore Sun*, December 28, 1966.

13. George E. Curry, "Rights Case Grows over Measles Vaccinations," *Chicago Tribune*, March 25, 1991.

14. NJ Rev Stat § 18A:61D-10 (2013); NJ Rev Stat § 18A:62–15.2 (2015).

15. CT Gen Stat § 19a-131e (2013).

16. Sharon Bernstein, "California Limits School Vaccine Exemptions," *Globe and Mail*, July 1, 2015; Ginia Bellafante, "Vaccine Fear Goes Viral," *New York Times*, October 12, 2014; Elizabeth Picciuto, "Twisted Anti-vaxxer Parents Choose Fatal Diseases over Autism," *Daily Beast*, July 1, 2014; Lena H. Sun, "California Vaccination Rate Hits New High after Tougher Immunization Law," *Washington Post*, April 13, 2017; Gabriela Capurro, Josh Greenberg, Eve Dube, and Michelle Driedger, "Measles, Moral Regulation and the Social Construction of Risk: Media Narratives of 'Anti-vaxxers' and the 2015 Disneyland Outbreak," *Canadian Journal of Sociology* 43, no. 1 (2018): 25–47; Paige Winfield Cunningham, "Who Are the Anti-vaxxers?," *Washington Examiner*, March 2, 2015.

17. Kayla Epstein, "Hundreds of Anti-vaxxers Flood New Jersey Capital to Protest Bill That Would End Religious Exemptions," *Washington Post*, December 13, 2019; Lena H. Sun and Ben Guarino, "Anti-vaxxers Target Communities Battling Measles," *Washington Post*, May 20, 2019; Marci Hamilton, "Children Have a Right to Live and Be Vaccinated, and Two Legal Reforms Are Needed," *Verdict*, April 28, 2019.

18. Craig Timberg, Elizabeth Dwoskin, and Moriah Balingit, "Protests Spread, Fueled by Economic Woes and Internet Subcultures," *Washington Post*, May 1, 2020. A network analysis of 1,300 Facebook pages with nearly one hundred million followers found that antivaccination groups discussed a wide range of topics that, the researchers speculated, made them "more responsive to diverse concerns and [made] undecided people feel listened to." Meredith Wadman, "Vaccine Opponents Are Gaining in Facebook 'Battle for Hearts and Minds,' New Map Shows," *Science*, May 13, 2020.

19. Sarah Pulliam Bailey, "How NIH Chief Francis Collins Is Trying to Get People of Faith to Wake Up to Coronavirus Realities," *Washington Post*, April 3, 2020; Stephanie Weaver, "Evangelical Doctors' Group Urges Churches to Halt In-Person Services amid COVID-19 Surge," *Fox News*, November 24, 2020; Sarah Pulliam Bailey, "What NIH Chief Francis Collins Wants Religious Leaders to Know about the Coronavirus Vaccines," *Washington Post*, December 12, 2020.

20. Among reports of budget reductions and staff layoffs, one example was a 24 percent reduction in operating budget reported by LifeWay Christian Resources, the supplier of most materials for the Southern Baptist Convention. Jeff Brumley, "LifeWay Cutting Staff, Expenses," *Baptist News*, April 29, 2020. The price of shares in Salem Media Group, the supplier of religious programming to more than three thousand radio stations, fell from six dollars in 2018 to eighty cents in May 2020. Daniel Silliman, "Largest Christian Radio Company Faces Financial Crisis Due to Coronavirus Downturn," *Christianity Today*, May 14, 2020.

21. Sarah Mervosh and Elizabeth Dias, "From Seattle to Kentucky, Churches Cancel Religious Services," *New York Times*, March 13, 2020; "Coronavirus: News, Reflections, Analysis," *America*, March 12, 2020; Michael J. Mooney, "One of Trump's Evangelical Defenders Wrestles with Flattening the Curve," *Politico*, March 22, 2020; Tad Walch, "First Presidency: All Church Meetings Temporarily Canceled Worldwide," *Deseret News* (Salt Lake City, UT), March 12, 2020; Sarah Pulliam Bailey, Kevin Schaul, Lauren Tierney, and Kevin Uhrmacher, "Cellphone Data Shows Coronavirus Kept Churchgoers at Home in Every State on Easter," *Washington Post*, April 17, 2020. Although in-person worship services were canceled, comments posted to a digital archive revealed that some church members attended at special times or met with clergy or lay leaders in homes to receive the sacraments. Pandemic Religion: A Digital Archive, pandemicreligion.org.

22. Jeff Brumley, "Some Churches Find Missional Niche in Health and Wellness," *Baptist Standard*, February 9, 2015; Annette E. Maxwell, Rhonda Santifer, and Cindy L. Chang, "Organizational Readiness for Wellness Promotion: A Survey of 100 African American Church Leaders in South Los Angeles," *BMC Public Health* 19, no. 1 (2019): 1–10; R. Marie Griffith, *Born Again Bodies: Flesh and Spirit in American Christianity* (Berkeley: University of California Press, 2004), 240.

23. First Congregational Church, Winchester, Massachusetts, fcc-winchester.com; Arcola United Methodist Church, arcolachurch.org.

24. "Resources for Catholics during COVID-19," United States Conference of Catholic Bishops, usccb.org; Lutheran Senior Life, lutheranseniorlife.org; Baptist Community Ministries, bcm.org; Virginia Interfaith Center, virginiainterfaithcenter.org; Idaho News 6, kivitv.com.

25. "Resources for NGUMC Churches," June 2020, North Georgia Conference, ngumc.org.

26. "CHS Urges Administration and Congress to Provide Continued Critical Financial Support," Catholic Health Association, April 20, 2020; Dennis Sadowski, "Catholic Leaders Urge Congress to Address Shortcomings in CARES Act," *Crux*, April 8, 2020.

27. Kristy Nabhan-Warren, *Cornbelt America: The Work of Faith in the Heartland* (Chapel Hill: University of North Carolina Press, 2020); Assemblies of God chaplain Brian K. Pounds as quoted in "On the COVID-19 Front Lines," U.S. Missions, April 26, 2020, usmissions.ag.org.

28. "Congress Debates Economic Priorities and Response," Evangelical Lutheran Church in America Advocacy Action Alert, April 15, 2020, support.elca.org; Kurt Adams, "Seminar Program Launches Virtual Series on COVID-19," Church and Society, May 4, 2020, www.umcjustice.org.

29. "Statement from the AME Church regarding the Racial Impacts of the COVID-19 Pandemic," Religion News Service Press Releases, April 8, 2020, religionnews.com.

30. "Letter to Congress on Priorities for Fourth COVID Supplemental," Catholic Health Association, May 11, 2020, chausa.org.

31. "Catholic Partners Letter: Removing Barriers to Care during the Novel Coronavirus (COVID-19) Global Pandemic," Justice for Immigrants, March 18, 2020, justiceforimmigrants.org.

32. Lynn Tramonte, "Outraged by Trump's Latest Immigration Ban? 3 Ways to Take Action," Interfaith Immigration Coalition, April 28, 2020, interfaithimmigration.org.

33. Allison Grossman, "Congress Must Protect the Vulnerable during This Public Health Emergency," Religious Action Center of Reform Judaism, March 13, 2020, rac.org.

34. "Investor Statement on Coronavirus Response," Interfaith Center on Corporate Responsibility, March 26, 2020; iccr.org.

Conclusion

1. James Madison, "The Same Subject Continued: The Union as a Safeguard against Domestic Faction and Insurrection," *New York Daily Advertiser*, November 22, 1787; George F. Will, "Religion and Politics in the First Modern Nation," John C. Danforth Center on Religion and Politics, Washington University in St. Louis, December 4, 2012; revised as "Religion and the American Republic," *National Affairs* 37 (Summer 2013), nationalaffairs.com.

2. *Zorach v. Clauson*, 343 US 306 (1952).

3. Commission on the Practice of Democratic Citizenship, *Our Common Purpose: Reinventing American Democracy for the 21ˢᵗ Century* (Cambridge, MA: American Academy of Arts and Sciences, 2020), 47. Robert Audi makes a similar argument in introducing the *Daedalus* collection of essays on religion and democracy; he writes that religious groups can be "a source of diverse elements that can bring to civil society ideas and values that might not otherwise be recognized or given due consideration. "Religion and Democracy: Interactions, Tensions, Possibilities," *Daedalus* 149, no. 3 (Summer 2020): 5–24, quote on page 7.

4. Isabel Wilkerson, *Caste: The Origins of Our Discontents* (New York: Random House, 2020); Joe Feagin, *Systemic Racism: A Theory of Oppression* (New York: Routledge, 2006); Khyati Y. Joshi, *White Christian Privilege: The Illusion of Religious Equality in America* (New York: New York University Press, 2020).

5. Chantal Mouffe, "Religion, Liberal Democracy, and Citizenship," in *Political Theologies: Public Religions in a Post-secular World*, ed. Hent De Vries and Lawrence E. Sullivan (New York: Fordham University Press, 2006), 318–26.

6. Chantal Mouffe, "Democratic Politics and Conflict: An Agonistic Approach," *Política Común* 9 (2016): 1. On misconceptions of agonistic democracy, see Andrew Schaap, "Agonism in Divided Societies," *Philosophy and Social Criticism* 32, no. 2 (2006): 255–77; Mark Wenman, "'Agonistic Pluralism' and Three Archetypal Forms of Politics," *Contemporary Political Theory* 2, no. 2 (2003): 165–80; and Mark Wenman, *Agonistic Democracy: Constituent Power in the Era of Globalization* (New York: Cambridge University Press, 2013).

7. Like Mouffe's focus on agonistic democracy, the literature on deliberative democracy acknowledges the benefits of encouraging adversarial debate; see, for example, Bernard Manin, "Political Deliberation and the Adversarial Principle," *Daedalus* 146, no. 3 (Summer 2017): 39–50.

8. Jeffrey Stout, *Democracy and Tradition* (Princeton, NJ: Princeton University Press, 2005); Douglas W. Rae and Michael Taylor, *The Analysis of Political Cleavages* (New Haven, CT: Yale University Press, 1970). On racial and ethnic variation, see the essays in *Religion Is Raced: Understanding American Religion in the Twenty-First Century*, ed. Grace Yukich and Penny Edgell (New York: New York University Press, 2020).

9. Peter L. Berger, "The Good of Religious Pluralism," *First Things* 262 (April 2016): 39–42, quote on page 41.

10. Manon Westphal discusses the institutional mechanisms of conflict regulation that must be present for agonistic democracy to maintain order. "Overcoming the Institutional Deficit of Agonistic Democracy," *Res Publica* 25 (2019): 187–210.

11. Paulina Tambakaki, "The Tasks of Agonism and Agonism to the Task: Introducing 'Chantal Mouffe: Agonism and the Politics of Passion,'" *Parallax* 20, no. 2 (2014): 1–13.

12. On the necessity of institutional constraints, see Dana R. Villa, *Politics, Philosophy, Terror: Essays on the Thought of Hannah Arendt* (Princeton, NJ: Princeton University Press, 1999), 107–27; and Steven Levitsky and Daniel Ziblatt, *How Democracies Die* (New York: Crown, 2018), 101–102. On unproductive forms of argumentation, see Deborah Tannen, "The Argument Culture: Agonism and the Common Good," *Daedalus* 142, no. 2 (Spring 2013): 177–84, and her lengthier treatment in *The Argument Culture: Moving from Debate to Dialogue* (New York: Random House, 1998).

13. See the discussions of these assumptions in Philip Pettit, *Republicanism: A Theory of Freedom and Government* (New York: Oxford University Press, 1999); James Tully, *Strange Multiplicity: Constitutionalism in an Age of Diversity* (New York: Cambridge University Press, 1995); and Mark Wenman, "William E. Connolly: Pluralism without Transcendence," *British Journal of Politics and International Relations* 10, no. 2 (2008): 156–70.

14. John Danforth, *The Relevance of Religion: How Faithful People Can Change Politics* (New York: Random House, 2015); see also John Danforth, *Faith and Politics: How the "Moral Values" Debate Divides America and How to Move Forward Together* (New York: Viking, 2006); John C. Danforth, "Onward, Moderate Christian Soldiers," *New York Times*, June 17, 2005; and John C. Danforth and Matt Malone, "A First Step toward Loving Our Enemies," *Wall Street Journal*, September 4, 2020.

15. Michael Gerson and Peter Wehner, *City of Man: Religion and Politics in a New Era* (Chicago: Moody Publishers, 2010).

16. Among various overviews of these developments, see Andrea Kendall-Taylor, Natasha Lindstaedt, and Erica Frantz, *Democracies and Authoritarian Regimes* (New York: Oxford University Press, 2019), and the essays in *Authoritarianism Goes Global: The Challenge to Democracy*, ed. Larry Diamond, Marc F. Plattner, and Christopher Walker (Baltimore: Johns Hopkins University Press, 2016).

17. Andrew L. Whitehead and Samuel L. Perry offer quantitative and qualitative data on this tendency. *Taking America Back for God: Christian Nationalism in the United States* (New York: Oxford University Press, 2020).

18. The evidence for this claim is most clearly presented in Michael Hout and Claude S. Fischer, "Why More Americans Have No Religious Preference: Politics and Generations," *American Sociological Review* 67, no. 2 (April 2002): 165–90. They argue that the "political part of the increase in 'nones' can be viewed as a symbolic statement against the Religious Right" (165).

19. For a treatment of the ill effects of political polarization, see Suzanne Mettler and Robert C. Lieberman, *The Recurring Crises of American Democracy: Four Threats* (New York: St. Martin's Press, 2020); for these effects on religion, see David E. Campbell, "The Perils of Politicized Religion," *Daedalus* 149, no. 3 (Summer 2020): 87–104.

INDEX

Abbott Laboratories, 203

abolitionists, 11

abortion, 132, 208, 211, 231

Abrams v. United States, 64

ACLU. *See* American Civil Liberties Union

ACORN. *See* Association of Community Organizations for Reform Now

Action Center of the Evangelical Lutheran Church in America, 244

Adalberto Methodist Church, 177–78

Addams, Jane, 32, 67

Adrian Dominican Sisters, 203

Affordable Care Act, 209, 231

African American churches: Faith-Based Initiative and, 142–43; and welfare, 127, 131, 134–36

African Americans: Baptists, 30; and New Deal, 36, 49; racial equality advocacy of, 49

African Methodist Episcopal Church, 244

African Methodist Episcopal Speaker's Club, 33

African Methodist Episcopal Zion church, 33

agonistic pluralism, 7, 254–59

agonistic religious practice, 256–62

Ahlstrom, Sydney, 85

Aid to Families with Dependent Children, 121, 137

Alinsky, Saul, 220

Allen African Methodist Episcopal Church, 135

Almond, Gabriel, 113

America (magazine), 111, 237

America First Party, 268n68

America Forward Movement for Religion and Americanism, 43–44

American Academy of Arts and Sciences, Commission on the Practice of Democratic Citizenship, 253

American Association for Economic Freedom, 31

American Baptist Convention, Commission on Christian Social Progress, 105

American Civil Liberties Union (ACLU), 32, 67, 110, 151, 181, 225, 251

American Friends Service Committee, 105, 113

American Humanist Association, 77

American Jewish Congress, 77, 143; Commission on Law and Social Action, 105

American Jewish Joint Distribution, 113

American League Against War and Fascism, 32

American Liberty League, 41–42

American Lutheran Church, 38–39

American Public Relations Forum, 112

American Recovery and Reinvestment Act (ARRA), 207

Americans United, 151

American Union Against Militarism, 56, 62

American Unitarian Association, 30

America's Voice, 171

Anabaptists, 11

Anarchist Exclusion Act, 62

Angelus Temple, 34

Anti-Defamation League of B'nai B'rith, 105

freedom. *See* individual freedom7

Freedom Club, 112, 122

Freedom Coalition, 210

freedom of assembly: civil right movement
and, 13, 104–7; First Amendment and, 86,
100; local statues concerning, 100–104;
networks as aspect of, 107–12; overview
of, 13; privacy and, 104–6; for religious
groups, 102–3; voluntary association and,
100–104. *See also* voluntary association

freedom of conscience: constraints on, 73–83;
as democratic principle and value, 55, 71, 83;
historical role of, 54, 62–63; justifications
of, 13, 62–64; meanings of, 13, 54–56, 83;
military service as exercise of, 76; in war
matters, 55. *See also* conscience; conscientious objection

freedom of religion: and COVID-19
pandemic, 228, 231; COVID-19 pandemic
and, 15; First Amendment and, 80, 86;
government as threat to, 15, 28, 30, 38, 41,
43–44, 46; in New Deal era, 26–28, 30, 36,
38, 41; Tea Party ideology and, 209; true
private choice and, 149–51; vaccinations
and, 234–36

freedom of speech, 64

Friedman, Milton, 201

Fuller, Charles E., 48

Gans, Herbert, 173

Gaston, Healan, 95

Gates, Bill, 215, 216

General Electric, 202

General Federation of Women's Clubs,
93, 96

General Foods, 201

General Motors, 201

General Tire and Rubber, 200

German Baptists, 61

Gerson, Michael, 258–59

GI Bill, 88

Gilded Age, 188

Gingrich, Newt, 144–45

Glide Memorial Methodist Church, 111,
133

God: conscientious objection and, 69–70,
72, 74, 77–80; "death of," 86, 144–45;
freedom linked to, 92; government as
embodiment of authority of, 229–30;
government as subordinate to authority
of, 26, 39, 42, 47, 48, 230

Goldman, Emma, 62–63

Goldstein, Jared, 42

Goldwater, Barry, 108, 119, 121–22

Good Neighbor League, 35, 36

government: COVID-19 role of, 15–16;
expanded powers of, as threat to democracy, 12, 19, 27–29, 45–46, 50, 65, 88–89,
120, 207–12, 259–60; in New Deal era, 12,
19, 25–53; skeptical attitudes toward, 15,
27, 36, 38–40, 42, 119–20, 195, 229; social
welfare role of, 14, 15, 28, 118–30, 145–46,
196; as subordinate to religious authority,
15, 28, 30, 36, 38, 43–44, 46, 66; Tea Party
criticisms of, 207–12; as threat to individual
freedom, 27, 39, 46, 47, 65, 119–20; as
threat to religious authority, 26, 40–41.
See also small government

Graham, Billy, 48, 92, 130, 190

grassroots participation: in community
organizing, 220–21; democratic role of,
171, 220, 223, 226; freedom of assembly
and, 87; and fundamentalism, 193; in
immigrant issues, 171; and New Deal,
35, 42, 52; and religious political
participation, 93, 112, 132, 133, 188–89;
in Tea Party, 207, 212; and wealth gap,
220–21, 223

Greater New York Conference of Presbyterians, 33

Great Society, 207

Greek Orthodox, 98

Greene, Alison Collis, 40

Griffith, Marie, 239

Groundswell, 225

Gulf Oil Corporation, 173, 202

A NOTE ON THE TYPE

This book has been composed in Arno, an Old-style serif typeface in the classic Venetian tradition, designed by Robert Slimbach at Adobe.